# SCHOOLS THAT ROCK

## THE

## COLLEGE GUIDE

# SCHOOLS THAT ROCK

# THE

# RollingStone

# COLLEGE

# GUIDE

## JENNY ELISCU

WENNER
BOOKS

WENNER BOOKS, NEW YORK

Published by
Wenner Media
1290 Avenue of the Americas
2nd Floor NY, NY 10104
(212) 484-1696
www.wennerbooks.com

Cover design by Fabrizio Moretti, Brett Kilroe, Mayapriya Long
Cover photo by Michael Waring
Editor: Nicholas Weir-Williams
Assistant Editor: Elizabeth D. Goodman
Research Assistants: Brian Orloff, Arielle Baer
Designer: Mayapriya Long, Bookwrights Design

Researchers: Jessica Adams, Andy Greene, Erin Hall, Joel Hoard, Joey Hood,
Adam Jardy, Brent Johnson, Alix McAlpine, Jeremy Schmidt, Vanessa Schneider,
Eddie Shoebang, Jeffrey Terich, Chris Tucillo, Harold Valentine, Sam Weiner,
April Williamson

Contributors: Steve Appleford, Ricardo Baca, Kimberly Chun, Eric Danton,
Dominic Devito, Zach Dundas, Kelly Fitzpatrick, Steve Forstneger, Peter
Gershon, Richard Gintowt, Caralyn Green, Eric Grossman, Chris Hassiotis,
Matt Hendrickson, Gil Kaufman, Jeff Klein, Ryan Lenz, Jennifer Maerz, Melissa
Maerz, Bob Massey, Bret McCabe, Kyle Munson, Randall Roberts, Micah
Salkind, Craig Seymour, Ryan Sult, Gemma Tarlach, Otis Taylor, Sanden Totten,
Nathan Turk, Carl Young

Printed in the United States of America

Library of Congress Cataloging-in-Publication Data

Eliscu, Jenny.
  Schools that rock : the Rolling Stone college guide / by Jenny Eliscu.
    p. cm.
Includes bibliographical references and index.
ISBN 1-932958-53-3 (alk. paper)
1. Universities and colleges—Curricula—United States. 2. Music in universi-
ties and colleges—United States. 3. Rock musicians--Education (Higher)—
United States. I. Title.

MT18.E45 2005
780'.71'173--dc22
                                        2005015199

# Contents

# Introduction

When you're deciding which college to attend, there are plenty of important factors to consider: which school has the best academic programs, the most affordable tuition, a favorable student-faculty ratio, a wide array of extracurricular activities, and so on. But what good will those perks do you if there's not a good student-rock ratio? The last thing you want is to arrive on campus and discover that there's nowhere in town for a music geek such as yourself to get his or her ya-yas out. Now, your parents will likely tell you that rock & roll should not be a consideration when you're making—imagine a stern, parental voice—THE MOST IMPORTANT DECISION OF YOUR LIFE. But can you imagine surviving through four years of exams, term papers, shitty roommates and even shittier food without seeing concerts or going record shopping?

Of course, *Schools That Rock: The Rolling Stone College Guide* also has a genuine academic purpose. If you aspire to be a professional musician or to work in a music-related field—whether as a teacher, producer, A&R person, etc—this book will help you figure out which schools have the best programs. The focus is not solely on technical training, but also on unconventional offerings that will teach you how to make music for films or how to manage a band, and classes with a challenging or unusual theoretical focus (on gender, race, or pop culture), as well as ones that treat music from the rock era with as much serious consideration as they give to canonical classical works. Universities such as Hampshire, Evergreen, and Antioch are featured because they encourage free-thinking types to build their own course of study. These are places you're likely to meet similarly minded individuals who would rather download songs from iTunes than crush beer cans on their heads. As weird as you think you are, you can be assured not to be the lone music junkie on campus.

This country is full of great music scenes, from Athens, Georgia (where R.E.M. started out) to Seattle (Nirvana. Duh) to Los Angeles (Mötley Crüe) to Minneapolis (Prince, the Replacements, Soul Asylum) to Omaha, NE (Bright Eyes, Cursive) to Washington, DC (Fugazi, Good Charlotte). *Schools That Rock: The Rolling Stone College*

*Guide* will help you figure out whether the college you're considering attending will provide access to one of these—or dozens of other—thriving scenes. And, once you move in, you can use *Schools That Rock* to figure out where to go see shows and buy records.

The criteria for inclusion in *Schools That Rock* is admittedly subjective and idiosyncratic. I have lived in New York City my entire life, so I hold pretty high standards for what counts as a good place to live, breathe, and hear rock & roll. I've tried to include venues and record shops specializing in genres other than rock & roll, but the bent of *Schools That Rock* is distinctly, well, rock—particularly indie, alternative, and punk.

A word regarding venues: Many of these places are 21+, and a lot are pretty strict about that rule. Far be it from me to condone underage drinking or the procurement of a fake ID just so you can see Sleater-Kinney at the Mercury Lounge. However, I would be loath not to include these places. How you get in is your business.

For those of you who do aspire to a music-related career, my best advice is to keep an open mind, try to land internships, and don't think studying music at college will assure you much of anything other than a diploma to hang on the wall. There's nothing that can compare to experience: Get involved with booking shows on campus or deejaying at your college radio station to make contacts within the industry and to learn how this shit works in the real world—outside your university bubble. Indulge your passions, go see shows and buy records and let's not worry for now what the hell you're gonna do when you graduate. College is all about becoming who you will ultimately be—not just as a professional, but as a human being with passions and a well-rounded worldview. And sometimes, you might even discover that the cute boy or girl from your Psych 101 class likes the Strokes just as much as you do. That's the kind of thing you have to leave campus to learn.

Feel free to email me at SchoolsThatRock@yahoo.com if you have suggestions, questions, comments, or even—gasp!—complaints. We aim to update this book in the coming years, and I'm counting on you to help make the next edition of *Schools That Rock* even better than this one.

—Jenny Eliscu

# SCHOOLS THAT ROCK

# THE Rolling Stone COLLEGE GUIDE

# What To Do With That Degree

Now that you've waded through all about B.A.s and B.M.s and so on, you're probably wondering whether any of these degrees have real world applications, or whether your parents' money will have gone to waste on a pretty piece of paper in a frame on your wall. Sweat it not: We spoke to an assortment of esteemed professionals who actually make a living off of music—either theirs or someone else's. Here's how they did it, and how you might do it, too.

**Name:** Alan Turry

**Job:** Music therapist and co-director of Nordoff-Robins Center for Music Therapy at NYU

**Studied:** Music Therapy at New York University

**Responsibilities:** Leads therapy sessions with patients that struggle with communication and speech. "Through the music we start to engage in a dialogue, which would be very difficult for the patients to do verbally," explains Turry. "It's the first step to building communication and a relationship. It's very rewarding to see how music can be so meaningful to people."

**How he got his job:** An improvisational musician by trade, Turry was invited to participate in a unique training session at the Nordoff-Robins Center, focusing primarily on improvisational therapy. "I was actually hired while I was doing the training. I became the first person to formally have the capacity to run a training course in the Nordoff-Robins approach."

**How you can get his job:** "Unfortunately, there are so many new disabilities that there is going to be a need for creative approaches to treatment," says Turry. "And I think music therapy is one that is continuing to move into the radar screen of public consciousness."

**Salary range:** $20,000-$200,000 but average is $42,000

**Name:** Angelica Cob

**Job:** Publicist/ VP of Media at Columbia Records

**Studied:** Political Science at University of California, Los Angeles

**Responsibilities:** Acts as liaison between artists and the press, securing interview opportunities and—God forbid—overseeing damage control in the event of a public controversy. "It's my job to come up with a media campaign and plan to not only launch an album but also to maintain an artist's career," says Cob, who has worked with artists such as John Mayer, System of a Down, the Raveonettes, Kid Rock, and Sugar Ray, among others. "It's nurturing an artist from a very early stage all the way up to the point where they get to be on the cover of *Rolling Stone* or win a Grammy."

**How she got her job:** Originally interested in music law, Cob began interning at Elektra Records while still in college, in order to get a feel for the music business. It was there that she fell in love with PR. The people at Elektra helped her get an entry-level position in the publicity department of Atlantic Records.

**How you can get her job:** Internships are the quickest way in, says Cob. "You have to start from the bottom. There is no other way to enter the music business," she explains. "You have to eat, breathe, sleep music. Because it's a really tough profession and if you don't have passion for the music, you'll never survive."

**Salary Range:** Starts at around $30,000, but can go into six figures once you're high up in the ranks

**Name:** Steve Mackey

**Job:** Composer and co-director of the Composers Ensemble at Princeton

**Studied:** Music at UC, Davis, then got his masters at SUNY, Stonybrook and his Ph.D. in composition at Brandeis

**Responsibilities:** Writing music. Or as Mackey puts it: "Sitting at home alone, letting your fantasies take over, imagining sounds and music and trying to capture it onto a page. It is the quintessentially creative job."

**How he got his job:** Mackey began his career writing music for anyone who was willing to play it, usually for free. "If I could find a good performer that I thought could bring my songs to life, I would just brown-nose them until they would play my music," says Mackey, who has composed pieces for the Los Angeles Philharmonic and the Chicago and San Francisco Symphonies. "And it just grew from there. At a certain point you get busy enough that you can't just write all these pieces that people are asking for, so you have to start charging money to limit the territory."

**How you can get his job:** "The product of a composer is only meaningful if it's unique to that individual," says Mackey. "It may take time to catch on, but a composer's best chance at success is by doing something that only he or she can do. So that means you really have to trust your vision and follow it."

**Salary range:** $20,000-$50,000

**Name:** Patrick Daughters
**Job:** Music video director
**Studied:** Film at New York University
**Responsibilities:** Directing music videos. "I get paid to create something based on my own idea," says Daughters who has made videos for the Yeah Yeah Yeahs ("Maps"), Kings of Leon ("Bucket"), and Death Cab for Cutie ("Title and Registration").

**How he got his job:** "My friend's band wanted to make some music videos. It had been something we talked about before they were signed to a label and when they were signed we stuck with it," explains Daughters. "The second video that I did for them was really well received and became kind of a hit single, so that led to a lot of other work." Modesty! He's talking about the YYYs' gorgeous "Maps" video, which was nominated for four MTV Video Music Awards.

**How you can get his job:** "It would be great to have a friend in a really good band that's going to break," jokes Daughters. But if your friends aren't the Bon Jovi type, here's some extra advice. "You can approach bands that you like and offer to do videos for free," suggests Daughters. "I still do videos for free, for bands that I like. A lot of really great music isn't going to have a big video budget."

**Salary range:** Average $60,000-$80,000, but like any creative field, you'll start off making nothing (or losing money) before settling into a stable income.

**Name:** Edward Smaldone

**Job:** College professor and director of the Aaron Copland School of Music at Queens College

**Studied:** Music at Queens College, then got his Ph.D. in composition at the CUNY Graduate School

**Responsibilities:** "What they pay me for is to teach classes," says Smaldone. But he says he really gets his kicks "watching students discover stuff. I've been teaching in a college for twenty-five years and I still get a charge out of that."

**How he got his job:** Smaldone went through the regular application process. "There are places where all the college jobs get listed, such as the College Music Society, which has a very thorough listing of all the openings in college music programs across the country."

**How you can get his job:** "You need to love teaching. Being a good classroom teacher is a very important piece of the puzzle," says Smaldone. "If you're Beethoven, you don't need to have a good classroom manner. Anybody short of that needs to know how to present the material; not just know it, but understand how to present it so your students will be able to figure it out."

**Salary range:** $45,000-$60,000; tenured professors can make close to six figures.

**Name:** Marina Sturm

**Job:** Second clarinetist for the American Symphony Orchestra

**Studied:** Got her masters in music from Victoria University in New Zealand, and went to Stonybrook for a Ph.D. in performance.

**Responsibilities:** Performing with the ASO at about ten concerts a year, along with additional freelance work

**How she got her job:** Sturm, who comes from a musical family, has been performing since she was twelve. Most of her jobs were landed through auditions, but many, including her current position with the ASO, came through references. "If you're on the New York freelancing scene, no one cares if you send a resume and say 'Hey, I'm this big deal.' They're more concerned about colleagues recommending you and saying you're a good player."

**How you can get her job:** It's all about your attitude, explains Sturm. "Have a good attitude and people will want to work with you. You have to be a really good colleague. If you're a friendly person that shows up on time and plays great, they want you. It's all part of the package."

**Salary range:** $50,000-$80,000 for freelancers

**Name:** Shelli Silberman

**Job:** Music teacher at PS 135 in Queens Village, NY

**Studied:** Elementary education and music therapy at the University of Michigan, then got her masters at Hofstra

**Responsibilities:** "We learn very basic music, about low and high notes, about beat and melody," says Silberman. "I introduce them to some of the composers and the different groups of instruments. It's an outlet from their academic day. They really enjoy it and I try to make it fun."

**How she got her job:** A kindergarten teacher for fifteen years, Silberman always incorporated music into her curriculum. "I always had a piano in my room and my principal always heard us singing. There's another music teacher in our school who teaches the older children and the principal asked if I would like to teach the younger kids."

**How you can get her job:** "Keep on pursuing it and loving what you do," offers Silberman. "Prepare a really good portfolio with your work and references. Just be persistent."

**Salary range:** $40,000-$81,000

**Name:** Michael McDonald

**Job:** Artist manager for John Mayer and Ray LaMontagne; president of Dave Matthews' label, ATO Records

**Studied:** Double-majored in Portuguese and Latin American history at the University of Wisconsin, Madison

**Responsibilities:** Oversees all major business aspects of an artist's career, helping the artist execute his or her vision. "You're the hub in the wheel of the artist's career," says McDonald. "You deal with the attorney, the A&R person, the marketing, sales and promotion departments at the label, the agent who books the live shows, and so on. My job is to funnel all this information, present it to the artist, and let them get back to their creative space as soon as possible."

**How he got his job:** McDonald's degree may not be music-oriented, but his social circle certainly was. After a stint selling t-shirts for the Dave Matthews Band, he became DMB's tour manager. He was later introduced to Mayer by DMB producer John Alagia.

**How you can get his job:** "Get into music however you can," says McDonald. "The point of entry is less important than what you do with the opportunity. You never know who you're going to meet, and when, so put yourself in a position to make your 'lucky break' more likely."

**Salary range:** Since managers make their money as a commission on the artist's income, their salary can range from zero to high six-figures. "More often than not, the first year it's in the negative," says McDonald. "Hopefully things improve after that."


**Name:** Jenny Eliscu

**Job:** Contributing editor, *Rolling Stone*

**Studied:** I got my B.A. in English at Queens College, and stayed there another couple years for my masters, also in English.

**Responsibilities:** Interviewing artists and writing feature stories, reviews, news pieces, and so on. People always ask me if it's anything like the way the job is depicted in Cameron Crowe's *Almost Famous*, and I'm happy to say that it often is very similar—without the romantic subplot, of course. Journalists nowadays have considerably less access to artists than they did in the good ol' days when there weren't a zillion publicists and managers interfering. But the crux of the job is the same: Find an artist you're passionate about or intrigued by, get them to sit down with you (and, usually, a tape recorder) and ask them whatever you need to ask to figure out what makes them tick.

**How I got my job:** I worked for five years at a small publication called *CMJ New Music Monthly* as a writer and editor before I started working on staff at *Rolling Stone* in 1999.

**How you can get my job:** We probably sound like a broken record, but intern, intern, intern! There's no substitute for the connections you'll make by interning for a real magazine or newspaper. And, more importantly, just keep writing. Go to as many shows as you can, know your rock history, and try pitching reviews or feature articles to your local paper and/or college paper. The only way to become a good writer is to start off as a bad one and then keep writing until you find your voice.

**Salary range:** For freelance writers, it can vary wildly. With a staff gig, expect to start around $30,000. Top level editors make upwards of $200,000.


**Name:** Leigh Lust

**Job:** Vice president of A&R for Atlantic Records

**Studied:** Communications (radio, TV, and film) at New York University

**Responsibilities:** "Signing acts is first and foremost," says Lust, who signed Jet, the Avalanches, and Remy Zero, among others. "Once you sign them, you oversee everything from the choosing of the producer to the making of the record and mixing and mastering, and then you're instrumental in working with the label on marketing and radio. As the band progresses, it's your job to make sure the label understands the artist's vision. You're like a mother bearing a child." Lust says his favorite part of the job is going out to hear live music, and he does a lot of it: On average, he sees about twenty bands a week.

**How he got his job:** In the Eighties, Lust worked his way up from interning at his college's radio station, WNYU, to being music director. There, he developed a strong working relationship with his current boss, Craig Kallman. "It's important to hang out with likeminded people," he says. "There's always the chance one of 'em will get a job and lift the whole community with them."

**How you can get his job:** "You just gotta live it," Lust says. "Be as aggressive as possible about educating yourself so that you're hearing as much music as possible. Go out there and see shows, listen to college radio, or check out bands on MySpace.com or Purevolume. com. That's how you'll discover an artist before anybody else, and that's what makes you an asset to a label."

**Salary range:** A low-level A&R job can pay from $30-$40,000. Top A&R execs—the kind who sign their share of multiplatinum acts —can make as much as $700,000, or more.

—Arielle Baer and Jenny Eliscu

# Ann Arbor, MI

## UNIVERSITY OF MICHIGAN
1100 Baits Dr.
Ann Arbor, MI 48109
www.umich.edu

Everything about the University of Michigan is big—its enrollment, its campus, its reputation—and the School of Music is no exception, with about 1,000 students and expansive course offerings: concentrations include composition, musical theater, conducting, musicology, music theory, voice, jazz and improvisational studies, and performing arts technology. Within the bachelor of music program, students focus on the standard components of a performer's education, including composition, theory, and the mastering of a specific, traditional instrument such as piano, flute, or clarinet. The bachelor of fine arts degree is designed more for those looking to study music from an interdisciplinary perspective by integrating, for example, the study of dance, piano, and computer programming. U Mich also offers a bachelor of science in sound engineering.

The university's music program is one of its strongest academic departments, and here's where size does matter: because U Mich has more than 200 different degree programs, there is an almost unlimited array of interdisciplinary options for students who want to combine their music studies with other interests. In addition, with a university community this large comes a multitude of performances each year. The School of Music itself features more than 300 musical events per year, and the University Musical Society—a 120-year-old organization—hosts a variety of musical and theatrical acts as part of the longest-running performing arts series in the country. UMS frequently brings top-notch touring artists to Ann Arbor for master classes and residencies. Recent performers have included the Berlin Philharmonic, Philip Glass, Joshua Redman, the Guthrie Theatre Company, and the Lincoln Center Jazz Orchestra. And of course, Ann Arbor—with its quirky jazz clubs and eclectic coffee house scene—brings its own variety of musical education to those students fortunate enough to study here.

# VENUES:

### The Blind Pig, 208 S. 1st St.,
### www.blindpigmusic.com

Founded by University of Michigan students Tom Isaia and Jerry Delguidice in 1971, the Blind Pig has transformed from a blues café into Ann Arbor's foremost rock club. R.E.M., Sonic Youth, and 10,000 Maniacs all performed here during the mid-Eighties, and the Blind Pig was ahead of the curve in booking grunge groundbreakers such as Soundgarden, Pearl Jam, and Nirvana several years later. In fact, Kurt Cobain once told MTV that this was his favorite venue anywhere. Today, the dank dive-bar puts on shows by heavily buzzed indie and alt-rock acts (Straylight Run, Gore Gore Girls, Wolf Eyes), as well as welcoming local punk, hardcore, and hip-hop artists to its stage. Another perk at the Blind Pig: no backstage area means you're more likely to bump into the headliner during the course of the night.

### The Ark, 316 S. Main St.,
### www.theark.org

Located in the heart of downtown Ann Arbor, this forty-year-old venue is where folk, blues, and acoustic acts stop when they're passing through town: Arlo Guthrie, Ani DiFranco, and Emmylou Harris have all graced the Ark's stage, and recent shows starred Leo Kottke and the Blind Boys of Alabama. A non-profit organization that relies on corporate and individual endowments, the club holds about 400 fans, and offers an open mic night once a month.

### Hill Auditorium, 825 North University Ave.

Owned and operated by the university, the 4,000-capacity Hill Auditorium hosts performances by the school's many bands and orchestras, as well as guest performers and touring rock acts including Wilco and Bob Dylan. The auditorium, situated on U Mich's Central Campus, has stellar acoustics that make even the rock acts sound hoity-toity.

### The Michigan Theater, 603 E. Liberty St.,
### www.michtheater.org

This 1,700-seat auditorium was originally erected in 1928 as a vaudeville and movie house. In the Eighties, it was fully restored—

thanks to a series of hefty endowments—so that it would retain the old-world architectural grandeur it had in its heyday. In addition to showing an assortment of artsier films—recent showings included *Hotel Rwanda* and *Vera Drake*—in a screening room with its original, ornate balcony, the Michigan Theater puts on shows by sit-down acts such as Elvis Costello, Brian Wilson, and Brad Mehldau. The theater also still houses the historic Barton Theater Pipe Organ, which was designed to accompany silent movies in the late Twenties.

**The Necto, 516 E. Liberty St.,**
**www.thenecto.com**

The number-one spot in Ann Arbor to get your groove on, this posh nightclub features local, national and international DJs spinning techno, trance, and other varieties of electronic music. In the past, acclaimed artists including Paul Van Dyk, Kevin Saunderson, and Juan Atkins have brought their turntable skills to the Necto. And every Friday, the club hosts "Pride: The One and Only Gay Night."

## RECORD STORES:

**Encore Recordings, 417 East Liberty St., Ann Arbor,**
**www.encorerecordings.com**

Encore Recordings, located only a few blocks off the campus of the University of Michigan, is an absolute must-visit for anyone who loves music. The store specializes in used media: CDs, vinyl, DVDs, sheet music, reel-to-reel tapes, audiocassettes, and, yes, even 8-tracks. This place is a little overwhelming at first, even for the seasoned collector. It's stacked from floor-to-ceiling, front-to-back with both CDs and vinyl, broken down by genre and alphabetically organized. Browsing is tough due to the sheer volume, but never fear, this ain't a corporate big box with sales assistants who know less about music than your ninety-year-old great aunt. With a fifteen-person staff made up of several notable indie rockers, the experts behind the counter at Encore can help you navigate through the hundreds of thousands of titles (literally!). Encore buys anything they don't have, even if you think it's worthless, so bring something to sell or trade to lower that bottom line.

### Wazoo Records, 336 1/2 S. State St.

For an indie store that's easier to browse without preparation (and perspiration), stop into Wazoo. Located on the upper floor of a downtown building directly across the street from the University of Michigan campus, Wazoo mixes used and new CDs and vinyl. The hottest new bands are regularly stocked while the walls are lined with amusing rare vinyl, making it a great place for getting your mind off that pesky chemistry exam. Random Wazoo lore: The logo on the awning outside Wazoo resembles an R. Crumb drawing. When Andrew W.K. was living in Ann Arbor, he sent Wazoo's owner a phony letter from Crumb's attorney, complete with a hand-drawn cancellation from San Francisco on the stamp, threatening to sue.

### Schoolkids Records in Exile, 332 S. State St., www.schoolkids.com

Two floors below Wazoo, in a basement crammed with new CDs and vinyl, Schoolkids stocks loads of indie rock, local acts, hip-hop, and jazz. Overall, the store has the best prices for new CDs on campus, with most albums selling for well below list price.

### PJ's Records & Used CDs, 617 Packard St., Ste. B

PJ's is like the U of M family business: it was opened in 1980 by alums/brothers Marc and Jeff Taras, and fellow U of M grad P.J. Ryder. The large space, which Jeff describes as a "chaotic musical garage sale" offers the largest selection of vinyl on campus, and their stock includes plenty of indie rock, hip-hop, and jazz.

## RADIO:

### WCBN 88.3, www.wcbn.org

U of M's freeform radio station allows its student DJs to play pretty much whatever the hell they want, in three-hour blocks. Expect to hear genres melt together and bang up against each other, rather than listening to the same old recycled specialty shows.

# Athens, GA

## UNIVERSITY OF GEORGIA
250 River Rd.
Athens, GA 30602-7278
www.uga.edu

**A**thens, GA, the town that houses state school University of Georgia, has quite a bit of rock & roll cachet. The quirky town is known primarily as the home of rockers R.E.M., and the band still maintains its offices and headquarters here. So, apart from a bevy of music stores and clubs, members of R.E.M. scour the town for future success stories. For aspiring musicians, that means Athens is a town where you may gain some exposure. The University's music program—which boasts a "mix of university and conservatory"—allows students to earn either a bachelor of music or a bachelor of arts. For the former, students can concentrate in composition, education, music therapy, performance, or music theory. Intriguing electives include the History of Popular Music, which covers music from a range of cultures, or the more specific African-American Music course. There's also the History of Rock and Roll, which considers rock music of all eras but also focuses on the rich history of the Athens scene. Think R.E.M. will show up in the classroom? The music school also offers classes for the community, including a variety of workshops and programs, offering UGA students the opportunity to interact and perform with the local community.

## VENUES:

**40 Watt Club, 285 W. Washington St.,**
**www.40watt.com**

If Athens is the consummate college music town, then the fabulous 40 Watt is the Platonic ideal of a college town venue. Not only is it the best venue in Athens, it's one of the best in the Southeast as a whole. Located in a former furniture store, the club—currently at its sixth location—is spacious enough to be comfortable but small enough that there's still a sense you're privy to a truly special event when artists such as Flaming Lips, Bright Eyes, Cat Power, and the Strokes roll through. The bar can be too chatty for quieter shows—it seems whenever Vic Chesnutt plays, more people show up to talk about seeing the show than to actually see the show—but the sound at the club has improved, thanks especially to Dan Korn, who mans 40 Watt's boards.

### Caledonia Lounge, 256 W. Clayton St., www.caledonialounge.com

Ignore the word lounge, because the Caledonia is anything but plush and velvety. Tucked away behind a parking lot, an eclectic consignment/thrift store and a wrought-iron gate, this smallish venue only recently got around to putting up a sign, even though it has inhabited the location since 1999. The club is solid indie rock territory and was home to two previous incarnations of the 40 Watt. This is the place where R.E.M. shot their video for "Turn You Inside Out" back in 1988. Today, the Caledonia is where you'll catch acts making their first inroads at college radio—national acts such as the Wrens, the Decemberists and David Dondero have stopped through—as well as established-but-still-growing locals like Iron Hero, Astra, and Phosphorescent. The wooden picnic tables set up in the courtyard to the left of the Caledonia's entrance make for a pleasant de facto beer garden, prime for when the weather's right and the band's too loud.

### Flicker Bar & Theater, 263 W. Washington St., www.flickerbar.com

Flicker's two halves are separated by wall and by curtain (a surprisingly effective way of keeping musical performance chatter free, and vice versa), and the performance space of this local musicians' watering hole seats a little more than thirty. Despite its size, Flicker is able to attract a stunning array of talent, including national acts such as Drive-By Truckers and local up-and-comers such as Circulatory System. Members of the waning Elephant 6 collective spend time communing here—from both sides of the bar—and the art on Flicker's walls has a strong chance of becoming your next favorite album cover. If your tastes tend more towards the accordion than the flying-V, swing by Flicker. Bartender Don Chambers, by the way, is one of Athens' most underrated songwriters, and deals out tales of whiskey, heartbreak, and woe with his banjo.

### Georgia Theater, 215 N. Lumpkin St., www.georgiatheater.com

If you watched MTV at all over the past couple of years, you saw John Mayer's video for "No Such Thing." And that means you've already seen the marquee for the Georgia Theater. What started as a movie theater in 1935 evolved into a music venue in the late seventies, right around the time the Athens music scene started kicking. The Theater, as it's succinctly known around town, is where Athens' biggest shows go down. Recent headliners have included David Byrne and former Athenians Sound Tribe Sector 9, with bills catering most frequently to the country-rock and hippie-jam audiences. A stroll past the famous marquee often offers a whiff of beer, patchouli, or something a little more pungent.

### Go Bar, 195 Prince Ave.

What's Athenian for hipster? While in most smaller cities the term "townie" is simply shorthand for the born-and-raiseds, 'round here it's used to denote the Eighties-T-shirt-and-shaggy-hair set. No place caters to this crowd better than Go, located in—oh the irony!—a former thrift store. The small bar with the surprisingly enticing blue pillar lights specializes in weekly events, from indie rock karaoke to DJs spinning international hip-hop or electroclash. High-profile locals (members of I Am the World Trade Center or Macha, for instance) often assume the reigns, matching tunes with the bar's resident burlesque troupe.

### Tasty World, 312 E. Broad St., www.tastyworld.net

Like many businesses here, this downtown club borrows its name from an earlier institution; Tasty World was an early-'Eighties Athens music magazine. Since 1997, the club has consistently boasted Athens' most diverse array of acts. Upstairs is as varied as it comes, ranging from weekly jazz events to experimental video/music sampling to private parties. Downstairs, things go a little more predictably along college rock lines, although anything from bluegrass to rap to metal is possible. Tasty World's sound guys like to turn the volume UP, and when the bass gets kicking, the setup works to the venue's disadvantage, but it's nice to know there's a spot in town actively cultivating multiple audiences.

**Tight Pockets, Northeast corner of Hancock St. and Pope St., www.tightpockets.org**

Though the name comes from a poolhall that once occupied the humble brick building, the phrase Tight Pockets applies well to the overarching low-budget aesthetic of this under-underground DIY/ punk venue. The Tight Pockets group is close-knit, but also strongly community-minded; you'll find the singer of Friday night's screamo five-piece offering up her floor as sleepspace to Saturday's touring band and distributing food to the homeless with the local Food Not Bombs chapter come Sunday morning. Tight Pockets lacks the more traditional venue trappings (PA systems, a stage, legal permits, etc.) so the best way to find out about a show is to look for flyers around town.

**X-Ray Café 261 W. Washington St.**

X-Ray is so much more than just a café. It's also an experimental music venue, and all-purpose hangout for eccentric owner/musician/ artist Paul Thomas, and a store with a labyrinthine collection of books, records, and miscellaneous crap. If you're down with the idea of a dude tapping a cymbal and making clicky noises with a laptop while a randomly spliced montage of 8mm video spools in the background, this is the spot for you. Performers at the X-Ray range from young locals like Green Lawns stepping out of the bedroom for the first time to internationally prominent artists off Chicago's Kranky label. As with anything experimental, a success rate is sketchy and unpredictable; while the final product may not be the most accessible music, it's the process of creating it that appeals to X-Ray regulars.

# RECORD STORES:

**Low Yo Yo Stuff Records, 285 W. Washington St., www.lowyoyostuff.com**

Squeezed into an area the size of a large kitchen, this record store takes full advantage of every possible nook and cranny. Because it's adjacent to the 40 Watt, Low Yo Yo caters to a show-going crowd— you're more likely to find the place open at 2 A.M. than you are at 2 P.M. Overall, it's a great place for music geeks to shop: The categories make sense, you can listen to pretty much any album, the staff's excellent about special orders, and the store has a huge selection of hard-to-find bootlegs and box sets.

### Schoolkids Records, 264 E. Clayton St., www.schoolkidsrecords.com/athens.html

The Athens location of this North Carolina-based indie chain still uses those annoying plastic holder things to display all their CDs, but that's okay—the huge selection more than makes up for it. Staffed primarily by local musicians—is there ever a day when Glands guitarist and Schoolkids manager Ross Shapiro isn't working?—Schoolkids has downtown Athens' healthiest hip-hop selection as well as the newest in mainstream stuff. And, to lure in release-day business, Schoolkids has regular Tuesday sales on used CDs and jazz albums. Nice!

### Wuxtry Records, 197 E. Clayton St., www.wuxtryrecords.com/athens.html

Not only is this where R.E.M.'s Michael Stipe first met Peter Buck (who was clerking at the store at the time), but it's managed to maintain its indie rock cred over the years: The Olivia Tremor Control's John Fernandes is just about the happiest guy you'll ever meet, and the fact that Wuxtry's got him on as a full-time clerk is one of the longtime downtown record store's major selling points. Competitively priced and offering a broad selection of CDs and vinyl, Wuxtry's also stocks videos, DVDs, and random memorabilia. Though the store—for some strange reason—moved its local selection into a glass case, Wuxtry is still the best place to find the record of a band whose show you caught last night. Ask the clerks about Extra Records, the new Wuxtry annex over by the 40 Watt where they sell vinyl by the pound. And check out Wuxtry's Athens Music Museum on the corner to ogle posters and such relating to the B-52's, Pylon, Neutral Milk Hotel, Love Tractor, Widespread Panic, and other Athens scene luminaries.

## RADIO STATIONS:

### WUOG 90.5 FM, www.wuog.org

Although it's fairly ridiculous, staffers at the University of Georgia's radio station like to affectionately pronounce the name of their mouthpiece "woo-og." Many a local musician, writer and scene heavyweight got started sifting through 90.5's bins and pulling 4 A.M. DJ shifts, and it's a testament to the town's musical vitality that WUOG has such a strong presence. The jocks absolutely kill it when it comes to enthusiasm, often promoting downtown shows with ticket giveaways. Every Tuesday and Thursday WUOG puts together "Live in the Lobby," a show focusing on local acts; also check "Sounds of the City" and "Odd Man Out" for excellent Athenscentric and gynocentric music, respectively.

**WUGA 91.7/97.9 FM,**
**www.wuga.org**

Also based out of UGA, Athens' home for National Public Radio goes for an older crowd than WUOG. In addition to national programming, the station has a strong local focus. From its "Invitation to Jazz" program to its "Athens New Matters" local talk roundup, WUGA's programming is as diverse as it is well thought out. Listen out for the special treat that is "Just Off the Radar"; curated by local radio host, writer, and promoter JoE Silva, the hour-long program's like getting a brilliant mixtape from your eclectic best friend—but augmented by commentary, live performances, interviews, and other surprises.

# MISCELLANEOUS EVENTS:

**Athfest,**
**www.athfest.com**

The local music and arts festival celebrates its tenth year in 2006. While the daytime offers attendees a chance to eat corndogs and funnel cakes, check out art, and listen to musicians and scene folk give panel discussions, the real treat of Athfest is the benefit of the wristband. For less than the price of a new CD, you'll gain entry to all participating clubs over the three-day period, giving you the chance to check out more than 100 bands. Though Athfest primarily features Athens bands, Atlanta-based and regional acts will occasionally snag a slot. Every year, Athfest and local Ghostmeat Records release a compilation CD that's guaranteed to contain some treasures; if you've got a spare coupla dollars, pick up some of the past ones for exclusive B-sides and the like.

**Nuçi's Space, 396 Oconee St.,**
**www.nuci.org**

Although officially called a "musician's resource space," it's hard to pin down Nuçi's Space. When Athens musician Nuçi Phillips took his own life in 1996, his mother Linda decided to honor his memory by creating an establishment that would give back to the music community. Since 2000, Nuçi's Space has served as an invaluable part of the scene, offering musicians counseling, legal aid, affordable practice and performance space. Unlike anything else in the country, Nuçi's Space is the epitome of what creates community. Stop by. Volunteer. Love music and those who make it.

*— Chris Hassiotis*

# Atlanta, GA

## EMORY UNIVERSITY
1804 North Decatur Rd.
Atlanta, GA 30322
www.emory.edu

Unlike many distinguished liberal arts colleges, Emory does not offer the option of receiving a bachelor of music. However, students pursuing a bachelor of arts in music have access to many of the same perks as B.M. students do at other schools: private instruction, ensemble performances, and background course work in music history, theory and literature. (Students working toward a jazz or guitar concentration within the major have additional require ments.) Individual lessons are free—whereas many other universities charge extra. Emory's music program is serious, and is well designed for similarly serious music students, but the school also ensures that those dabbling in the subject are able to do so. Seminars of interest to the casual student have included topics like Performing Shakespeare's Music, Music of India, and The Beatles: Form, Style, and Culture.

# VENUES:

### Eddie's Attic, 515-B McDonough St., www.eddiesattic.com

Quite possibly, John Mayer owes his career to this club, where as an upcoming singer/songwriter, he often tested out new tunes, as well as his arsenal of contorted facial expressions. It's the place to be if you want to hear a lot of acoustic six-string strumming and earnest, heart-on-the-sleeve emoting. Plus, a weekly open-mic night gives you the chance to both catch a rising star and maybe even become one.

### Variety Playhouse, 1099 Euclid Ave., www.variety-playhouse.com

Located in quirky, boho Little Five Points (L5P for those in the know), this club, which has hosted Death Cab for Cutie, Sleater-Kinney, Bright Eyes, Magnetic Fields, and the Arcade Fire, is quite simply one of the best places to hear live music in Atlanta. It feels cozy and never cramped with a balcony, a floor seating area, and a place to stand in front of the stage. And the great acoustics make you feel like you're listening to the show on your iPod.

### MJQ Concourse, 736 Ponce de Leon Ave., www.mjqatlanta.com

This club is so underground that it's literally located beneath a parking lot. You enter through what looks like a backyard shed, then you descend down some scary, worn steps, hoping you won't be buried alive. Once inside, however, the fun begins. DJs, depending on the night, pump out everything from Brit-pop to deep house, and when you see professional rockers like Jet boogying on the dancefloor following their show, you'll feel like a wimp for being so scared to come inside.

### Roxy Theater, 3110 Roswell Rd., www.atlantaconcerts.com

It seems that nearly every city has a Roxy, but this one is special because it's housed in an old Art Deco movie palace located in Atlanta's ritzy, bustling Buckhead neighborhood. Keane, Interpol, and the Scissor Sisters have all done their thing at this theater, which holds about 1,000, including some upstairs in the balcony. One great feature is the club's slanted floor, which means that just about any spot in the house is a decent one.

### Swayze's Venue, 2543 Bells Ferry Rd., #650 Marietta, www.swayzesvenue.com

Despite its movie star namesake, this suburban hub for all things hardcore, emo, and death metal—located about thirty miles outside of the city—doesn't feature any dirty dancing. In fact, all of the club's pictures of Patrick Swayze have long since been ripped from the walls. But, not surprisingly, that hasn't stopped the club from pulling in crowds of kids who are anxious to rock out.

### Apache Café, 64 Third St., www.apache.info

If you're into neo-soul, this is a spot that you immediately want to add to your mental cache of favorite places. Not only will you get to see R&B up-and-comers, you can also find big guns like Erykah Badu, India.Arie, and Jill Scott showing up for impromptu, down-low gigs. The cozy club serves a menu of tacos, burritos, and quesadillas, and also hosts art shows, spoken-word performances, and open mic nights.

### Club 112, 1055 Peachtree St NE

"112, where the playas dwell," the Notorious B.I.G. once spit in a rhyme, immortalizing this infamous hip-hop nightspot. It has recently changed locations from a grungy, remote strip mall to a warehouse-like compound in trendy Midtown. But the party is still jumping; the lines are still long; and more lyrical shout-outs are likely to come.

### Drunken Unicorn, 736 Ponce de Leon Place, www.thedrunkenunicorn.net

Adjacent to the MJQ, this small room offers some of the best underground rock shows for all ages at really cheap prices ($5-$10). It's the place to see under-the-radar national acts like Cex, Panther, and Death From Above, 1979, plus hordes of local punk, garage, and alternative bands. If you are—or aspire to be—cool in a trendsetting, indie rock kind of way, you need to make this your home away from home away from home.

### The Earl, 488 Flat Shoals Ave.,
### www.badearl.com

This is one of those spots that obviously wasn't originally designed to be a rock club. The stage is in the corner of what feels like a back room and it only stands a few feet from the floor. But somehow this works, making you feel like you're actually a part of the show. The music is good and loud; the energy is high; and if you can avoid one of the foundational beams in the room, the sight lines are pretty good.

### The Fox Theater, 660 Peachtree St. NE,
### www.foxtheater.org

Ever wanted to rock in a certified National Historic Landmark? The Fox Theater gives you that chance with shows by acts such as the Pixies, Wilco, and Jane's Addiction. Originally designed as a mosque in the 1920s, the Fox, which is a structural mix of ornate domes, arches, and temples, plays host to touring Broadway productions and vintage and current films when it's not being used for concerts.

### Lenny's, 307 Memorial Dr.

A bonafide rock & roll dive bar, Lenny's is entirely unpretentious yet full of character and attitude. The set-up is simple: a bar, a pool table, an outdoor patio, and a smallish stage/dancefloor. Lenny's features live music Thursday through Saturday and karaoke and DJ sets (hip-hop, break beat) during the week.

### Tabernacle, 152 Luckie St.,
### www.atlantaconcerts.com

Another of Atlanta's best venues, the Tabernacle can be found downtown in a cathedral-like building that was once a proper church. Everything about this place is elegantly quirky and cool, from its sprawling staircase to its hanging black and white vintage rock & roll photos to its exotic collection of art, tapestries and rugs displayed throughout the building. The club is full of interesting nooks and crannies, but the concerts by acts such as Yellowcard, Ryan Adams, Elton John, and Morrissey take place in "the Sanctuary." Overlooking the room is a massive balcony where even more people can gather in this grand house of musical worship.

### 10 High, 816 N. Highland Ave., www.tenhighclub.com

This basement joint, beneath the Dark House Tavern in Atlanta's upscale but artsy Virginia-Highlands neighborhood, offers a spot to catch young, scrappy, and scruffy local rock bands. One of the club's best features is what it calls "Metal-some Mondays," where you can live out your hair-band fantasies—karaoke-style—in front of a live band.

### Vision, 1068 Peachtree St. NE, www.visionatlanta.com

What do Usher, Andre 3000, Nelly, P. Diddy, and Ludacris have in common? In addition to being some of the biggest names in rap and R&B, they have all partied at Vision—singularly the premier place to stargaze in Atlanta. With its white walls, glowing fluorescent lights, and shining red and blue bars, the club, which occupies an almost block-long chunk of Midtown, resembles one of those sleek, minimalist nightspots that you most often see on TV and in movies. There's a massive dancefloor, several intimate lounge areas, and a stage where you can catch performances by acts such as Floetry and Young Buck.

### Chastain Amphitheater, 4469 Stella Dr.

Less a basic music venue than a full-blown cultural phenomenon, this outdoor amphitheater becomes one massive picnic site during its summer concert series. Ticket holders arrive hoisting giant coolers and big bags of gear from which they set up elaborate dining tables complete with candles, tablecloths, real silverware, and a wide assortment of food not normally found at concerts: steamed lobster, shrimp cocktail, barbecued ribs. It can be fun chowing down while watching folks like Elvis Costello, Alicia Keys, Norah Jones, and Mary J. Blige, but there's one major caveat. When it rains—which it often does during Atlanta's long steamy summers—there's no shelter from the storm. You'll get drenched; your food will become soup; and the show will go on with no refunds.

# RECORD STORES:

### Criminal Records, 466 Moreland Ave. NE, www.criminal.com

Yeah, this sounds corny, but it really would be a crime to miss out on this store, which has the best indie rock selection in the city. The prices are competitive; the abundant staff is knowledgeable; and the store also carries a full line of DVDs (including hard-to-find artsy and foreign fare), comic books (from underground stuff to the more traditional dudes-in-spandex), and magazines (from music 'zines to imported fashion rags). One more plus? Criminal often hosts free outdoor concerts by groups such as the Polyphonic Spree.

### Earwax Records, 565 Spring St. # 200

Centrally located downtown, this is a retail shrine to the music that drives Atlanta hip-hop and R&B. The shop offers a full selection of the latest CD and vinyl 12-inch releases. Plus, you can also cop the hottest DJ mixtapes and, if you're an aspiring producer or rare grooves type, you can browse the extensive selection of used vinyl soul oldies.

### Ed's Records, 1875 Piedmont Ave., www.edsrecords.com

So, you were at a dance club on Saturday night, heard a hot song, and now you want to find a dozen mixes of it. This is the place to go, especially for more mainstream fare. The store carries both vinyl and CDs, and the staff lets you listen before you buy.

### Moods Music, 1130 Euclid Ave., www.moodsmusic.net

Atlanta boasts a strong underground neo-soul scene and this is singularly the best place to buy the music. The store—located in an indoor urban bazaar—stocks a limited but impressive range of independent and foreign releases that you're unlikely to find at any other shop in the city. And the way the CDs are displayed, tucked into a web of metal wiring, makes you feel like you've stepped into a funky military camp.

**Satellite Records, 421 Moreland Ave. NE,**
**www.satellite-records.com**

Trance, techno, electro, tribal, deep house, drum and bass, progressive: this store stocks an impressive array of the latest releases on vinyl. (Beware: the CD selection is paltry.) There are listening stations so that you can try before you buy, and the shop also carries record bags, needles, headphones, and just about everything else you need to live out your turntablist dreams.

**Tower Records, 3232 Peachtree Rd., Suite B,**
**www.towerrecords.com**

You love Franz Ferdinand; your roommate digs T.I.; and her friend gets all hot for Kenny Chesney. Tower is one of the few places where you can all find what you're looking for. They boast the largest selection of CDs across genres (including reggae, jazz, blues, and classical) and they're open pretty late if you need a post-library music fix.

**Wax 'n Facts, 432 Moreland Ave. NE**

Almost every city has a dark, dusty used record store full of treasures and this is Atlanta's. Overstuffed crates of oldies—from all genres—cover the tables and floor, and if you're trying to kick it Eighties-style, there's a whole wall of used cassettes. In addition to the back-'n-the-day stuff, the store also has a small selection of new vinyl, as well as, used rock books and CDs.

## RADIO STATIONS:

**WRAS 88.5,**
**www.wras.org**

With a playlist including the Futureheads, Elliot Smith, the Fiery Furnaces, and Parker and Lily, this station, run by current Georgia State University students, is the best place to hear new indie rock. Specialty programs at night and on weekends provide a dose of everything from Japanese music to reggae.

**WREK 91.1,**
**www.wrek.org**

Transmitting from the Georgia Tech campus, WREK offers perhaps the most eclectic mix of music by showcasing classic rock, new wave, blues, world music, spoken word. The station also transmits live over the Internet.

**WNNX 99.7,**
**www.99x.com**

99x, the area's leading new rock station, plays all of the usual suspects: Green Day, the Killers, Snow Patrol, Interpol, Jimmy Eat World, etc., but a weekly show called "Sunday School" veers off the main road with imports, album cuts, and local music. And, if you need to bone up on your rock history, there's a daily hour of Nineties alternative and weekly serving of Eighties new wave.

## MISCELLANEOUS EVENTS:

**Music Midtown,**
**www.musicmidtown.com**

This three-day, outdoor festival—recently moved from spring to summer—allows you to see more than 100 bands for about fifty bucks. Each year, it draws 300,000-plus people to a forty-acre area behind the Atlanta Civic Center. OutKast, No Doubt, Fountains of Wayne, Joss Stone, Hoobastank, Courtney Love, and Twista have all played here, making it one of Atlanta's coolest events.

*—Craig Seymour*

# Austin, TX

## UNIVERSITY OF TEXAS, AUSTIN
John Hargis Hall
Austin, TX 78712-1157
www.utexas.edu

**U**T is the largest single-campus university in the U.S., with 52,000 students occupying its sprawling terrain. The university is not known for its music department, but the lure is the city itself—one of the best music towns in the country, behind New York, Los Angeles, and Chicago. A relatively affordable public institution, UT is worth the cost of admission just to be in Austin every March, when the South-by-Southwest music and film festival brings hundreds of up-and-coming artists to town for four nights of rock & roll, country, punk, bluegrass and jazz.

UT does, however, offer a strong music program that awards a bachelor of music in the categories of performance, composition and music studies. The latter is designed to train students who want to become music teachers, or to pursue careers in music therapy or the music business at large. The music studies major is a performance-intensive program, requiring four semesters of training on an instrument as well as classes in conducting, ensemble work and either choral music or instrumental music techniques.

The university includes a Center for American Music whose stated goal is to "advance the teaching, scholarship, and performance of American music from all traditions, including concert, folk and popular musics." The Center began in 2002, but it already has big plans to start up new programs in recording technology, music business and to launch a University of Texas record label. Since the Center opened, new classes offered by UT's music department have taught about the history of Texas music, taking advantage of the school's access to archival recordings and photos from the Center for American History.

UT's communications program includes a Radio, Television and Film Department whose course offerings include Radio Station

Management—a business class that teaches about regulatory developments, the role of audience research and radio formatics, among other aspects of the field. Another RTF course worth waiting for is called Gender and Rock Culture; the class description cautions that "music and song lyrics will not be our only or primary objects of study," but rather offers a socio-cultural approach to examining how gender constructions in the world at large have affected rock and pop music.

## VENUES:

### Emos, 603 Red River,
### www.emosaustin.com

Emos, which is located downtown, off of Sixth Street, is Austin's most reliable source for great live shows, cheap drinks, and hipster eye-candy. Seven days a week, the venue hosts national and/or up-and-coming regional punk rock, indie rock, electronica, and new wave acts. It's not unusual to see Blonde Redhead one night, followed by De La Soul the next night. This is also the club where bands such as Spoon and You Will Know Us By The Trail of Dead got their start. The bigger stage is technically outdoors, but sheltered by a patio that keeps it suitably dark. The smaller stage is in the club's front room, which is spacious enough for the crowd that storms Austin during South by Southwest to see acts such as Pretty Girls Make Graves. Between the two halves of the club is a courtyard where you can take a break from the music, grab a beer at yet another one of Emos' bars, or just sit at a picnic table and scope out your fellow indie rockers. There's definitely a strong sense of community at Emos, and most nights it's hard to pick out who's actually in the band, who's a patron, and who works there. It's also the only all-ages venue downtown, so make sure you check her ID before you bring home a girl you met at the Death Cab for Cutie show.

### Stubbs BBQ, 801 Red River,
### www.stubbsaustin.com

Stubbs doubles as one of Austin's best tourist-friendly BBQ joints. (Mmmmm... Pulled pork po'boy!) The outdoor portion is pretty huge, so it's perfect for acts as diverse as the Pixies and Keith Urban. Those shows can get a bit pricey, but the sound and sight-lines are consistently great. Bands on their way up tend to play on the other stage, which is in a small room (with a bar) downstairs that has the vibe of a rustic old cabin. The constant smell of BBQ doesn't hurt, either. During SXSW, this is where the biggest and best parties usually happen. And, if you don't feel like eating BBQ, there's an amazing Mexican joint across the street called Jaime's that serves the most sinfully cheesy plates imaginable, for real cheap.

### The Continental Club, 1315 South Congress Ave.

The Continental Club has been around since the late Fifties, and not a lot about it has changed. The first thing you notice when you arrive is the cadre of classic cars parked in front. Inside, the club still has pretty much all of its original artwork, which makes for a unique blend of swank and punk. There are even the remains of a shoeshine station, and a motorcycle hanging from the wall. Here you'll find a mix of tattooed greasers, Bettie Page-hairdos, blue-collar townies, and college kids all listening to live retro roots, country, rockabilly, swing, bluesy rock, and alt-country music on a nightly basis.

### Antone's, 213 West 5th St., www.antones.net

One of the more historical venues—and one of the best-sounding ones in town—Antone's is Austin's home of the blues, and they showcase plenty of rock and country, too. This is the club that helped give birth to such acts as Stevie Ray Vaughan and Doug Sahm. These days are a bit more eclectic: On an average week you can catch Buckwheat Zydeco, Eric Johnson, Lucinda Williams, and Evan Dando all under the same roof.

### The Back Room, 2015 East Riverside Dr., www.backrm.com

Heavy Metal is alive and breathing in the heart of Texas. If you were aching to see that Jackyll reunion or felt like you were missing something if you didn't see Dangerous Toys in '92, now's your chance. Also home to some of the best-named local acts, just in case you're wondering what Front Butt or the Oklahomos sound like.

### Austin Music Hall/The Backyard, 208 Nueces St., www.austinmusichall.com

Located on the outskirts of Austin, the Austin Music Hall hosts big-time stars such as David Bowie and Bob Dylan. The Backyard, which is basically just the Hall's, um, backyard is a sweet place to see an outdoor show once the weather heats up. It holds about 4,000 people, but make sure to get there on the early side, because parking is a bitch.

## RECORD STORES:

### Waterloo Records, 600A North Lamar, www.waterloorecords.com

There aren't a lot of record stores in Austin anymore and one of the reasons is because Waterloo is all you need. Think Empire Records meets High Fidelity. You can find almost anything you're looking for: new and used CDs, vinyl, imports, DVDs, magazines, and even those kitschy Kelly Osbourne dolls. The selection is impressive and so are the really nice hipster music geeks who work there. Its also really easy to find what you're looking since everything is placed alphabetically and not by genre. That way you don't have to be embarrassed when looking for that Hilary Duff CD that's "for your girlfriend." The best part of Waterloo, though, is the in-stores. Most popular acts that roll thru town with a new album end up playing a free afternoon show at Waterloo, or at the least, a record signing. One of the first weeks I moved here, I saw Elliott Smith put on an in-store and they had to turn away hundreds of screaming fans. And before you leave you can buy your concert tix to most any show in town.

### Sound On Sound, 106 E. North Loop Blvd.

Austin's newest record shop resembles an old school mom-and-pop operation. Though it's closer to the size of an office cubicle than a store, this place has the one thing most lack: Passion. Looking through the collection of new and used vinyl, you get that electric feeling of scavenging for records at a garage sale and finding gold. Genre is thrown out the window as that Kiss picture disc you've been looking for is snuggled up against a rare Miles Davis.

### Cheapo Discs, 914 North Lamar Blvd., www.cheapotexas.com

Just as important as where to buy your music is where to sell it. Everyone needs beer money and to this day, I still haven't found a CD that Cheapo wouldn't buy from me. Hell, one time I think I sold them a half-cracked empty case for a quarter. You can also kill a few hours going through their flea-market-style bins of thousands of used CDs and DVDs. One man's trash is another man's treasure.

## RADIO STATIONS:

**KVRX 91.7FM,**
**www.kvrx.org**

Student-run from the ground up, KVRX is so punk rock that it doesn't even have its own station. It shares the frequency with KOOP, which lords over the day shift. The music is eclectic and the DJs are... well, they're learning. KVRX also hosts on-air concerts by "buzz" bands in their studio every Sunday. And since they're only on the air at night, they're allowed to be a lot bawdier than daytime jocks.

**KGSR 107.1FM,**
**www.kgsr.com**

Alongside Waterloo Records, the other famous Austin staple is KGSR. Their playlist ranges from folk to country to alternative rock. They tend to use their own judgment when it comes to what they play, support local music, and play a big hand in community events, from sponsoring shows to promoting music and arts festivals to donating time and money to hundreds of worthwhile causes. Even better is their ability to book celebrity on-air performances and interviews from such artists as Elvis Costello and R.E.M..

**KROX 101.5,**
**www.krox.com**

Most of the time, KROX is your average "new alternative station," which means it pretty much plays the same hard-edged modern rock as everyone else. But every Sunday, 101X showcases the best in local and new music. This is your chance to hear that new Franz Ferdinand song three months before the album is released, or some weird demo that never has—and maybe never will—come out as a record. This is where you'll find the band you'll be telling your friends about, smarty pants.

## MISCELLANEOUS ATTRACTIONS:

**South By Southwest,**
**www.sxsw.com**

SXSW is supposed to be a music industry convention, but it's oh-so-much more than that. For four nights every March, hundreds of bands from around the country descend on Austin, playing shows in any corner of town where they can find or build a stage. During the day, record biz types mill around getting drunk on someone else's dime at various barbecues and afternoon showcases. At night, downtown bustles with activity as strains of rock, country, punk, met blues, folk, jazz—you name it—fill the sidewalks outside the venues. It will cost you a few hundred bucks to buy a laminate that will get you into any show you want (provided you get there early enough or are willing to wait in line), but the price of admission will get you a year's worth of music in one blur of a weekend.

*—Jeff Klein*

# Baltimore, MD

## JOHNS HOPKINS UNIVERSITY
The Peabody Institute
One East Mount Vernon Pl.
Baltimore, MD 21202
www.peabody.jhu.edu

**M**usic students at Johns Hopkins come in many forms. Because the University as a whole does not offer a bachelor of arts degree in music, students must choose from one of several options: enroll at the Peabody Institute and study music full-time, pursue one of Johns Hopkins' rigorous dual degree programs and study music in addition to another subject, or enroll as a Johns Hopkins student and dabble in courses from the Peabody Institute but leave thoughts of a liberal arts degree in music behind. Keep in mind that students interested in the dual-degree options must be accepted to both the School of Arts and Sciences or the School of Engineering, AND the Peabody Institute. The Institute also offers, to a particularly qualified group of music students, a five-year bachelor of music and masters of music dual-degree program. Those undergraduates who are deemed qualified are given the option of completing both degrees with only one additional year of study.

Peabody undergraduates pursue the bachelor of music degree and concentrate in one of several areas including keyboard instruments, early music instruments, voice, and composition. Some students, who take the accompanying education courses, can graduate with a degree in music education combined with a Performer's Certificate.

One of the most compelling of the Peabody Institute's offerings is the school's bachelor of music in Recording Arts and Sciences program. This relatively unique double-major program (the Peabody/ Hopkins degree) combines course work and requirements from the Peabody bachelor of music program with courses in the Recording Arts and Sciences department. In addition, relevant courses in subjects like electrical engineering and math are taken at Johns Hopkins' G.W.C. Whiting School of Engineering. So basically this is a music, recording arts, and engineering program all rolled into one. Students are encouraged to intern in the fields they are training to enter such as radio production, television, and recording technology.

## VENUES:

**The Ottobar, 2549 N. Howard,**
**www.theottobar.com.**

This lower Charles Village club, located a few blocks south of Johns Hopkins, is Baltimore's hipster haunt for all stripes of live music. From the indie rock of Deerhoof and Secret Machines to the backpack hip-hop of Jean Grae and Grand Buffet, from the hardcore of Senses Fail and Kylesa to the electronic motion of Solex and Baltimore's own Cex, the Ottobar is a friend to the guitar and the laptop, the turntable and the drum machine. The Ottobar's ample concert room holds up to 450 people, but it really only packs that many bodies in when marquee names such rapper Slick Rick, college-radio fave Blonde Redhead, or underground metal heavyweight Dillinger Escape Plan hit the stage.

### Talking Head, 203 Davis St.,
### www.talkingheadclub.com

Tucked away off a side street in downtown Baltimore, a few blocks north of the Inner Harbor tourist trap, the Talking Head is kind of like the Ottobar's little brother. Located in same space where the Ottobar opened in 1996, the Talking Head has remodeled the space into a lively alternative club for smaller national touring bands, local indie rock bills, and those flowerings of avant noise-rock that don't need a big club to sound in-brain close. Monday nights at the Talking Head are devoted to Taxidermy Lodge, an indie rock dance party that starts working for the weekend as the week itself has just begun.

### Sonar, 407 E. Saratoga,
### www.sonar.us

Modeled on the expansive dance clubs of Chicago, Los Angeles, and New York, Sonar is a big-city venue with Charm City's homey vibe. In essence three dance floors housed in one former industrial downtown building, Sonar brings in global DJs to spin drum'n'bass, techno, house, trance, jungle, and every new style bubbling out of DJ booths from Montreal to London, Berlin to San Francisco. Sonar's large room with the bumping system has sweated to the sounds of Scott Henry, hometown hero Charles Feelgood, Goldie, and Aphrodite, as well as DJ and MC acrobatics from Kid Koala, the Invisibl Skratch Piklz' Q-Bert, and MC Skillz.

### Sidebar Tavern, 218 E. Lexington,
### www.sidebartavern.com

The Sidebar Tavern is Baltimore's home of punk rock, from '77 revivalists and psychobilly freak-outs to hardcore metal heads. A long room with the bar running along one side and the stage at the far end, the Sidebar is a haven for local and regional punk bands just entering the East Coast club circuit and seasoned veterans such as the U.K. Subs and Iron Cross' Sab Gray. Just don't let the leather jackets and tattoos scare you off. The Sidebar is home to some of the friendliest clientele with facial piercings and studded wristbands you'll ever meet.

### Funk Box, 10 E. Cross St.,
### www.thefunkbox.com

Don't let the name fool you. Though the Funk Box sounds like a place that's gonna smell like a boy's locker room, it's one of the swankiest clubs in town. The club remodeled two adjoining rowhouses in the Federal Hill neighborhood just south of the Inner Harbor into an upscale place to catch the likes of Raphael Saadiq, southern-fried rockers North Mississippi Allstars, emerging singer/songwriters such as Donovan Frankenreiter, and party-ready bands from Robert Walters 20th Congress to Big Bad Voodoo Daddy. All shows are eighteen and over, and the Funk Box boasts Baltimore's only "spring-loaded dance floor," something you won't notice until a crowd really starts jumping up and down.

### Rams Head Live, 20 Market Pl., www.ramsheadlive.com.

Baltimore's newest live-music hall is a multi-level, futuristic expanse of sleek comfort. Tucked into the weekend nightlife corridor called Power Plant Live, across the street from the Inner Harbor, Rams Head Live is a 1,400-capacity hall for big-name national touring acts. Its two bars, numerous flat-panel monitors, and balcony space with unobstructed sight lines make it a ideal venue for the older crowd that comes for grassroots singer/songwriter Phil Vassar, honky-tonk hero Robert Earl Keen, and blues legend B.B. King. But it also brings in a few cool-kid acts like indie-country vixen Neko Case, the Constantines, and the roof-raising antics of George Clinton and the P-Funk Allstars.

### Fletcher's, 701 S. Bond St., www.fletchersbar.com

This Fells Point bar with a small upstairs concert stage caters primarily to a rotating cast of local rock bands with its Monday night, local-radio station-sponsored "Noise in the Basement" series. But Fletcher's has also been the entry stage for buzz bands coming through Baltimore on their early tours. The Darkness threw their guitars into the air at Fletcher's, and Van Hunt got down in the joint before his 2004 debut album even came out. If you're coming on a Friday or Saturday night plan to arrive early. Weekend Fell's Point parking is extremely limited during the school year.

### Charm City Space, 1749 Maryland Ave., www.ccspace.org

Even in little American cities that lack youth-oriented clubs, the punk or indie rock show still happens somewhere—be it at the pizza parlor, the coffee shop, the community recreation center, a Unitarian church, or somebody's basement. A gaggle of enterprising Baltimore DIY twentysomethings got together and decided to have that space without all that other stuff. The Charm City Space is a collective-run art gallery with a basement performance space that reaches out to the punk, emo, indie-folk, and rock bands running through the Philadelphia, PA, to Richmond, VA, corridor, as well as under-the-radar national bands such as the Thermals, and Washington's girl-powered Partyline. Neither smoking nor drinking are allowed, shows usually start at 6 or 7 P.M. so you can get home at a reasonable time, and most are a very affordable five to six bucks.

**Recher Theater, 512 York Rd., Towson,**
**www.rechertheater.com**

The Recher Theater looks like a refashioned movie house with its marquee announcing upcoming acts. Inside it's a large rectangular space that can easily house a standing-room-only crowd of 700 for MTV2-friendly pop and rock acts from Rusted Root and Citizen Cope to Mötörhead and Aaron Carter. Its close proximity to the Towson campus means the Recher maintains a very college-friendly crowd, bringing in both the guys in white baseball hats and gals in thrift-store cute, people hitting the shows or bopping into the attached Rec Room poolroom and bar.

## RECORD STORES:

**Sound Garden, 1616 Thames St.,**
**www.cdjoint.com**

This Fell's Point shop was, for the longest time, the only place to satisfy all your music needs. From the indie rock coming out on Matador, Touch and Go, and Saddle Creek to the electronic tweaking of Sasha and Digweed, from obscure free-jazz and improv to white-label 12-inch singles, and from classics by Pavement and Pearl Jam to the newest U2 and Bright Eyes, Sound Garden stocks it. It also maintains an extensive and wide-ranging stock of used CDs and DVDs to flip through, meaning you can pick up those old Slint discs and try to figure out why your older brother says Mogwai is just ripping them off. (The store also readily buys used CDs and DVDs for when you realize you could use some book money.) The store stays open until midnight Thursday through Saturday. And if you're wandering around Fell's

Point and can't find it, one word of advice before asking directions: You're in Baltimore, hon, and the street isn't pronounced like the river running through London. It rhymes with "games."

**Dimensions in Music, 233 Park Ave.**

Larry Jeter's Dimensions in Music is the only place you need to go to for R&B, soul, and funk. This local institution on the west side of downtown is a place you could visit a few times a week and keep finding things you didn't know you wanted. Everything is reasonably priced, the dreadlocked Mr. Jeter is usually the easygoing man sitting behind the counter, and the store itself is only two blocks away from Baltimore's Lexington Market: an indoor food court that's been around since 1782 where you can score deli sandwiches on the cheap and homemade cookies by the pound. And few midday treats are quite as nice as picking up the new Cam'ron and then grabbing a crab cake sandwich, all for less than $20.

**Reptilian Records, 403 S. Broadway, www.reptilianrecords.com**

Baltimore scenemaker Chris X has helmed this shop since 1990: Over the years he has established a peerless reputation as a straightshooter and his store is the only place in town for underground punk, hardcore, metal, noise, and all combinations thereof. The shop occupies a bright green storefront on the north end of Fell's Point, and Reptilian packs a motherlode of stuff in its narrow store. Records, CDs, 7-inch singles and EPs, videos, DVDs, books, and magazines run around the room and climb the walls, and Mr. X or any of the other quick-witted staff is always ready to point you in the right direction or offer a snappy comment, whichever response the situation requires. Reptilian is not the place to go looking for the new Hoobastank or Jet, but if Pig Destroyer, Dillinger Escape Plan, Converge, or Kylesa mean anything to you, then you'll fit right in.

**Once.Twice Sound, 519 N. Charles St., www.oncetwicesound.com**

Baltimore's newest independent record store is a suave pad of minimal cool. And proprietor Jason Urick takes the independent part of that tag literally. Once.Twice carries only CDs and vinyl from independent labels, and if you're a music geek or an aspiring music geek you can waste an entire afternoon at Once.Twice exchanging esoteric musical knowledge with your brethren in the store, or checking out something at the listening booth so you can decide before you buy. The selection is extensive, but it's all good stuff. So if you come across something on the Sun City Girls' Sublime Frequencies label that you've never heard about before and are wondering if it's worth trying out, chances are there's something about it that's just going to curl your toes.

### True Vine, 1123 W. 36th St.,

Hampden is a northwest Baltimore neighborhood, home to a healthy kitsch streak, and its main drag is West 36th Street—affectionately called the "Avenue" by the locals. Cute coffee shops, diners, cafes, and restaurants, hip shoe and clothing boutiques, and thrift stores dot the Ave's four blocks like Christmas lights, and near its west end terminus is the True Vine, Baltimore's most enthusiastically offbeat record store. If it goes buzz, zap, zoink, weeeee, the good men at the True Vine can name that tune in four notes, and then proceed to tell you every tangential, behind-the-scenes anecdote that went into making that particular kind of zoink. And that's really the True Vine's charm: It's not just a record store; it's an education.

### Joe's Record Paradise, 5001 Harford Rd.

Joe's Record Paradise is what you imagine record stores looked like before CDs came along. Sprawling over two rooms are rows and rows of LPs, protected inside shrink-wrap if new or a plastic sleeve if used, and the entire place feels like a neighborhood library. While Joe's tends to stock some new releases on vinyl, it specializes in used copies and reissues of soul, jazz, funk, R&B, as well as new mainstream. And don't sweat it if you don't have a turntable yet. Joe's also repairs and sells refurbished turntables and stereo equipment at very affordable prices, and for fifty dollars you could go home with a turntable, two speakers, and an LP to play.

## RADIO STATIONS:

### 92Q WERQ FM,
### www.92qjams.com

One of the coolest things about Baltimore being a predominantly African-American city is that black radio options are much, much more interesting than the usual classic or alternative rock same old-same old. WEAA (88.9 FM) is the National Public Radio affiliate run out of the historically black college Morgan State University, and its daily jazz programs and Friday night "Strictly Hip-Hop" show are always quality listens. But in WERQ-FM 92Q, Baltimore has a small miracle: a corporate urban radio station that overflows with personality. Sure, you do get a fair share of the latest hot cut from Snoop Dogg or Cam'ron or the silky new slow jam from Ashanti or Destiny's Child that's overplayed everywhere, but 92Q's jocks don't just run through the playlists. Afternoon and evening personalities are DJs who also work the clubs around town as well, and whole hours turn into on-the-fly mixtapes.

**WTMD 89.7 FM,**
**www.new.towson.edu/wtmd/**

WTMD is the public radio affiliate licensed through Towson University, and while its daytime hours do contain NPR staples such as World Café and Jazz at Lincoln Center, its afternoon jocks steer closer to singer/songwriters, folk pop, and indie rock from the likes of Norah Jones, the Killers, Modest Mouse, Wilco, Jem, Cat Power, and Ani DiFranco. Sometimes it sounds like WTMD has tapped into some strange 1980s portal and goes through long stretches of the Police, Tom Petty, Blondie, and Camper Van Beethoven, but it's all very innocuous, and it's, like, the perfect piped in sound for any Starbucks.

## MISCELLANEOUS EVENTS:

**Artscape,**
**www.bop.org**

Baltimore is a bastion of outdoor festivals during the spring and summer, and Artscape is the granddaddy of them all. Sponsored and funded by the city, Artscape is a Friday- through-Sunday celebration of the performing, visual, and literary arts, blocking off the streets of the Mount Royal Cultural District near the Mary Institute College of Art. Exhibits are strewn outdoors and through MICA's galleries, vendors lines the streets, and you can find more fried foods and grilled meat on a stick than you can shake a, uh, stick at. And over these three days local and national bands and artists—Blues Traveler, Al Green, De La Soul, the Violent Femmes, Galactic, Isaac Hayes, and Wyclef Jean have played in recent years—perform for free. Parking is beyond impossible, so leave the car at home, hop on a bus or the light rail, or pedal on over.

**Sowebo Arts Festival,**
**www.soweboarts.org**

If Artscape is Baltimore's civic heart, then Sowebo is Charm City's quirky soul. The festival takes place in the west side neighborhood called Sowebo that surrounds Hollins Market, and is where local musicians and bands of all kinds perform and visual artists display their latest works. It also frequently turns into a very long day of conviviality that ends in jubilant street dancing and laughs. Get good directions before you head down, though, because it's a part of the city that can be hard to navigate if you've never been before.

*—Bret McCabe*

# Berkeley/East Bay, CA

## UNIVERSITY OF CALIFORNIA, BERKELEY
104 Morrison Hall # 1200
Berkeley, CA 94720-1200
www.berkeley.edu

Aside from offering students access to the vibrant music community in Berkeley and neighboring San Francisco, UC Berkeley provides pre-professional training and a strong liberal arts curriculum to students interested in performing, composing or merely analyzing music of the past and present. Core curriculum requirements ensure that students master Western music and theory but also insist that music from various cultures be considered too. In addition to History of Jazz in America, there are also internationally minded offerings such as Sonic Culture in China. For future producers and engineers, Berkeley gives a class called Music Culture and the Digital Media Environment that consider the effects of technology and computer-mediated music on the creative and recording process.

# VENUES:

### Yoshi's, 510 Embarcadero West, Oakland, www.yoshis.com

The sushi is excellent, but the jazz at this—the finest venue of its kind in the Bay Area and indeed the entire West Coast—is truly outstanding. When it comes to the lineups, sightlines, acoustics, and comfort, Yoshi's is hard to beat. Expect international and local jazz greats such as McCoy Tyner, Cecil Taylor, Charlie Haden, Gonzalo Rubalcaba, Brad Mehldau, Omar Sosa, and Berkeley High School grads-made-good such as Joshua Redman and Benny Green as well as soul/hip-hop divas such as Goapele and Sakai, jazz vocalists Dianne Reeves and Abbey Lincoln, and blues, roots, and world music performers such as Ruth Brown, Mose Allison, Orchestra Baobab, and Maria Muldaur. Also look out for the jazz house's annual events such as their harmonica and B3 organ summits and the holiday residency by Berkeley High alum and eight-string guitar wiz Charlie Haden (a show that has pulled such local ax-wielding heavyweights as Metallica guitarist Kirk Hammett).

### Paramount Theater, 2025 Broadway, Oakland, www.paramounttheater.com

Come early to take in the lavish art deco beauty of this movie palace. Beck, Tom Waits, Elvis Costello, Jill Scott, Air, and Flaming Lips have performed amid the ornate metalwork and jewel-tone motifs of this beautifully preserved retro stunner. The theater also screens classic Hollywood movies such as *The Maltese Falcon*, preceded by concerts on the house's Mighty Wurlitzer organ.

### 924 Gilman, 924 Gilman St., Berkeley, www.924gilman.org

The blueprint for anarchist cooperative music venues was laid down here, with many of the punk and hardcore bands that make it into *Maximumrocknroll* and onto Lookout! Records initially finding their footing in the clubhouse for the "Alternative Music Foundation." These days groups including Erase Errata, From Ashes Rise, Pitch Blank, Enemy You, Mirah, Babyland, Fleshies, and Phenomenauts mix it up where Green Day, AFI, Bikini Kill, Operation Ivy, Mr. T Experience, and the Swingin' Utters once raged. All shows are seven dollars with a two-dollar membership, which is valid for a year.

## RECORD STORES:

**Amoeba Music, 2455 Telegraph Ave., Berkeley,**
**www.amoebamusic.com**

This is the O.G. of the chain. Legend has it that the best and biggest independent music store in the country found its start here in the hands and heads of disgruntled Rasputin employees, toiling further down the street. Regardless, the joint still exudes a cozy, crazed air with a huge range of new and used music, vinyl, posters, DVDs, and videos—the aisles tend to get tight on the weekends on this happening corner, located in prime real estate on this active stretch of Telegraph Avenue.

**Mod Lang, 2136 University Ave., Berkeley,**
**www.modlang.com**

Discerning Anglophiles and connoisseurs of obscuro rock, pop, and folk will dig the high-mod European imports and indie recordings at this downtown Berkeley storefront. Pluses include a knowledgeable staff, in-store performances by groups such as the Thrills and Stereolab, and giveaways such as posters and memorabilia with certain purchases. Check their email newsletter for a healthy list of new releases in addition to upcoming shows of note.

*—Kimberly Chun*

# Boston / Cambridge, MA

## BERKLEE COLLEGE OF MUSIC
1140 Boylston St.
Boston, MA 02215
www.berklee.edu

Located in Boston's posh Back Bay neighborhood, Berklee's campus offers one of the city's finest, intimate concert spaces: the Berklee Performance Center, a wood-paneled, acoustically perfect theater. Apart from campus shows, major touring acts have come through including Icelandic iconoclasts Sigûr Ros and jazz singers such as Cassandra Wilson. The school is also a quick walk from Newbury Street, a ritzy shopping district. If the location and course offerings weren't an immediate selling point, consider some of the school's alumni: Quincy Jones, Melissa Etheridge, guitarist Steve Vai, among others. And, in 1999, David Bowie received an honorary doctorate.

Berklee is hard to beat when it comes to educating and training aspiring performers: If you think you want to pursue a music career, if you live and breathe music, then this might be the place for you. Though highly selective, Berklee enrolls 3,800 students, matches them with 460 faculty members and takes an international approach (students come from all over the world) to create an interactive, personalized experience. Apart from mastering performance or composition, the school offers technical courses in recording and production and guidance in surviving the business.

As a major, you can focus your studies on performance, composition, music production and engineering, film scoring, music business/management, music synthesis, music education and music therapy. Students are expected to come to Berklee with ample knowledge, passion and scholastic ability. Any of the above concentrations (for a bachelor of music) require not only the fundamentals in terms of music courses, but also stress a broad, liberal arts education with courses in literature, history, math, philosophy, and languages.

Other, more specialized majors, including one in songwriting, stress melody, song structure, lyric writing, and developing an original style. Similarly, a "professional music" major begins with a close relationship with one faculty member and culminates in the creation of an original project that demonstrates enough depth to survive in a professional setting. The "music synthesis" major focuses on sound design, digital media and sound effects. Berklee also boasts an impressive, heralded jazz program.

The school deserves its reputation as one of the country's foremost music programs, however you should bear in mind that the training you'll receive at Berklee may be better suited for musicians interested in technical expertise than for those who want to rock out. Notably, John Mayer dropped out of Berklee after just a couple semesters because he felt the course work was too traditional and didn't encourage enough creative thinking.

## HARVARD UNIVERSITY
Music Building
North Yard
Harvard University
Cambridge, MA 02138
www.harvard.edu

**H**arvard University's academic standing really needs no explanation. The Ivy League institution is located in Cambridge, an engaging town immediately outside of Boston proper, with shops, restaurants, and a rich cultural life. Expect to work hard, but academic achievement need not come at a price so steep that all fun is sacrificed. In fact, Harvard recognizes that its students need to let loose; the school recently created a position, the "fun czar," which, stuffy title aside, is dedicated to planning parties and activities for students.

As for the music program, studies are very focused and serious. The music program is one division of the undergraduate college, which houses all concentrations (as opposed to other schools that subdivide their undergraduate programs into various colleges). Students receive a B.A. with a concentration in music. For some, even more focused and driven students, there is a B.M. program in performance practice, a degree suited to those seeking careers in teaching or performing. Apart from housing a music building with abundant resources—a music library, practice rooms, a concert hall, the Harvard University Studio for Electroacoustic Composition, and an early instrument room—the school promises an intimate program of study. Check out this ratio: fifty music students to twenty-one fulltime faculty members.

# BOSTON UNIVERSITY
855 Commonwealth Ave.
Boston, MA 02215
www.bu.edu

**B**oston University—in the heart of Boston with an urban campus that sprawls along the Charles River—is a large, private institution whose music program dates back to 1872. In fact, BU has the oldest, degree-granting music program in the country. The school's philosophy is in tune with its founder, Eben Tourgee, who believed the program should "enable students to more intelligently interpret and perform the works of the masters, render their services as instructors more valuable, and qualify them to do far more towards elevating the art to its true position in the estimation of the public."

Students working toward a bachelor of music will adhere to a curriculum that includes the standards (music theory, history and musicology) but makes certain you will be able to master your instrument—from voice to cello to euphonium. Musicology and music educations majors must audition on a particular instrument, though the curriculum is historically focused. Outside the music program, students looking for courses involving pop culture and music can find relevant offerings in a variety of departments including Women's Studies, American and New England Studies, Mass Communications and Sociology.

## BOSTON CONSERVATORY
8 The Fenway
Boston, MA 02215
www.bostonconservatory.edu

## NEW ENGLAND CONSERVATORY
290 Huntington Ave.
Boston, MA 02115
www.newenglandconservatory.edu.

The New England Conservatory and the Boston Conservatory give classically inclined musicians the chance to study in an intimate setting where private instruction is emphasized. This focus also means stressing versatility—from mastering an instrument to performing regularly in recitals and ensemble performances. Founded in 1867, the Boston Conservatory offers concentrated study in music, dance, theater and music education. Apart from the standard, and expected, array of courses, the conservatory offers classes tailored to students pursuing careers—and that means lives—as professional musicians. Witness: Career Skills for Musicians, a class which is conceived as an introduction to the life of a musician; skills honed range from resume writing to how to survive financially to tips for gigging. A course called American Music looks directly at twentieth-century music and not just classical composers; expect to study jazz and other popular compositions.

## VENUES:

The Middle East, 472/480 Mass. Ave., Cambridge, www.mideastclub.com

Cambridge's premier all-purpose club offers three distinct stages in which to enjoy everything from local folk collectives to national rock acts. The downstairs room (capacity: 575) was once one of the oldest candlepin bowling rooms in the Boston area and has hosted high-profile acts like Modest Mouse, Death Cab For Cutie and Queens of the Stone Age. The smaller upstairs room holds nearly 200 and is home mostly to regional and local acts starting out. This being Cambridge, the Mid East enjoys later curfews than Boston's clubs (headlining acts on the weekends often don't take the stage until 11 P.M.), and drink prices are generally cheaper than what you'd find across the river.

### TT The Bear's, 10 Brookline St., Cambridge, www.ttthebears.com

For anyone who's always wanted to be close enough to taste a rock star's sweat, TT's is the place. This diminutive club puts fans right in the middle of the action, with nothing separating those at the front from the low stage. Because of the room's limited size, noise levels are prohibitive (bring earplugs or tomorrow's lecture will be a blur). Most shows are 18+, and with room for only 300, many shows sell out. TT's is renowned for being the first area venue to host the likes of Franz Ferdinand, Scissor Sisters, and Snow Patrol.

### Paradise Rock Club, 969 Commonwealth Ave., Boston, www.thedise.com

Located on the edge of Boston University's campus, the Paradise has long been a local institution. With a high stage and a roomy balcony, the club is one of the city's most unique and rewarding venues. Though the capacity is around 500, you can bet that thousands claim they were there when the likes of U2, Coldplay, and the Police appeared on stage. The front lounge offers a relaxed spot for a cheap meal and hosts smaller acts on most nights.

### Avalon, 15 Lansdowne St., Boston, www.avalonboston.com

Befitting Beantown's largest club, Avalon attracts only the cream of the crop when it comes to national touring acts. It's a true Boston experience to hit a sold out show and wade through 2,000 concertgoers in search of a drink or a place to stand. On weekends, shows tend to start remarkably early in order for the club to be emptied in time for 10 P.M., when a whole new crowd pays $20 to groove along to world-class DJs. Almost all concerts are 18+, so leave your fake ID at home.

### Club Passim, 47 Palmer St., Cambridge, www.passimcenter.org

Since 1958, Harvard Square has been home to Passim, one of the country's truly seminal folk clubs. The intimate venue, which seats only 125, was the scene of the Northeast's first hootenanny and everyone from Bob Dylan to Joan Baez has passed through its doors (other notable acts have included Jimmy Buffett and Bonnie Raitt). Recent years have seen a subtle shift towards contemporary acts like Howie Day and Josh Ritter. Befitting Passim's earthy-crunchy vibe, no alcohol is served and food is provided by Veggie Planet, an in-house restaurant that's one of the area's best for vegetarians. The club has been non-profit since 1995, with proceeds going towards kids' programs and a music school.

### Johnny D's Uptown Restaurant and Music Club, 17 Holland St., Somerville, www.johnnyds.com

Somerville's Davis Square is home to Johnny D's, one of the area's most multifaceted music clubs: Many a patron has stumbled unexpectedly onto a hillbilly jam or a Latin funk artist. Sundays prove popular thanks to a jazz brunch that's followed by a lively open blues jam. Most evening shows are 21+, much to the chagrin of the numerous Tufts students who call the neighborhood home. The club, which opened in 1969, holds just over 300 and has welcomed then-unknowns like Phish, Ben Harper, the Dixie Chicks, and Jeff Buckley.

### Harpers Ferry, 158 Brighton Ave., Allston, www.harpersferryboston.com

Allston Center's top spot for live music offers plenty of distractions (pool tables, dart boards, video games, foosball) for the tone deaf. With so many students and young professionals living within a stone's throw, it's no surprise that the beer is cheap and the covers are low (a few bucks for local bands, more for national touring acts). While most acts veer towards the mainstream (think Rusted Root, Fishbone, Pat McGee Band), the club hosts its fair share of blues and funk acts like Buckwheat Zydeco and Susan Tedeschi.

### The Roxy, 279 Tremont St., Boston, www.roxyplex.com

Boston's "other" mega-club hosts the occasional big-time concert, as crowds of over 1,500 have filled the Roxy's floor and wraparound balcony to see the likes of the Arcade Fire, the Shins, and the Flaming Lips. Like the Avalon, the Roxy makes its name by hosting some of the city's most raucous club nights, with world-class DJs and gaggles of scantily-clad scenesters. Matrix, Roxy's smaller club space, hosts shows as well.

### Orpheum Theater, 1 Hamilton Pl., Boston, www.boston.cc.com/venues.asp?venueID=832

In a city chock full of historical sites, the Orpheum stands out as the oldest concert venue that's still in use. The original home of the New England Conservatory dates back to 1852 and serves as Boston's premier venue for acts that are too big for the clubs but can't quite fill an arena. Located next to Suffolk Law School, the theater holds 2,800 over two levels and is a favorite stop on the jam band circuit. While the sightlines are above average, the venue loses major points for having a no food or beverage policy in the stands (concertgoers are forced to enjoy their overpriced beers in the stuffy lobby).

### Berklee Performance Center, 136 Massachusetts Ave., Boston, MA 02115, www.berkleebpc.com

As one would expect from one of the nation's most respected schools of music, Berklee's main performance center provides the city's best acoustics and sightlines. Seating 1,220 over two levels, the auditorium hosts everything from big band revues to contemporary acts like Sigur Ros and Travis. Faculty and student shows are held frequently and offer tremendous value (some are free).

### Wally's Café, 427 Massachusetts Ave., Boston, www.wallyscafe.com

Tucked away on a nondescript stretch of Mass. Ave. resides Wally's, one of the city's true hidden gems. This atmospheric jazz club hosts live music 365 days a year, and there's never a cover (although on weekends, there's usually a line). Cooing couples and grizzled jazzhounds—Wally's is 21+—fill the narrow room to nod along to the aspiring musicians who take the stage most nights. Professionals pop up every now and then, but most acts are local students and amateurs, though you'd never know it from the enthusiastic manner in which most crowds respond.

## RECORD STORES:

**Newbury Comics, Four locations in the Boston area:**
**332 Newbury St., 1 Washington Mall,**
**36 JFK St., 211 Alewife Brook Parkway,**
**www.newburycomics.com**

Area students have one of the nation's best independent retailers at their disposal. Each and every location is well-stocked with rare, hard-to-find CDs, including an unrivaled indie section. Best of all, prices across the board can't be beat, with most best sellers coming in at under $13. Newbury's also the go-to spot for offbeat pop culture items like bobbleheads, action figures, and lunchboxes. Need to decorate your room? The poster selection's killer. Want to fit in like a local? Pick up a "Yankees Suck" t-shirt.

**Virgin Megastore, 360 Newbury St.,**
**www.virginmega.com**

The city's largest record store takes up 40,000 square feet of the Frank Gehry building that keeps watch over Newbury Street. Dozens of listening stations are spread out over the store's three floors, and special kiosks allow customers to preview every single CD in the house. Serious types enjoy an unrivalled classical section, and those in need of a break find refuge in the third floor café.

**Nuggets, 486 Commonwealth Ave.,**
**www.nuggetsrecords.com**

If you're dying to hear Ryan Adams's cover of "Wonderwall," but don't want to pay $10 for *Love is Hell, Part 1*, chances are Nuggets has a cheap, used copy somewhere in its huge library. This virtual museum of pop culture sells decades worth of music, promo glossies and rock mags, all on the cheap (on Red Sox game nights, ticket holders receive a discount). Due to its Kenmore Square location, the shop is popular with B.U. students in search of old-school vinyl and 45s.

**CD Spins, Multiple locations: 324 Newbury St., 58 Winter St.,**
**235 Elm St., 54 Church St., 668 Centre St.,**
**www.cdspins.com**

Looking to unload your old Good Charlotte CDs? Swing by any one of CD Spins' conveniently located outlets, where used discs are the name of the game. The city's premier spot for buying, trading, and selling used CDs offers chart-toppers of today and yesterday, plus lots of rare gems. Those looking to sell receive cash on the spot (expect to get about $3-$4 for high-profile titles), and those looking to trade get a 25% bonus on top of the cash value.

**Skippy White's, 538 Massachusetts Ave., Cambridge**
**www.skippywhites.com**

The Boston area's Mecca of old soul, R&B, disco, and jazz lures music aficionados from far and wide. And Skippy's provides those looking to go old-school with ample opportunity, as the selection of 45s and 8-tracks is amazing.

**In Your Ear Records, 957 Commonwealth Ave.,**
**www.iye.com**

This straightforward B.U. record shop carries an adequate selection from all genres and formats, including both new and used LPs, 8-tracks and 7-inch singles. Local artists are well represented, and there are plenty of bargain boxes for the budget minded.

# RADIO STATIONS:

**WERS 88.9,**
**www.wers.org**

One of the country's most acclaimed college radio stations provides Bostonians with one of the most eclectic options on their dials. From blues to sports talk, gospel to a cappella, every genre under the sun makes an appearance in ERS's weekly format. And who knows, that overnight blues DJ may be the next Jay Leno, who is just one of the school's many successful alumni.

**WBCN-104.1**
**www.wbcn.com**

**WFNX-101.7**
**www.fnxradio.com**

While every major city now has an alternative rock station, Bostonians get to brag of having two of the most influential in the land. Among its many claims to fame, WBCN proudly boasts of having been the first station in the U.S. to play U2, in 1980. (The song? "A Day Without Me.") While it now veers more towards modern rock territory, BCN's counterpart, WFNX, stays the alternative course by being committed to breaking new artists. FNX, one of the nation's few true alternative stations, was the first station in the city to play the likes of the Postal Service, the Mars Volta, and Razorlight.

## MISCELLANEOUS EVENTS:

### NEMO Conference,
### www.nemoboston.com

One of the country's premier music conferences envelops the Hub every year, providing students with a weekend full of live music (most shows are open to the public). Over thirty venues host everyone from international acts trying to break the American market to unsigned local artists, and many shows are free.

### CollegeFest,
### www.collegefest.com/boston.htm

Every year, thousands of students fill the Hynes Convention Center to stock up on free swag (one can never have enough crappy keychains) and check out local and national artists (past performers include Maroon 5 and Lil' Flip). When a generic teen act takes the stage, attendees pass the time by getting makeovers or auditioning for WB dramas.

—*Eric Grossman*

# Boulder, CO

## UNIVERSITY OF COLORADO, BOULDER
301 UCB
Boulder, CO 80309
www.colorado.edu

The Boulder branch of the University of Colorado not only offers the benefit of proximity to this hip college town, but also a strong music program. Although none of UC Boulder's three music majors reside in the schools list of most-declared undergraduate majors (psychology is no. 1, journalism no. 2, biology no. 3, and English no. 4), they're still popular.

The music department grants qualified students either a bachelor of arts in music, or a bachelor of music in performance (in a variety of instruments), composition and theory, conducting, jazz studies, music education or musicology. For music education majors, your courses will even prepare you for your teaching licensure; that means you'll be taking a hefty dose of education courses. And on the degree front, you can also earn certificates in jazz studies and music technology.

If classical music isn't your thing, don't fret: UC Boulder offers plenty of contemporary courses both in and out of the music school. For instance, Music in American Culture focuses on the social and historical elements of U.S. musical forms. Rock & roll fans will want to sign up for Music of the Rock Era, a class that studies the evolution of rock from the Sixties through grunge's early Nineties heyday. Outside of the music program, the media studies curriculum incorporates film, music and popular culture in ways that ought to appeal to any serious music geek.

## VENUES:

Fox Theater, 1135 13th St.,
www.foxtheater.com

Boasting some of the best sound in the state, an epic location on Boulder's University Hill and a love affair with hip-hop that would make the Reverend Run jealous, the Fox is, as Beck would say, where it's at. If you're wondering where the hot new Anticon/Sub Pop/Def Jux/Saddle Creek/Ninja Tune/Merge band plays in Boulder after graduating from the club circuit, the Fox is the likely answer. But it's also the home to jam culture in Boulder, the place where String Cheese Incident and Leftover Salmon and Yonder Mountain String Band cut their teeth and broke beyond the theater's limited capacity.

### Club 156, basement at the CU-BUniversity Memorial Center , www.colorado.edu/programcouncil

It's undergone countless incarnations, but everyone knows this generic space as the joint in the basement of CU-Boulder's University Memorial Center. It's home to familiar indie rockers as frequently as it is to obscure punk rock, and its central location in the university's student union makes it a favorite for the dormed up. CU-Boulder's Program Council operates the venue, and while they could do a better job filling it up with bands from Boulder, Denver, Fort Collins, and beyond, they do get a little help from area promoters (including Denver folk at the Larimer Lounge and Rock Island) who lend the venue credibility by bringing in bigger, buzzier, more in-demand names.

### Boulder Theater, 2032 14th St., www.bouldertheater.com

A few blocks away from campus and the Hill is the Pearl Street Mall—home to the historic Boulder Theater, which originally opened in 1906 as the Curran Opera House. Sure, there's the occasional jam band or indie act, but the Boulder Theater is mostly where locals go to hear world music, blues, folk, traditional bluegrass, and jazz. It's also the home of e-town, a nationally syndicated public radio program that focuses on roots artists such as Ani DiFranco, the Del McCoury Band, and Greg Brown.

### Acoustic Café, 95 E. 1st St. in Nederland, www.acousticcoffeehouse.com

About fifteen miles up Canyon Avenue, west of Boulder, is the small township of Nederland, which has in recent years become the primary hub for the Denver and Boulder jam band community. String Cheese Incident, Leftover Salmon, and Yonder Mountain String Band all have some roots in this canyon, and members from each band have also played the Nederland coffeehouse, an institution for roots, bluegrass, and folk music in the foothills between Boulder and Central City. A recent renovation has the intimate venue feeling more comfortable and sounding a lot more professional, but non-compete "radius clauses" in other area venues' contracts are hampering the café's style. (For example, a contract will say: "If you play the Boulder Theater, you can't play anything within sixty miles of us.") Still the café thrives via the supportive and grass-roots community that surrounds it in Boulder Canyon.

## RECORD STORES:

**Albums on the Hill, 1128 13th St.**

This University Hill regular lost all of its nearby competition in 2004 when both Wax Trax and Second Spin closed because of sagging CD sales. That's not saying it's easy sailing for Albums and its owner Andy Schneidkraut, but of the three, Albums was the more important store. (There's still Wax Trax's Denver store, and Second Spin was a national chain.) This downstairs joint across from the Fox Theater has the personality and the youthful staff required of a proper college music store.

**Bart's CD Cellar, 1015 Pearl St.,**
**www.bartscdcellar.com**

Boulder is all about the jam bands, but while Bart's embraces that, it's more indie rock than anything else in the surrounding scene. For instance, their in-stores tend to star underground acts such as the Unicorns, Supersuckers, Broken Social Scene, and Nellie McKay. The Bart's staff is also well versed in underground hip-hop, as it would have to be with the nearby CU-Boulder maintaining its "I'll-buy-anything-with-a-Def-Jux-sticker!" reputation.

## RADIO STATIONS:

**KVCU/Radio 1190-AM,**
**www.radio1190.org**

1190 revolutionized Boulder radio when it first started making waves in the Nineties. Finally there was an independent voice, a station with college kids calling the shots, something on the air with weird, edged-out niche shows at 1 A.M. on Mondays that blew your mind, a morning show that mattered and taught you something, a locals-only show that was a tastemaker and a true and respected supportive force in the scene. This is college radio, yeah, but sadly the area went without for so long that we forgot the way it was supposed to be. Now you can hear Party of Helicopters (and Del tha Funkee Homosapien and Thee Shams and Planes Mistaken for Stars) on Colorado radio, and for this we thank Radio 1190.

## MISCELLANEOUS EVENTS:

### Gavin AAA Convention

This annual festival, which takes over the Hill for a long weekend every August, draws music makers, scene shakers, and dealmakers from all over the country—while still setting aside a few tickets for the fans. Past artists who have played the convention include Dave Matthews, Lyle Lovett, Chris Isaak, Willie Nelson, Bonnie Raitt, and Julian Lennon, and beyond the fact that these are industry showcases, they're also special because these artists wouldn't otherwise be playing the intimate Fox Theater (or, in some cases, even smaller venues).

—*Ricardo Baca*

# Burlington, VT

## UNIVERSITY OF VERMONT
392 South Prospect St.
Burlington, VT 05405-0144
www.uvm.edu

Nestled between Lake Champlain and the Green Mountains, Burlington is a city of 60,000 that brings together the best qualities of small-town life and big-city cosmopolitanism. The temperature may dip below freezing for a substantial part of the year, but one can't help but get a warm feeling from the place that brought you Phish, Ben and Jerry's ice cream, and Howard Dean. Music is only one facet of a bustling, homegrown arts community that encompasses grassroots theater, painting and sculpture, and such quirky outlets for political activism as the whimsical Bread and Puppet Theater.

Burlington's music scene was already thriving by the time the members of Phish arrived in town as University of Vermont undergrads in the early 1980s. Guitarist Trey Anastasio credits nights spent in now-defunct Main Street clubs such as Hunt's and the Front watching local talent including the late Big Joe Burrell and the Unknown Blues Band as the inspiration that sparked his own group's early efforts. Many of the musicians who tutored Anastasio—guitarist Paul Asbell and banjo player Gordon Stone, for instance—are still living in town; if you want a lesson, often times all you need to do is approach them after a gig or look them up in the phone book.

Music students at the University of Vermont should enjoy performance, because the school emphasizes it regardless of which concentration students elect. You will be expected to perform with peers and faculty in ensembles and recitals throughout your time at UVM. Students can earn either a bachelor of music, bachelor of arts in music, or a bachelor of science in music education in a setting with small classes and high-level instruction. Internships are recommended with local arts organizations (of which there are many). Students are also encouraged to pursue individual projects and tailor these interests to an independent study opportunity. The school has a study abroad program established in Cuba where students can go to Havana for two weeks and study local music by steeping themselves in the country's groovy Afro-Cuban sound.

But you don't have to go that far south—or leave campus at all—to find live tunes. Billings Student Center and the adjoining Ira Allen Chapel regularly host small-to-midsize local and touring acts such as Charlie Hunter, Leo Kottke, and the Yonder Mountain String Band. And the denizens of Slade Hall (another early Phish venue) routinely open their basement to hometown bands and as many listeners as are willing to squeeze their way inside. Meanwhile, acts including Primus, Jurassic 5, and Bob Dylan have played to capacity crowds at the roomy, if acoustically less desirable, Patrick Gymnasium.

# VENUES:

### Nectar's, 188 Main St.,
### www.liveatnectars.com

This Main Street grill is famous for two things: making the city's best French fries smothered in turkey gravy, and being the first venue to offer the members of Phish a regular gig. Operated for decades by Greek fry cook-cum-entrepreneur Nectar Rorris, the tavern changed hands in 2003 and has enjoyed a recent facelift, most notably the installation of a booming sound system and roomier dance floor. Gone is the longstanding policy of free music every night of the week, but with the imposition of a small cover charge, the quality of the bands has improved.

### Club Metronome, 188 Main St.,
### www.clubmetronome.com

Upstairs from Nectar's is Burlington's longest-running rock venue, Club Metronome. Opened in 1993 by Anne Rothwell, the Metronome was the first local spot to book such Nineties up-and-comers as the Counting Crows, Ani DiFranco, and the Dave Matthews Band. Things cooled a bit by the late Nineties, when "Retronome" (picture hippies awkwardly dancing to lame Eighties tunes) replaced live music in large part, but the club's gotten its second wind under new management and now offers a mix of styles from jam bands plus frequent visits from the A-list DJs of Montreal's Ninja Tune label. Even "Retronome" has been revamped, and is now under the thoughtful direction of MC Fattieboombalattie, the class clown of Burlington hip-hop scene.

### Red Square Bar and Grill, 136 Church St.

Around the corner from Metronome, just across the street from City Hall, you'll find Red Square, a hole-in-the-wall pub with a big attitude and one of the tiniest stages in town. However, something's always afoot here, whether it's the weekly jazz of local legend James Harvey or regular appearances by saxophonist Dave "the Truth" Grippo and his funk band. Both men schooled the members of Phish on their way up, and now they're raising a new generation of jazz-funkateers. One caveat: Unlike some other Burlington venues, you need to be twenty-one to get in.

### Higher Ground Music Hall, 1214 Williston Rd., www.highergroundmusic.com

For larger touring acts requiring more elbow room, South Burlington's Higher Ground Music Hall is the natural choice. Formerly located across the river in neighboring Winooski until an urban renewal project turned the club out, Higher Ground reopened in a decommissioned movie house only a short walk from the UVM campus. Bookings over the years have included Medeski, Martin & Wood, Lisa Loeb, Ween, Herbie Hancock, Yo La Tengo, Steel Pulse, and Soul Coughing. If your favorite band hasn't been there yet, it's probably just a matter of time.

### Flynn Center for the Performing Arts, 153 Main St., www.flynncenter.com

This beautifully restored theater houses Burlington's serious arts programming. From the symphonic sounds of Vermont's Youth Orchestra jazz, blues, and world music, dance troupes and spoken word, a night out at the Flynn is always special. Perhaps you've heard of Mikhail Baryshnikov? Wynton Marsalis? Garrison Keillor? Willie Nelson? They've all graced the Flynn stage, as have artists such as Phil Lesh and Friends, Jethro Tull, the String Cheese Incident, Bela Fleck, and countless others. In 2001, the Flynn Center expanded to include an underground theater, the Flynnspace, which regularly hosts cutting-edge jazz, dance and theater projects.

## RECORD STORES:

### Pure Pop, 115 S. Winooski Ave.

Pure Pop is THE record store in town, independently owned and operated since 1980 by former UVM college radio DJ-turned-concert promoter Jay Strausser. Pure Pop offers the area's best selection, whether you're looking for popular, edgy, and/or local music. The staff is extremely knowledgeable, with a passion for music bordering on the compulsive, and convenient listening stations and the funky décor of their underground digs will make you feel so at home that you might never leave.

**Downtown Discs, 198 College St.**

If you're looking for used music at bargain prices, this is a place not to be missed. Thousands of CDs are neatly alphabetized and conveniently displayed, and in recent years the store has expanded to offer used vinyl, stereos, and videogame equipment. Whether you're selling a collection or building one, Downtown Discs deserves a look, and since it's across the street from Pure Pop, there's no reason not to visit both in one afternoon.

## RADIO STATIONS:

**WRUV 90.1,**
**www.uvm.edu/~wruv/**

Home to the most cutting edge sounds on Burlington's radio dial by far, WRUV is also home to a great community of music geeks. If you're a joiner, there's always room for one more (as long as you're willing to start out on the graveyard shift and alphabetize some CDs once in a while). Nobody tells these DJs what to play, and they follow their noses, mixing rap and reggae with avant-garde jazz, world music, left-field rock and even spoken word : A few years back, one DJ took to reading long passages from Herman Melville's Moby Dick.

**WBTZ 99.9 "the Buzz",**
**www.999thebuzz.com**

If your listening tastes tend toward the mainstream, you might not even mind the fact that the Buzz plays all the same stuff as whatever corporate radio station commands your airways back home. Modern rock (both hard and light), R&B make up a fairly balanced diet of popular commercial music. One saving grace, however, is WBTZ's "Homebrew" hour, dedicated solely to local music.

## MISCELLANEOUS EVENTS:

**Champlain Valley Expo**

Vermont is mostly farm country—the humble cow its unofficial mascot—so it should come as no surprise that the annual Champlain Valley Fair is the state's largest entertainment event, drawing 300,000 annually to this late-summer festival of music, amusements and livestock. The 84th annual festival starred Tim McGraw, but previous expos have been visited by the Allman Brothers Band and Yes. Try your hand at carnival games and marvel at oversized vegetables before the concert!

### Discover Jazz Festival

After more than twenty years, Burlington's annual Discover Jazz Festival has earned a reputation as one of the strongest and most diverse of its kind, drawing internationally renowned talent such as Branford Marsalis, Sonny Rollins, B.B. King, and Luther. But the free events are often the week's most popular attractions, including meet-the-artist discussions and other educational opportunities, a jazz parade ending with a picnic in City Hall Park, and a block party on the Church Street Marketplace, where every restaurant and street corner seems to come alive with music.

*—Peter Gershon*

# Chapel Hill / Raleigh / Durham, NC

## DUKE UNIVERSITY
Box 90665
Durham, NC 27708-0665
www.duke.edu

Two words: Free iPod. In 2004, Duke University made that unbelievable perk available to all incoming freshman. I shit you not. At press time, the university was still deciding whether to continue the giveaway. But any school that would give 1600 kids free iPods can't be all bad, eh? If that's not reason enough to consider applying to Duke, consider the fact that the university unofficially dubbed "the Harvard of the South" allows music majors to study everything from composition and theory to ethnomusicology and music history, participate in one of thirteen different performing groups, and take advantage of a low student-faculty ratio, a magnificent music library, and a cool collection of rare musical instruments dating from as far back as the eighteenth century.

If you are looking for an innovative program in which to study the cultural relevance of pop music, or if you want to supplement your business degree with a course or two on the history of rock & roll, Duke may not be the place for you. If, on the other hand, you have a particular interest in world music, or are seeking a music degree that allows you to merge the study of theory and performance with music history, Duke is an excellent choice. And, if you feel like mixing things up a little, electives include Music and Modernism, African-American Music in the Twentieth Century, and World Music: Aesthetic and Anthropological Approaches. Graduates of the program have gone on to hold many distinguished positions in including president of the New York Philharmonic and chair of the National Endowment for the Arts.

And even non-music students get to enjoy on-campus concerts on a regular basis. Over the past few years, the Duke University Union, a student-run programming group, as well as the Last Day of Classes chairs in Campus Council have brought a number of popular bands and artists to Duke. In 2004, the Union brought Nappy Roots and Dierks Bentley with Cross Canadian Ragweed to campus. Duke also has an annual free concert on the Clocktower Quad on West Campus on the last day of classes in spring. The 2004 concert was headlined by Kanye West. The concert in 2003 featured Wilco and opening act Better than Ezra.

## UNIVERSITY OF NORTH CAROLINA, CHAPEL HILL
Department of Music
CB #3320 Hill Hall
Chapel Hill, NC 27599-3320
www.unc.edu

Students interested in majoring in music at the University of North Carolina seek one of two degrees: the bachelor of arts degree in music and the bachelor of music degree. As with other schools offering similar degrees, UNC's B.A. is best for students who really want to focus on music as the epicenter of a broader education in the liberal arts, while B.M. students are looking to specialize in music performance, composition, or education. UNC's music department has a core curriculum that all enrolled students must complete, which consists of four courses in music history, four in music theory, and four semesters of ensemble participation. B.A. students can emphasize composition, history, jazz, or even popular music, while B.M. students can focus on music education, composition, or performance.

The UNC Department of Music does offer a music minor, which allows students to dabble in the music program with limited investment, but for any student looking to sample music courses without committing to total immersion, UNC is a particularly great place because the department offers an array of courses specifically designed for non-majors. The list of "non-majors only" courses includes: Great Musical Works, Jazz Innovators, Popular Song in American Culture, Beethoven and His Era, Musical Modernism, and Music as Culture among many others. Plus, many of the department's other music courses handle topics interesting to a wide variety of students like Gongs, Punks, and Shadows: Performance in Southeast Asia, Analysis of Popular Music, Keyboard Skills, Analysis of Twentieth-Century Music, Introduction to Country Music, and Introduction to Rock Music.

## VENUES:

### Cat's Cradle, 300 East Main St., Carrboro, www.catscradle.com

The Cat's Cradle, located just down the road from UNC Chapel Hill, is the triangle's best-known venue thanks to the quality of the acts it draws. On any given night, some of the most hyped independent artists in the country may take the stage—everyone from the White Stripes (back when they weren't too big for the Cradle) to Le Tigre. The Cradle is a two-room venue—one large room contains the stage and most of the crowd and a back room houses the bar, games, and the more socially inclined concertgoers. Formerly a dark, smoky club, the Cradle is now simply dark as it has banned smoking. They list a capacity of 615, but even sold-out shows retain a high degree of comfort and intimacy.

### Local 506, 506 W. Franklin St., Chapel Hill, www.local506.com

Local 506 is an integral part of the famous Franklin Street scene at UNC-Chapel Hill. A membership to the club is required to get in, and those under twenty-one have to pay a small fee. This bar atmosphere works well for 506, a small venue (capacity is about 250) that enables its patrons to move easily between Pabst Blue Ribbons and the stage. Local 506 brings in a lot of local and regional indie rock and Southern rock acts, but also books cult favorites like Lou Barlow and the French Kicks.

### Disco Rodeo, 2820 Industrial Dr., Raleigh

Formerly known as the Ritz, Disco Rodeo is a large warehouse-like building with strobe lights and dance floors. Disco Rodeo has focused heavily on the Latino market, with Latino music and dance parties on the weekends. As the Ritz, the location was a staple for popular indie-minded bands (Sonic Youth, the Strokes), but this reputation seems to be waning in recent years. The venue (capacity 2,500) is basically one large, open room with a balcony. Because of its size, it's simply not as intimate as the Chapel Hill hotspots, but it's still better than going to some sterile arena.

### Carolina Theater, 309 West Morgan St., Durham, www.carolinatheater.org

The Carolina Theater in Durham has the kind of refined, elegant atmosphere that naturally lends itself music. The venue doubles as a movie theater, showing independent films and documentaries. As a music venue, the Carolina is a great place to catch a jazz show or laid-back rockers such as Lambchop or the Magnetic Fields. It's fancy and ornate, and if you're looking for smoky bar appeal, then the 1,000-seat Theater is not for you.

### Kings Barcade, 424 S. McDowell St., Raleigh, www.kingsbarcade.com

Beer, bands, and video games? Sign me up! Kings Barcade, owned by three music aficionados, books local talents on select nights and leaves the rest of the time open for slurping PBR and playing Pac-Man. The Barcade also hosts trivia nights, movie screenings and drink specials. The club is pretty local minded, and only holds a couple hundred people, but national rockers such as Broken Social Scene and Ted Leo have actually hit the stage at Kings.

### The Coffeehouse at Duke University

In the Seventies, Eighties, and Nineties, the Coffeehouse on Duke's East Campus was frequented by local bands and well-known indie rock outfits. It's an extremely cozy venue that holds about 150 people. Recently revamped, the Coffeehouse is kicking better than ever, and now plays host to several local acts and popular regional and national acts. When the Coffeehouse is not staging a concert, it is, naturally, a great place to get a cup of coffee and hit the books.

## RECORD STORES:

### Schoolkids Records, 142 E. Franklin St., Chapel Hill
### www.schoolkidsrecords.com/chill.html

There are two FYEs and a Borders in the Raleigh-Durham-Chapel Hill triangle, but the best small record store is Chapel Hill's Schoolkids, which stands on the edge of the UNC campus. And it's still easily accessible to Duke students, since Duke provides a free bus to UNC as part of the Robertson Scholars Program. (Pose as a scholar and then do some record shopping instead!) One of the country's foremost indie stores, Schoolkids has a wide enough selection to appeal to hipsters and mainstream shoppers alike. Their stock includes everything from indie favorites like Rilo Kiley and Postal Service to R. Kelly, Alicia Keys, and Eminem. The store also features a wide selection of local bands and musicians, such as the Rosebuds and Camera Obscura, who are both on Merge Records, a legendary local label. Aside from CDs, Schoolkids also carries an extensive selection of both new and used vinyl, and sells tickets to shows at Cat's Cradle, which is right down the block.

### CD Alley, 405 W. Franklin St., Chapel Hill

It would be hard for any store in the triangle to compete with Schoolkids, but CD Alley does an admirable job of it. The smallish shop is packed to the gills with CDs, vinyl, 7-inch singles and DJ platters—all from a variety of underground favorites, broken down into highly specific subgenres like "Japanese Punk" and "Krautrock." It's a bit cramped and stuffy, but at least there's a couch where you can rest when your fingers get sore from flipping through CDs, and the store offers a listening station where you can sample a record before you buy it. And to get 10 percent off your purchase, be sure to look at the chalkboard outside CD Alley: Every day it has a music trivia question, and if you get it right, you get the discount.

## RADIO STATIONS:

### WXYC 89.3,
www.wxyc.org

One of the country's most cutting-edge college stations, WXYC proved how forward thinking it is in 1994, when it became the first station ever to rebroadcast its signal over the Internet. The programming at this student-run station is freeform, which gives DJs the chance to be more adventurous in their selections. Or, as station manager Jason Perlmutter described it: "[O]ur mission is to illustrate the relationships between seemingly disparate types of music. Our disc jockeys harness the almighty power of the segue to draw musical linkages across time, culture, and pure sound. For example, you might be humming along to the chorus of your favorite Jay-Z monster, only to hear it followed by the very Bobby "Blue" Bland mega-hit from the Seventies from which the sample was lifted." WXYC hires new DJs at the beginning of each semester, and once you're hired you can remain on-staff indefinitely.

### WXDU 88.7,
www.wxdu.duke.edu

Duke's college radio station is run by a subcommittee of the Duke University Union, and the DJs include both Duke students and non-students. The station plays a diverse, and typically DJ-selected, mix of independent music, as well as specialty programs devoted to live local music, urban music, jazz, world music, Americana, comedy, and sports.

# Charlottesville, VA

Though Charlottesville's nickname, "the Hook," derives from its spidery geographical layout, the moniker's musical connotation is also apt: Like the chorus to a song that you can't get out of your head, this small town has one of the most irresistible, hard-to-leave scenes in the country. With a population of 40,000, Charlottesville—rated the best city to live in by Frommers last year—is primarily driven by university affairs. Consistently ranked among the top five public universities in the U.S., the **University of Virginia** (www.virginia.edu) has an undergraduate student body of 13,000 and a respected liberal arts and sciences program. The school offers a B.A. in music and houses the Virginia Center for Computer Music, which seeks to expand the scope of modern composition.

There are also a number of fine vocal and instrumental ensembles to be found on "grounds" (the campus), and an impressive calendar of jazz and classical events has brought musicians including John Zorn and Meredith Monk to C-ville.

Of course the most famous contemporary artist affiliated with Charlottesville is Dave Matthews, who has turned his worldbeat-influenced folk-pop into staggering record sales and concert numbers. Not bad for a South African-born C-ville resident who started playing in Miller's, the bar where he used to mix drinks. Matthews' hybridization and acoustic music has deep roots here—a lefty haven surrounded by serious bluegrass country. Good music, in the ears of C-ville, is generally laid-back, groovy, and fun. As such, "rock" is not necessarily at the top of the food chain, but there are plenty of hooks to be had.

Charlottesville includes two cultural hubs: Located across from UVa, the Corner district includes a number of bars, coffeehouses, restaurants, and boutiques. For those with wheels, the Downtown Mall on the east end of town is an idyllic pedestrian thoroughfare paved with brick and host to movie theaters, trendy clubs, restaurants, bookstores, novelty shops, and the occasional street urchin. Both areas are great for people watching and barhopping, but you're more likely to drop serious coin on the Mall.

There have been numerous major changes in Charlottesville's musical landscape since the mid-Nineties, but the future is promising. Several popular rock venues, namely Trax, Tokyo Rose (a legendary stop for indie bands in the late 1990s) and the Pudhouse (a quasi-legal club for noise bands in the early 2000s), have closed, with a few fresh ones springing up to pump new blood into local offerings. The main mover and shaker for music in town is Coran Capshaw, manager of the Dave Matthews Band, who runs several enterprises, including merchandising, ticketing, and concert promotions. **Starr Hill Music Hall** (www.starrhill.com), a 400-capacity club owned by Capshaw, has brought a variety of talent to C-ville since 2000, mostly in the jam-band or acoustic/bluegrass vein. There have also been occasional stops by breaking rock acts or underground legends such as Death Cab for Cutie and Jonathan Richman. Capshaw is developing a large outdoor amphitheater on the Downtown Mall, which bodes well for larger, louder shows in the future.

**The Prism Coffeehouse** (www.theprism.org) is situated amongst a row of fraternity houses but has been home to some of the finest musicians in the world since 1966. This smoke- and alcohol-free venue seats 140 and features quality acoustic music performed by acts from diverse international locales such as Cape Breton and Mali. Two newer venues in town look to pick up the slack left from the closing of Tokyo Rose: **Gravity Lounge** (www.gravity-lounge.com) is a sit-down venue with a modern bookstore/gallery feel welcoming singer/songwriter talent and local literary types, while **Twisted Branch Tea Bazaar** (www.teabazaar.com) combines a hippie/socialist vibe with irregularly scheduled avant-garde music and serves tasty vegan fare plus a wide array of teas. And **Miller's** (www.millersdowntown.com) on the Downtown Mall (where Matthews used to bartend) has hosted quality live local jazz in a cozy setting for years, featuring former Miles Davis sideman John D'Earth and Robert Jospe.

There are a couple good options for record shoppers, too. Boasting two Charlottesville locations (one on the Corner and the other on Rt. 29 North), **Plan 9 Music** (www.plan9music.com) offers a huge selection of reasonably priced new and used CDs, DVDs, and vinyl, plus novelties. The Corner location carries the current underground and mainstream hits, features an in-store coffee bar and lounge, and offers listening stations for previewing music. **Sidetracks Music**, located off the Downtown Mall, is small, but always has the right titles in stock, supplemented by a stellar assortment of artwork by painter Steve Keene, who's done album covers for Pavement and the Apples in Stereo.

Being a culturally high-minded town, it should come as little surprise that Charlottesville features one of the highest per capita ratios of public radio stations in the country. Owned by UVa but supported in large part by the community, **WTJU-FM** (www.wtju.radio.virginia. edu) is the area's premier tastemaker for eclectic listeners, featuring rock, jazz, folk, classical, roots, blues, world, techno, news, and children's programming, with the occasional in-studio appearance and lively interview. Famous station alumni include Stephen Malkmus and Bob Nastanovich of Pavement, David Berman of Silver Jews, James McNew of Yo La Tengo, and John Beers of the Happy Flowers. Today, the station, while not quite freeform, continues to evolve with the adventurous ear in mind. WTJU's hold on the rock landscape receives healthy competition from upstart **WNRN** (www.wnrn.rlc.net). Founded in 1996, WNRN is the place to hear programmed college rock with an emphasis on breaking artists, adult alternative, and local flavor.

*—Dominic J. DeVito & Carl Young*

# Chicago, IL

## COLUMBIA COLLEGE
600 S. Michigan Ave.
Chicago, IL 60605
www.colum.edu

C hicago's Columbia College is located in the city's south Loop area, downtown and nestled into the city's cultural network, only minutes from the Art Institute, Symphony Center and the city's countless theaters and rock venues. The school specializes in media arts and performing arts and its music program offers three major programs of study: composition, jazz studies, and vocal/instrumental performance. Columbia also offers a music business degree, and students in the program get hands-on experience working for the school's very own record label, AEMMP, which records, releases, and markets albums by student bands and solo artists.

Rock & roll fans will be pleased to know that, in addition to the jazz curriculum, Columbia introduces rock and popular music terms, vocabulary, and styles into the curriculum. Sample electives and courses demonstrate the range of programs available for study. Take Chant to Zappa: Music Through the Ages, Popular Contemporary Music, Black Pop Music in America, or Life and Music of Duke Ellington if you're looking to whet your appetite for pop culture studies.

Columbia also puts on an assortment of its own music events, including the annual Manifest, where students are encouraged to showcase their bands, contribute their art, writing, performances, and school/personal projects. Student organizations set up tables and tents to talk to students about joining in the next year and provide instruction on how to become involved with extracurricular groups that will give them experience for their major and career path. Every month, the school hosts Big Mouth, an open mic/talent show for Columbia students who aspire to be poets, MCs, singers, instrumentalists, comedians, actors and dancers. And various Columbia buildings put on performances each week by student musicians who sign up to play free gigs.

## UNIVERSITY OF CHICAGO
116 East 59th St.
Chicago, IL 60637
www.uchicago.edu

The University of Chicago has carved out a reputation as one of the country's best research institutions, and its music program hews to that reputation: It's primarily research-based and stresses theory, historical study, analysis, and ethnomusicology, though its composition program is also well regarded. But you don't need to be a music major to take advantage of the department's offerings. U of Chicago allows all students to sample classes such as Music Analysis and Criticism or Women and Music, Opera: Its Divas, Queens and Enchantresses.

# DEPAUL UNIVERSITY
One East Jackson Blvd.
Chicago, IL 60604
www.depaul.edu

**D**ePaul University is located in Chicago's Lincoln Park, a quaint neighborhood that houses shops, restaurants, brownstones, and the majority of the city's nightclubs. The school's music program takes advantage of its location and the city's resources: students are encouraged to join institutions like the Chicago Symphony or the Lyric Opera. Undergraduate music students will spend their first two years focusing on a general curriculum and the final two on a specific concentration. Students can earn a bachelor of music in performance, composition, jazz studies, music education or arts management. The management concentration prepares you for the business side of the industry—and you don't need to focus only on non-profits such as opera companies or classical music institutions. The major will prepare you for jobs in the commercial world including merchandising, promotion, and other aspects of the record business. DePaul also offers a bachelor of science in sound recording technology that will train you as a producer or engineer.

# ROOSEVELT UNIVERSITY
430 S. Michigan Ave.
Chicago, IL 60605
www.roosevelt.edu

**O**riginally called Chicago Musical College, Roosevelt University's conservatory is among the top programs in Chicago. The school's Auditorium Theater has become a favorite performance spot for classical acts and rockers alike, drawing Elvis Costello, Wilco, and R.E.M. for on-campus gigs. Roosevelt offers a bachelor of music in composition, jazz studies, music education, orchestral studies, or performance. Expect to take a spate of courses—everything from theory to music history—along the way. Some courses include Music of Today, which highlights trends in late modern and post-modern music. Or for those interested in studying the music business, or gearing up for a career in pop music, take Commercial Music, which promises a break from the classical curriculum.

## VENUES:

### Metro/Smart Bar, 3730 N. Clark St., www.metrochicago.com

The Metro is Chicago's most venerated rock institution. Situated ironically across the street from the World's Largest Frat Party, a k a Wrigley Field, it is relatively uncommon for a band to achieve national acclaim without playing here first. In twenty years, the 1,000-capacity venue has seen performances by R.E.M., Red Hot Chili Peppers, Nirvana, Smashing Pumpkins (who played some of their first gigs here), Weezer, the Strokes, and the White Stripes. It still breaks the city's biggest bands as well as hosting multi-night runs by Sonic Youth, Guided by Voices, and Built to Spill. Downstairs in Smart Bar, late-night dance parties—occasionally deejayed by the bands who took the stage earlier in the evening—frequently pay tribute to Chicago house if live DJs like Paul Oakenfold or Afrika Bambaataa aren't behind the decks themselves.

### Double Door, 1572 N. Milwaukee Ave., www.doubledoor.com

By virtue of its Wicker Park address, the Double Door has retained its reputation as Chicago's hipster stronghold in the wake of the early-Nineties Liz Phair/Urge Overkill/Local H boom. Now a home for indie acts like Spoon and the Soundtrack of Our Lives, the club's biggest asset is the downstairs safety hatch/pool room, where you can escape the city's chattiest clientele and catch the band you paid to see on a number of televisions with live feeds.

### Empty Bottle, 1035 N. Western Ave., www.emptybottle.com

The best compliment we can pay the dilapidated bathrooms at the Empty Bottle is to say that the music onstage is just as adventurous. Slightly off the beaten path, Bruce Finkelmann's dive is the city's experimental jazz Mecca. Underground hip-hop, angular post-punk, and European art rock stick to the grungy walls, and while you're sampling the scene's cheapest drink menu—$2 cans? In Chicago? In 2005?—Jeff Tweedy can occasionally be found chatting up the regulars about the next Wilco record.

### Schubas, 3159 N. Southport Ave., www.schubas.com

The stage at this sixteen-year-old club feels almost too nice to be in an indie rock bar, and a healthy dose of singer-songwriters helps enhance the cozy aesthetic. But in case you're worried that it's a glorified coffee shop, Schubas has been a springboard for Ben Kweller, Pete Yorn, Damien Rice, and Pedro the Lion.

### Bottom Lounge, 3206 N. Wilton Rd., www.bottomlounge.com

Since the fall of the vaunted Fireside Bowl—where no less than Alkaline Trio cut their teeth—the Bottom Lounge has picked up the slack and served a steady diet of punk rock from national acts and locals. Chicago-based Victory Records, one of the country's biggest indie labels and home to Atreyu, Taking Back Sunday, and Hawthorne Heights, uses the Bottom Lounge as a testing ground for new acts. While a number of pillars obstruct views and drink prices are too high, the Red Line of Chicago's train system lets you off right outside, and that's a convenience that's hard to beat.

### The Hideout, 1354 W. Wabansia St., www.hideoutchicago.com

For pure kitsch, the Hideout cannot be beaten. Stationed in an industrial park with nothing remotely hospitable surrounding it, the venue is home to Chicago's fertile alt-country scene. This two-story joint is nestled between warehouses where truckers and hipsters stop by to hear otherworldly jams and acoustic-guitar strumming from Billy Corgan, Jeff Tweedy, Neko Case, and the insurgent himself, Robbie Fulks. The Hideout's early-fall block party is also one of the city's best-kept secrets.

### Elbo Room, 2871 N. Lincoln Ave., www.elboroomchicago.com

Those in the know often joke that if your band can't get a gig at any of Chicago's loftier establishments, they can always get one at Elbo

Room. It's not entirely true: Rachael Yamagata used the room to solidify her pre-record deal fan base and some national acts—including the post-Morphine outfit Twinemen—have made the best of this intimate space. The Elbo Room is one of those rare clubs where you can get in without having to pay to see the band, and the music room's width can accommodate more than curious onlookers.

### House of Blues, 329 N. Dearborn Ave., www.hob.com

It's a credit to the Chicago House of Blues' staff that locals forgive the venue's franchise status. Frequently a pit stop for middle-of-the-road major label acts, it has also become a home for the metal underground (Hatebreed, Dead to Fall) and indie acts such as Modest Mouse and the Shins. While liquor prices and unbelievable overcrowding continue to plague the H.O.B., credit is due for the club's unwavering support of new and old, not to mention the fact that it has the leading hip-hop stage in Chicago.

### Buddy Guy's Legends, 754 S. Wabash St., www.buddyguyslegends.com

Owned by blues trailblazer—and Chicago native—Buddy Guy, this club's calendar is packed with a rotating cast of hometown bluesmen such as Willie Kent and Joe Moss. In January, Guy does his own month-long residency, and the venue is also a sort of home-away-from-home for the Rolling Stones, who often use this solitary club on the Near Southside for their personal after-party. Somewhere Howlin' Wolf is smiling.

### Abbey Pub, 3420 W. Grace St., www.abbeypub.com

The Abbey used to be merely a neighborhood Irish pub where locals would go to watch a Saturday soccer match. But when one of Chicago's best indie clubs, the Lounge Ax, shut its doors in 2001, The Abbey began to inherit some of the top independent touring talent in the country. Lately, the pub's bookings have focused on the local hip-hop scene, but leave room for singer-songwriters and quirky acts such as the indie rock orchestra the Rachel's. The Abbey's bookers also put on shows at another upscale Irish bar in town, Gunther Murphy's (www.gunthermurphys.com); their calendar is spotty, but worth checking out nonetheless.

**The Note, 1565 N. Milwaukee Ave.,**
**www.thenotechicago.com**

Chicago didn't have a grimy, balls-to-the-wall club so it had to invent the Note. On the weekends, garage bands from both the city and suburbs bang it out, but during the week this place is dominated by DJs and the unlikeliest of unlikely: samba.

**Uncommon Ground, 1214 W. Grace St.,**
**www.uncommonground.com**

As a true-to-life coffee bar, Uncommon Ground is the essential post-Sixties Chicago folk hangout. Triple bills occur nearly every night of the week, and this quiet neighbor (just north of the Metro) also hosts an annual Jeff Buckley Tribute.

**Logan Square Auditorium, 2539 N. Kedzie Ave.,**
**www.logansquareauditorium.com**

While Bottom Lounge has thrived, this 600-capacity venue in a borderline neighborhood —resistant to gentrification from a longstanding community—books tall acts (Urge Overkill, Arcade Fire, !!!), but has yet to conquer its awful acoustics. Post-Fireside spillover makes up most of the weekly fare and its high school auditorium vibe fits its teen skate patrons perfectly.

**Silvie's, 1902 W. Irving Park Rd.,**
**www.silvieslounge.com**

The Chicago music scene has a preternatural gift for picking up slack, and Silvie's is evidence of that. Barely months after the Lyons Den punk hangout shuttered itself, this new entry rolled out the carpet just down the block. Like Double Door and Bottom Lounge, you can fall off the CTA onto its doorstep, nixing taxis and giving you more money to budget for lick-uh.

**Martyrs', 3855 N. Lincoln Ave.,**
**www.martyrslive.com**

If there's a remaining hippie stronghold in the city, this be it. Martyrs' best offering is Tributosaurus, which, on the first Monday of every month, morphs into a different cover band from the Ramones to Steely Dan. And the place has recently become the stomping grounds of U.K. bands come Stateside such as Keane, Ed Harcourt, and the Delays.

**Old Town School of Folk Music, 4544 N. Lincoln Ave.,**
**www.oldtownschool.org**

Perhaps the city's most acoustically perfect room, Old Town School is the rare example of a venue that actually enhances performance. You're bound to remember where you were when you saw your favorite band, but no other Chicago location brings out sonic nuances of acts like this one. Linked directly to the Second City's deep folk lineage (John Prine, Steve Goodman), acoustic performances here (Steve Earle, Neko Case, Mavis Staples) are rites of passage for local folkies.

**Sonotheque, 1444 W. Chicago Ave.,**
**www.sonotheque.net**

Can and Kraftwerk outrank crunk every day and twice on Sundays at Sonotheque, a nightclub where "dance music" takes on a whole new meaning. The linear physique of this River North hangout welcomes high-profile DJs (TV On The Radio, Aluminum Group) spinning the kinds of electro-tinged tunes you won't hear on Top 40 radio.

**FitzGerald's, 6615 W. Roosevelt Rd., Berwyn,**
**www.fitzgeraldsnitclub.com**

It might only be close to UIC students—and a bit of a hike even for them—but FitzGerald's is like a tourist attraction for non-tourists. Most people have seen it before in films such as *The Color of Money, A League of Their Own*, and *Adventures in Babysitting*. But to be inside is like opening the wrong door in a movie and winding up in a veritable roadhouse. In a bit of role reversal, FitzGerald's doesn't rely on its historical cachet to recruit ancient artists like most Chicago blues clubs; this suburban outpost behaves as if it's the only ticket in town.

**U.S. Beer Co., 1801 N. Clybourn,**
**www.usbeercompany.com**

The last thing Northside yuppies wanted in their backyards was a metal club, but it's exactly what they got with U.S. Beer. It's not the best place to see a show—unless you're fond of sonic imbalance and a lead singer who's routinely mixed too high—but the bar has more than enough guts. During the summer's annual MOBfest local band celebration, U.S. Beer is known to book more than seventy bands in a single weekend. That's why the neighbors don't like them.

### The Aragon Ballroom, 1106 W. Lawrence Ave. and 4800 North, www.aragon.com

Named for a province in Spain, the Aragon was built in 1926 as high-scale ballroom full of crystal chandeliers and mosaic tiles. Today, the Aragon fills its 5,000 capacity floor and balcony by hosting alt-rock acts such as Interpol, the Used and the White Stripes on the nights when there isn't a Spanish-language act headlining. (Los Monstros de Rock en la casa!) The venue has great sightlines and acoustics, but its t-shaped barricade keeps crowds from getting as close to the stage as they might like.

### Riviera, 4746 N. Racine Ave.

With a huge floor and adjoining balcony and some of the best acoustics, the 2,300 capacity Riviera hosts mostly rock bands such Muse and Death Cab for Cutie before they're large enough to move to the UIC Pavilion. The floor is a little flat and not so easy to see the stage from if you're short. When a band plays the Riv, you know that it's your last chance to see them play close enough to be remotely visible.

### The Vic Theatre, 3145 North Sheffield, www.victheatre.com

Accommodating 1,400 people is no sweat for the Vic, which has seats for 1,000 in its upstairs balcony. The theater was designed in 1912 by architect John E.O. Pridmore and operated for years as an ornate, five-story vaudeville house. Easily accessible by train off the always-hopping Belmont stop in Lakeview, the Vic welcomes indie-rock bands (Le Tigre, the Gossip, Old '97s) weekly as well as holding "Brew and View" movie screenings.

## RECORD STORES:

### Reckless Records, 3157 N. Broadway, 1532 N. Milwaukee www.recklessrecords.com

Nick Hornby originally wrote *High Fidelity* to take place in London, but the Cusack film adaptation rests on stereotypes you might find at either locale of Chicago's notorious Reckless Records stores. Sure, record store clerks from Williamsburg, NY to Lawrence, KS are surly pricks but the Reckless store itself will intimidate you even before you ask someone if the new Q And Not U is any good. "What, are you a fucking asshole?" Actually (and perhaps unfortunately), this has never happened at Reckless, the greatest of Chicago's indie record sheds.

### Record Emporium, 3346 N. Paulina, www.recordemporium.com

Step into Mike Felten's Record Emporium and you won't know who's coming or going. Sure, you're inside, but for as long as the store has been there Felten has kept the appearance that he's either moving in or ready to break his lease. It's probably an ingenious business plan to make you buy that Sun Ra record you unearthed—almost literally—in the back: This store don't look like it'll be here tomorrow.

### Dusty Groove America, 1120 N. Ashland Ave., www.dustygroove.com

Dusty Groove is one of the best things about living in Chicago, and yet you don't have to live in Chicago to avail yourself of its awesome selection of funk, soul, hip-hop, jazz and world beat gems. All of Dusty's wares are available on its web site, which is updated daily with the newest rare albums the store has gotten its hands on. Of course, one benefit of proximity to the store is that you can order a pile of obscure Brazilian LPs online and then go pick them up at Dusty Groove's take-out window. No, seriously. The shop caters to DJs searching for original grooves to sample, or to the serious record collector who's dying to track down an original gatefold pressing of Kool & The Gang's *Love & Understanding*.

### Groovin' High Inc., 1047 W. Belmont, www.groovinhighinc.com

Raising the bird to business trends, Groovin' High actually OPENED as an indie record store in 2003. Aside from being the tidiest record shop you've ever been in, it's also not very intimidating and you'll have the courage to ask questions like "Which George Harrison album was the good one?" As a tip, check bins. Groovin' sneaks a gem in there occasionally whether they know it or not.

### Rock Records, 175 W. Washington

While Columbia, Art Institute, and downtown DePaul kids have their pick of Chicago's architecture and museums on their doorsteps, they can only count on a sole independent record store, and Rock

Records is it. The space feels like a Tower Records in that "I know there's money behind this, so why don't they spruce it up?" kind of way, but it's just as likely to carry a stack of Norah Jones discs for the bustling Loop as it is a T. Rex import for the rest of us geeks.

### Metal Haven, 604 W. Belmont Ave.,
### www.metalhavenchicago.com

That Metal Haven sits in the heart of Boystown is not hilarious, it's great. Their Top 20 is full of bands and album titles you wouldn't repeat to yourself in a dark moment and if we're to believe that metal is the real punk rock, then it deserves a spot like this.

### Dr. Wax, 5225 S. Harper,
### www.drwax.com

University of Chicago students, among other things, are renowned for slogans saluting their school such as "U of C: Where fun goes to die." Part of that wisecrack can be attributed to the fact that there's nowhere to see live music in the Hyde Park neighborhood, although it can lay claim to Dr. Wax, an essential record store if there ever was one.

### Gramaphone Ltd., 2843 N. Clark,
### www.gramaphonerecords.com

Even with the latest Euro remixes blaring on the in-store PA, everyone inside Gramaphone bobs their head to their own beat. That's because the city's DJs wear headphones in this Lincoln Park cubbyhole while trying to determine what to splice from the vinyl they're sampling. Prepare to be bumped while looking for something bumpin'.

### Jazz Record Mart, 444 N. Wabash,
### www.jazzrecordmart.com

The retail wing of Chicago's legendary Delmark record label, Jazz Mart is a collector's wet dream. Since 1959 (1965 at this location), Bob Koester has been the first person jazz and blues novices have looked to, and the store's collection of bootlegs, 78s, and, um, *everything* is unrivaled by anything else in the nation.

### Hi-Fi Records, 2570 N. Clark,
### www.hifirecords.com

Hi-Fi, which has a standalone and a spot underneath the Metro venue, specializes in vinyl and independent records along with the largest selection of crummy promo CDs you'll ever see. Elite without the added pretense of jerky clerks, DePaul kids call Hi-Fi an alternative to the slim pickings of Chicago radio.

## RADIO STATIONS:

### WXRT 93.1 FM,
www.wxrt.com

Once an independent holdout for progressive programming, XRT has aged—not well. Even as one of the few stations in town to take chances on new music (Flaming Lips, Modest Mouse), it struggles to break free from a 1965-85 time warp, and if you can listen for an hour without hearing a Pretenders tune...could be worse, though.

### WKQX 101.1 FM,
www.q101.com

Q101, as it's known, led Chicago radio into the alternative rock battleground during the nineties, set up camp, and hasn't budged since. Though its schedule is peppered with local music programs—all in the prime listening hours of Sunday night—its anchor is morning madman Mancow Muller, which pretty much says it all. Q101 is a guy's station with mask. The greatness of Q101 is its willingness to promote just about any show in town and its accessibility to youngsters looking to join street teams.

### WLUW 88.7 FM,
www.wluw.org

Loyola's WLUW is more like a community station than a college one, LUW—which also hosts an annual record fair—works with NPR to provide the city of Chicago a voice for their community. The most popular of any college radio station in Chicago, this is what the music elitists listen to whenever a Saddle Creek song isn't playing on their i-Pod. The show to listen to is Radio One Chicago. It's on every Thursday from 6:30 to 10:00 P.M. and is dedicated to the Chicago music scene. Chris Siuty and Mike Gibson have been doing the show in one form or another for almost five years and they do know their stuff. Every week has at least one live performance and every year they release a comp of the show.

WCRX, 88.1 FM,
www.colum.edu/crx/

Columbia's college station is targeted at the club fan, the dance addict, and the vinyl lover. If you are any of those, be sure to check out the station, staffed mostly by Columbia College radio majors. The main problem with the signal is that they're the lowest possible FM on the dial and they're located in the loop. In other words, it's like they don't have a signal. On the plus side, you can listen online.

## MISCELLANEOUS EVENTS:

### Wicker Park Fest
### Belmont/Sheffield Fest

Chicago is home to dozens of street festivals in the summer, but Wicker Park fest and Belmont/Sheffield have the best musical attractions. In 2004, the French Kicks, Wheat and the Ponys headlined Wicker Park Fest; two years ago, Interpol played the Belmont/Sheffield event and admission was a mere five bucks.

### Estrojam

Chicago's answer to Ladyfest, Estrojam is a weeklong gynocentric music and arts festival created by Columbia graduate Tammy Cresswell. In addition to hosting panels such as "DIY Filmmaking" and a breakdancing battle, Estrojam has welcomed grrrl bands including Pretty Girls Make Graves and Northern State.

### Mobfest

While not quite on par with SXSW or CMJ, Mobfest brings the music industry to Chicago on a smaller scale, booking dozens of bands—many unknown or unsigned—to venues around the city. Past acts have included the Killers, Rachel Yamagata, and Kill Hannah.

—*Steve Forstneger*

# Cincinnati, OH

## THE UNIVERSITY OF CINCINNATI
College Conservatory of Music
Mary Emery Hall
P.O. Box 210003
Cincinnati, OH 45221-0003
www.ccm.uc.edu

f you're a budding opera diva or you can just blow on the sax, Cincinnati might not jump to mind as the musical Mecca for getting your act together. But the University of Cincinnati's College Conservatory of Music has been pumping out virtuosos, professors, Broadway singers, and hot session players for nearly fifty years. Since its incorporation into the university's campus in 1962, the conservatory has grown into a mini-university of its own, with four on-campus halls (ranging in size) that host more than 1,000 performances per year—more than any other venue in the state. Though CCM doesn't officially offer co-op or internship programs, the stage experience—from solo recitals to full-fledged operas—and close ties with the Cincinnati Opera provide ample opportunity to get real-world experience on the stage and in the classroom. The musical theater program is considered one of the tops in the country and the voice and conducting programs are also nationally ranked.

In addition to dance and electronic media focuses, CCM has six academic divisions: composition, musicology/theory, opera/music theater/arts administration, ensembles/conducting, and keyboard and music education. Classes range from jazz saxophone and classical guitar to the history of jazz and pop, with more than a hundred possible choices of majors. Students can also learn about stage management and sound design.

## VENUES:

**Bogart's, 2621 Vine St.,**
**www.bogarts.com**

Located within walking distance of campus on "short Vine," a lively strip of tattoo parlors, restaurants, record stores, and other music venues, this 1,400-capacity club, formerly a movie house and restaurant, has a wide open (permanently sticky) floor and a balcony that offers a great vantage point for viewing the more than 200 shows a year. From metal to rock and jam bands, Bogart's has hosted a galaxy of stars over the years, some on their way up, some peaking and others just looking for an intimate place to play between Cleveland and Lexington. More than anything, it's a great place to see promising bands such as Chevelle, Kings of Leon, and Umphrey's McGee up close and personal before they graduate to more cavernous rooms. Among the illustrious alumni are: Red Hot Chili Peppers, the Strokes, Tracy Chapman, Sting, Goo Goo Dolls, Lenny Kravitz, Pearl Jam, and Limp Bizkit.

**Southgate House, 24 E 3rd St. Newport,**
**www.southgatehouse.com**

Worth the fifteen-minute drive from campus, this towering mansion on the Kentucky side of the Ohio River was built in 1814 and once hosted Abraham Lincoln. The birthplace of Brigadier General John Tariaferro Thompson, the inventor of the 1920s gangsta favorite Tommy gun, has been converted into one of the best and hippest music venues in the area. The main ballroom holds more than 500 people and has been filled by everyone from the Afghan Whigs, the Arcade Fire, Elliott Smith, Flaming Lips, and Guided by Voices to Little Richard, Modest Mouse, and the White Stripes. The first floor lounge has pool tables and a small area where bluegrass bands, singer/songwriters, and assorted oddballs entertain those bellied up to the bar. A third, more intimate parlor upstairs also presents a wide array of offbeat small shows and the third-floor gallery has a rotating display of local, regional, and international art works. On a good night, you can catch a mind-expanding array of acts on all three floors.

**The Mad Frog, 1 E. McMillan St.,**
**www.themadfrog.net**

With live music seven nights a week, this center-of-campus spot has a little something for everyone. Sunday is jazz night, Mondays boast the very popular Latin dance sessions with local salsa band Tropicoso, Tuesday's are DJ nights and budding CCM singers can try their pipes out at Wednesday night's Open Mic. The rest of the week is a mix of jam bands, rock, and lots of local acts.

**Sudsy Malone's Rock and Roll Laundry, 2626 Vine St.,**
**www.sudsys.com**

Another staple of the short Vine strip, this 15-year old venue/laundromat has undergone a number of facelifts over the years. With washers and dryers in the back and a small stage in the front window, Sudsy's has hosted up-and-coming local acts as well as national draws including Stone Temple Pilots and the Melvins, Faster Pussycat, and L.A. Guns. Before he blew up, Beck even did an unannounced show here. These days, the 18+ club has rock & roll karaoke every Monday and books an eclectic mix of metal, hard rock, more metal, and the occasional death metal rocker. Wear black, and preferably some chains.

**Top Cat's, 2820 Vine St.**

If you're too small for Bogart's and not metal enough for Sudsy's, Top Cat's is the place for you. It looks like something straight out of indie rock central casting, with a long bar along one side, a cramped merch area in the back and a cozy stage parked in the far corner. Alert hipsters can catch bands like Hot Hot Heat, Muse, and the Black Eyed Peas in this former mortuary before they graduate down the street, or roll the dice and see lesser-known national and local punk and ska acts.

## RECORD STORES:

**Everybody's Records, 6106 Montgomery**
**www.everybodysrecords.com**

It requires a fifteen-minute drive north of campus, but for more than twenty-five years, Everybody's has been a no-nonsense independent store with a fat collection of rap, reggae, rock, jazz, soul, blues, punk, indie, hardcore, country, bluegrass, gospel CDs and vinyl.

**Mole's CD and Record Exchange, 111 Calhoun**

For thirty years, Mole's has been a haven for music lovers. The small storefront is packed with thousands of new and used classic and prog rock, reggae, pop, folk, and punk CDs, as well as one of the best used vinyl collections in town.

**Shake It! Records, 4156 Hamilton Ave.,
www.shakeitrecords.com**

The best record store in town requires a short drive to the funky Northside neighborhood. A narrow storefront crammed with all the indie rock, reggae, punk, and electronic miscellanea you could want on CD and vinyl, old family-owned Shake It! is a soothing antidote to generic record stores. It also hosts in-stores and has its own record label. Plus, there's a magazine selection to make Barnes & Noble blush.

# RADIO:

**BearCast Radio, 2217 Mary Emery Hall, P.O. Box 2100,
www.bearcast.uc.edu**

This training ground for students studying communications is part of the College Conservatory of Music village. The Internet-only station has a broad range of programs, including Top 40 music, metal, oldies, garage rock and electronic.

—*Gil Kaufman*

# Cleveland, OH

## CASE WESTERN RESERVE
103 Tomlinson Hall
10900 Euclid Ave.
Cleveland, OH 44106-7055
www.case.edu

## CLEVELAND INSTITUTE OF MUSIC
11021 East Blvd.
Cleveland, OH 44106
www.cim.edu

The Case Department of Music offers a variety of degree programs, including a bachelor of science in Music Education and a bachelor of arts in music. Students in the B.A. program can focus their studies in several ways, by concentrating on performance, general musicianship, music history, music education, and audio recording technology. Case also allows music majors to participate in a joint program with the Cleveland Institute of Music (housed on the same campus), which permits students at both schools to take advantage of each other's facilities. For its part, CIM offers concentrations in performance, composition, eurhythmics, music theory, piano accompanying and Suzuki pedagogy. Both the Case music department and CIM require an audition as well as a music theory placement test.

Case encourages students to pursue a double major, which is particularly appropriate for those who want to take advantage of the school's Audio Recording Technology courses. For aspiring producers, a B.A. in music can be combined with a B.S. in engineering. The recording curriculum includes classes on studio techniques, multi-tracking, studio maintenance, and audio internships. There's also a course on Computers and Music, and the college's Center for Music and Technology includes Mac workstations equipped with MIDI keyboards for composing, sampling and music calligraphy.

Case and CIM students have access to the impressive Kulas Music Library, which boasts nearly 40,000 music scores, recordings, videos, periodicals, microforms and books. Case music majors, however, also get to use the CIM library, where they can refer to an even more specialized array of scores and musicological texts.

# VENUES:

### The Agora, 5000 Euclid Ave.,
### www.clevelandagora.com

One of the nation's best rock clubs, the Agora is Cleveland's preferred tour stop for punk and metal bands such as the Used, Taking Back Sunday, Slayer, and Satyricon. The Cleveland Agora originally opened in 1966 and moved to its current location in a dodgy part of downtown in 1985. The main theater holds 2,000, but there's also a smaller ballroom that holds 700 where local bands often perform. For an extra five dollars you can park your ride in the lot behind the theater.

### The Odeon, 1295 Old River Rd.,
### www.theodeon.com

Recently purchased by ClearChannel, the Odeon is a mid-size general admission venue located in the Flats. The club attracts acts like Staind, Hoobastank, the Donnas, and Papa Roach. The bathrooms are pretty gross, but there's a snack bar where you can buy chips and ice tea and other goodies. Area Top 40 station Q104 puts on its "Jingle Ball" holiday blow-out at the Odeon, and Cleveland teens go head to head at the Odeon during the annual High School Rock Off competition.

### The Grog Shop, 2785 Euclid Heights Blvd.

Oasis played here during their first American tour, but that's when nobody gave a damn about them. The Grog Shop is still putting on shows by bands on their way up—indie rockers such as Ted Leo and emo acts such as Midtown. When there's no band playing, the bar serves as a regular hang for local hipsters and punks. When there is a show, it's fairly affordable and easy to get right near the stage to see tomorrow's Oasis today.

### Peabody's, 2083 East 21st St.,
### www.peabodys.com

Located across the street from Cleveland State University, Peabody's often puts on shows that no one else will. So if you like seeing former Poison singer Bret Michaels do his solo bit, this is where you'll find it. But the venue, which has a large bar and a stage area out back, occasionally hosts a decent hip-hop or punk show by the likes of Bone Thugs N Harmony or Further Seems Forever. Locals say the shows never start on time, but at least they've got a good sound system.

**The Beachland Ballroom, 15711 Waterloo Rd., www.beachlandballroom.com**

A former Croatian social club, the building was converted into a rock venue in 2000 and has become a favorite club for many Cleveland music fans. The Beachland includes two stages—the Tavern and the Ballroom—with local bands playing the former and national acts the latter, both on the same night. The venue puts on an eclectic array of shows, including everything from Le Tigre and Los Straightjackets to Gogol Bordello, Richard Thompson and the Zombies. Plus, Beachland fans applaud the club's décor: poster-covered walls, old pinball machines and a jukebox that plays real 45 rpm vinyl singles.

**Blossom Music Center, 1145 W. Steels Corner, www.hob.com/venues/concerts/blossom/**

One of the nation's oldest amphitheaters, the Blossom opened its doors in 1968 with a show by Janis Joplin. The venue is located in Cuyahoga Falls, strategically accessible from both Cleveland and Akron. Though traffic jams en route to the venue detract from the overall experience, the Blossom is both visually and sonically arresting. Its wooden structure makes for great sound, and the theater itself is a beauty to behold. The pavilion seats around 5,000 and the other 17,000 sit on the lawn. This is THE place for most summer festivals—from Ozzfest to Jimmy Buffett's annual road show.

## RECORD STORES:

**Record Revolution, 1832 Coventry Rd.**

Duck into this record shop to avoid getting knocked down by local punks on skateboards whizzing by in the Coventry section of Cleveland. Around the corner from Little Italy and about ten minutes from downtown, Record Revolution houses the city's best-stocked local music section, as well as selling an impressive array of punk, thrash and classic rock records. The place has been around since the late sixties, but has adapted with the times: In the first of two large street-level rooms, you can buy t-shirts, incense, and chintzy "punk" jewelry. The second room houses new and used CDs and all the posters on the wall are for sale. Their bootleg selection tends to be overpriced, but the basement has tons of vinyl for sale.

### My Generation, 25947 Detroit Rd.

It may be located in a strip mall, but My Generation is a true blue record shop for bonafide music lovers. Its well-appointed selection includes jazz and classical, plus posters, t-shirts, imports, music magazines, and DVDs. The staff is knowledgeable and will order anything they don't stock in the store.

### Time Traveler, 2615 State Rd., Cuyahoga Falls

You'll have to schlep to Cuyahoga Falls—about twenty minutes away—to get to Time Traveler, but it's worth the trip. Cleveland music fans make frequent pilgrimages down there, and even stop by to hear local televangelist Ernest Angley broadcast his show—for free—across the street from the store. As one Clevelander puts it, "Drive down, get a Neil Young bootleg and get healed on local television." The store has all the requisite rock, jazz, and reggae, but "rare live imports" are Time Traveler's specialty. The Beach Boys section alone is larger then some entire record stores. There's a used CD bin in front where you might even find the Clash's *London Calling* for less than six bucks. Rare box sets are housed in a glass display case, worth ogling even just for fun.

### Bent Crayon, 11600 Detroit Ave., www.bentcrayon.com

Downtown Cleveland's only good stop for techno heads, Bent Crayon is a popular haunt for local DJs because of its selection of white-label vinyl.

## RADIO STATIONS:

### WBWC 88.3, www.wbwc.com

Baldwin-Wallace College's station was founded in 1958 as the first fully student funded station in the country. These days, its playlists include standard college radio fare. Punk and classic rock dominate the programming—but WBWC is still better than the average commercial station. And they often run eighteen-hour marathons of music by artists such as the Who, U2, and Yes.

**WCSB 89.3,**
**www.wcsb.org**

The student-run station at Cleveland State University plays a wide array of genres including folk, jazz, indie, techno, reggae, metal, and even a show called "Music of Macedonia." So it's no lie when they boast that it's not unusual to listen for a whole week and never hear the same song twice.

**WJCU 88.7,**
**www.wjcu.org**

The main event on John Carroll University's station is their Saturday rock show "Kick Out the Jams" with host Mitch Capka. Capka's a wild man who's been on the air for years and knows all there is to know about obscure garage and psych rock. The station as a whole has a strong reputation for playing only the best indie rock, in addition to specialty shows for reggae, electronica, and jazz.

## MISCELLANEOUS EVENTS:

**Rock and Roll Hall of Fame and Museum, One Key Plaza,**
**www.rockhall.com**

Open since 1985, the Rock and Roll Hall is the top tourist attraction in the state of Ohio. And for good reason: For $20, you get to spend the day perusing memorabilia from Robert Johnson, Jimi Hendrix, Britney Spears, and dozens of others. The bulk of the collection rests in the main exhibition hall on the ground floor of the pyramid-shaped glass building, designed by I. M. Pei. Exhibits constantly change, but priceless artifacts like Paul Simonon's smashed bass from the cover of *London Calling*, David Byrne's oversized white suit from *Stop Making Sense*, 3/4 of the Beatles original Sgt. Pepper's outfits (George was the lone holdout), John Lennon's grade school report grade, pieces of the plane that Otis Redding died in and countless more are on constant display. Two movie theaters in the main exhibit hall play documentaries on the history of rock. The higher levels usually are reserved for special exhibits that change about twice per year. Past exhibits have included: Lennon: A Life, In the Name of Love: U2, Reflections on the Supremes, The Psychedelic 60s, Got My Mojo Working: The Life of Muddy Waters and so forth. The hall of fame itself is located on the third and fourth floors. It has a multi-media presentation of the inductees' work as well as signatures on the wall of every inductee.

# Columbia, MO

## UNIVERSITY OF MISSOURI-COLUMBIA
Columbia, MO 65211
www.missouri.edu

Columbia, Missouri may seem like it's in the middle of "red state" nowhere—located almost exactly between St. Louis and Kansas City—but this small city is actually an oasis of rolling hills, left-leaning locals, and of course, higher learning. The flagship campus of the University of Missouri system calls Columbia home and, with its student population of more than 27,000, exerts a profound influence on life and culture in Columbia, a city with just 90,000 full-time residents.

Located just south of downtown, MU is best known for its life sciences and journalism schools, the latter rivaled only by Columbia and Northwestern in terms of stature. Befitting a top program, the J-school has vast resources with its own citywide daily newspaper, an NBC affiliate, and an NPR radio station among the outlets available to students.

The music school isn't particularly strong, but respectable with thirty-four full-time faculty and 220 majors, making it one of the larger areas of study in the Arts and Sciences college. Students must complete the basic liberal arts requirements before focusing on one of four major areas of concentration: performance, music theory, music history, and composition. Headquartered in the Fine Arts Building the department has an adequate number of practice rooms and studios for students to use. Scholarships are offered, though you must audition to be considered. Non-majors are welcome to take classes in the school with survey courses in jazz and rock history being two of the most popular.

## VENUES:

### The Blue Note, 17 N. Ninth St.,
### www.thebluenote.com

The epicenter of Columbia nightlife is the 9th and Broadway district, and venerable club the Blue Note—currently celebrating its twenty-fifth anniversary—is the clubhouse. During the Eighties college rock explosion, the Blue Note was one of the premier clubs in the country (Uncle Tupelo called it home and Hüsker Dü played their final show there in 1988). Now housed in an old vaudeville theater (it made the move downtown in 1994), the club still attracts artists such as the Faint, Ani DiFranco, and Wilco. A separate upstairs bar provides a respite from the crowd on the floor or a pit stop on the way to the balcony.

### Mojo's, 1013 Park Ave.,
### www.mojoscolumbia.com

Just down the hill from the Blue Note is Mojo's, a roadhouse-style bar that books buzzy indie acts (Arcade Fire, British Sea Power) as well as healthy contingent of local groups. The club also offers Cajun-influenced food on the weekends as well as a giant outdoor patio—the perfect setting for the free Friday happy hour or the Sunday night blues jam.

### The Music Café, 120 S. Ninth St.,
### www.themusiccafecolumbia.com

The quirky Music Café isn't the best place to see a show (the stage is immediately to your right as you enter making for a harrowing trip to the bar in the back when its crowded), but if it's beer you're after, you've found nirvana. More than 125 types are available, with everything from the most obscure Belgian ale to the old Missouri standby, Budweiser. The club features live music every night of the week (a lot of jam bands, local acts and the occasional national artist), but if the music is weak, check out the back where more than 7,000 used CDs are available for sale.

# RECORD STORES:

### Streetside, 401 S. Providence Rd.

This Missouri-based chain caters to the everyman record buyer in Columbia. The classical, jazz, and rock selections are particularly well stocked, and they have a nice bin of used CDs. (Added bonus: they pay the most in town for your own used selections).

### Apop Records, 807 Locust

The newest addition to the record store scene in Columbia feels like someone emptied out their dorm room and dumped it here. The place might be a mess, but they have a healthy collection of indie vinyl along with the requisite fanzines and alternative press.

### Whizz, 20 S. Ninth

While Apop has the market cornered on hipster vinyl, Whizz specializes in mainstream rock, country and funk. The knowledgeable sales staff will help you find some gems at a reasonable price (an *Exile on Main Street* LP with the actual zipper for $17.99).

### Slackers, 1020 Broadway

Slackers has the largest and best selection of used CDs in town, but also caters to the gaming set with a huge assortment of used and new xBox and Nintendo games available. They'll even buy those vintage Atari 2600 or Colecovision sets taking up space in your mom's basement.

# RADIO STATIONS:

Befitting a town with a major university, the MU radio station **KCOU** (www.kcou.mu.org) has quality varied programming (though locals bitch that it was better in the Eighties), with the Tuesday night flashback show "Same as It Ever Was" garnering a faithful following. The non-collegiate radio market is surprisingly fertile, highlighted by the lefty community station **KOPN** (www.kopn.org) and the rock station **KBXR** (www.bxr.com), which often dares to deviate from the standard corporate playlist.

*—Matt Hendrickson*

# Columbia, SC

## UNIVERSITY OF SOUTH CAROLINA
813 Assembly St.
Columbia, SC 29208
www.sc.edu

L ike many music departments associated with large universities, the one at USC provides its students with a complete music education but also ensures that graduates satisfy many requirements in separate subjects. Music students at USC can pursue either a bachelor of arts in music, or a bachelor of music degree, or they can minor in music if they've taken the necessary prerequisites, which include Introduction to Music Theory and Introduction to Music Literature. Particularly interesting courses offered by this department include Jazz and American Popular Music, World Music, and Theory of Twentieth Century Music.

B.A. students at USC must fulfill general education requirements in writing, the humanities, foreign language, and social sciences among others, as well as series of required major courses that include history of music, conducting, and ensemble work. In addition to these relatively standard requirements, bachelor of arts students must also satisfy two more unusual requirements: students must complete a minimum of twelve hours of cognate courses—advanced course work that is related to but outside the scope of the student's major, and a minimum of three cultural awareness courses, one pertaining to the culture of those who speak the foreign language studied by the student, one in North American studies, and one focused on a culture that is not American or Western European.

B.M. students must also fulfill the general education requirements but are held to fewer extra-music demands than B.A. students because they are busy with the ninety hours of major requirements they are expected to log! Bachelor of music students concentrate in one of four areas: performance, theory, composition, or jazz studies and, like bachelor of arts students, must take courses in topics like music theory and history.

# COLUMBIA COLLEGE
1301 Columbia College Dr.
Columbia SC 29203
www.columbiacollegesc.edu

**M**usic students at Columbia College study four main subjects: performance, music education, sacred music, and piano pedagogy. In addition to bachelor of music degrees in these areas, the college also offers a bachelor of arts degree in music, which is well suited to those who are drawn primarily to the academic study of music and not to music performance. The sacred music program is particularly uncommon; students enrolled specialize in organ or in vocal music, training which prepares them for careers as church organists or choir directors. Columbia College students who concentrate in piano pedagogy train to teach piano in their communities, music education students train to teach music in primary and secondary schools, and performance students focus on all phases of performance with respect to a variety of instruments.

## VENUES:

**New Brookland Tavern, 122 State St.,**
**www.newbrooklandtavern.com**

The longest-running rock club in town, New Brookland anchors the area locals call Vista West. Even though it's a capital city, Columbia is often skipped in the routing of bigger touring bands. But when an indie or punk band does decide to stop here, it's usually at New Brookland. Bands such as Iron and Wine, AnBerlin, Enon, Of Montreal, Rainer Maria, Rogue Wave, and Calla have played for drunken hipster gatherings. Locals and artists complain about the venue's size—a capacity of 300 with no backstage area—but New Brookland is the only rock-style club in town where kids with the latest pins on their jackets and white studded belts can act like rock stars while opening for rock stars. It's also the place where mall-core teenagers and metal heads get to rub elbows. But what makes New Brookland unique is its twice-a-year freestyle battles, where talented crunkdified MCs spit rhymes in front of a mixed crowd. Anywhere dreads and hipsters can drink beer together has got to be cool.

### Art Bar, 1211 Park St.,
### www.artbarsc.com

Just over a year ago, Art Bar was a dance-only spot frequented by people with alternative lifestyles, people into goth and people who like to get really smashed. But once local guitar teacher and player Marty Fort started booking area bands at the club, music fans looking for a new venue were more than happy to pay the two-dollar cover to hear the darkest of Columbia's live bands. With two stages (one with a wall of TVs), Art Bar has stretched its arm into town and is famous for its all day festivals. Recently, Fort started booking national bands such as the Woggles, the Close and Elf Power.

### Headliners, 700 Gervais St.,
### www.headlinerscolumbia.com

With a 900-person capacity, Headliners is the biggest rock club in Columbia. But the fact that it shares walls with a college dance club scares people away —especially the hipsters. For that reason, most of the live music is jam-oriented. Rock bands that are obviously bent on getting radio spins play here, too. Booking agent Charles Wilkie has attempted to draw indie kids to the club, but shows with bands such as Keane, the Sounds, Rooney and the Von Bondies have bricked.

### Hunter-Gatherer, 900 Main St.

Columbians who are particular about the company they keep frequent Hunter-Gatherer with its "hello, my friends" atmosphere. Don't ask for a domestic or import beer here; the pub brews its own beer. Tuesday and Wednesday nights are reserved for the dinner eaters, but on Thursday nights, HG turns into a rich man's juke joint. Attorneys, politicians and bankers mingle with servers, artists and college students. On Friday nights, one band gets the two-set treatment, with the music beginning around 11 P.M. Local jazzologist Ross Taylor has made Columbia a destination for touring Chicago freak-jazz scenesters such as Triage and Dragons 1976. While most bands bring more wattage than necessary, making it near impossible for conversation, HG remains one of the classiest places in town.

# *RECORD STORES:*

### Acme Comics, 2757 Rosewood Dr.

Acme Comics owner Randy Dunn quit his job at a local record store after it was bought out by one of the big chains. A career music geek, Dunn decided to open his own place on Rosewood Drive, where there's plenty of shoppers around. Dunn brought three employees from his old job over to Acme, and the result is a comic book heaven with indie rock cred. Dunn and others put up their own collections of discs, records, and posters to start inventory. How hard it must've been to sell some of that stuff, but when you don't want to work for the man, what can you do?

### Manifest Discs & Tapes, 1563 Broad River Rd.

For nearly twenty years, Manifest had been Columbia's best mom-and-pop record store. But last year it changed ownership, added DVDs and cheesy t-shirts and stickers to its inventory, and raised its prices. Nonetheless, this remains a great place to guy buy obscure rock albums, and it's comforting to know the new CD you want is a fifteen-minute drive away and not three days—depending on how it's shipped.

### Papa Jazz Record Shoppe, 2014 Greene St.

Prepare to lose a few hours of your life in this hole-in-the-wall shop. Don't go here if you're claustrophobic, because unless you're as skinny as Mary-Kate Olsen, you have to contort your body to get through the aisle if someone else is thumbing through crates. The arrangement of stock can be disorienting, and, oh, yeah, there's also no air-conditioning. But if you're a serious record collector, this place has an incredible selection worth wading through. The store doesn't carry new titles, but you can order them and within a few days a friendly voice will call you to tell you your stuff has arrived.

### Sounds Familiar, 4420 Rosewood Ext.; 7252 Parklane Rd.

Once with stores spread throughout the city, Sounds Familiar had to downsize because of an industry-wide drop in album sales. The store is still kicking, offering better-than-average prices on new discs. With a mall record store decor—big posters and lame, stand up cutouts—SF is unlike mall record stores because the family-owned business hires folks who can actually discuss music with you, and they're as well versed in Southern hip-hop they are in the latest cool New York underground bands.

## RADIO STATIONS:

### WARQ 93.5 FM,
### www.warq.com

The station bills itself as "the rock of your world." Really? Until the last year, WARQ played lame new-metal and sorry excuses for hard rock. Like the rest of the mainstream world (thank "the O.C.," car commercials and, begrudgingly, MTV), WARQ woke up and realized that there were cool subgenres of rock out there, and that people actually want to hear bands like the Killers, Franz Ferdinand and Modest Mouse on the radio.

### WHXT 103.9 FM,
### www.hot1039fm.com

It plays the best hip-hop during its mix shows, but what makes this station so good is loud mouth DJ Charlemagne the God. This guy keeps it gutter and grimy. He railed Yung Wun, who was so high he didn't realize he was getting clowned. Charlemagne also called out the Ying Yang Twins on the air, but again, they were too far gone to get it. Guess that's crunk.

### WUSC 90.5,
### www.wusc.sc.edu

The USC radio station plays not only the requisite indie rock, but gives plenty of airtime to jazz, new age, industrial, and electronic in an assortment of specialty shows that commercial radio can't compete with.

—*Otis R. Taylor, Jr.*

# Columbus, OH

For the musically inclined, **Ohio State University** (www. osu.edu)—only a short drive away from Cincinnati—offers a large assortment of potential concentrations and majors. Students can pursue a bachelor of music education, a bachelor of music in performance (this curriculum emphasizes training on an instrument, or, for singers, vocal lessons), and a bachelor of arts in music. If you opt for the B.M., you can concentrate on music history—or musicology, as it is known in academic circles—so that you will be equipped to study, perform and write about all types of music from any and all eras. From there, the options are only as limited, it seems, as your imagination. For example: study baroque music, American jazz or Brazilian popular music. Musicology requires intense writing, theory and music history courses, even world music. You can also work toward a concentration in Jazz Studies, where performance skills, aural skills, and arranging become more important. A concentration in music theory involves technical and analytical coursework, including intense work with structure, history of theory, aesthetics of music, and music theory pedagogy. You can also earn a concentration in music composition, where conducting and orchestration courses will come into play.

Outside the Music School, there are other opportunities to study popular culture and its relation to music, specifically pop music. Check out the Comparative Cultural Studies Program for a fascinating, interdisciplinary approach to culture. You might enjoy classes such as Survey of African-Derived Music in the Western World, or Baadasssss Yearning: Cinema and Black Power.

For the casual concert fan, look forward to the Ohio Union Activities Board's series of concerts, which are produced for students either on campus or in Columbus venues.

Most off-campus concerts are held at one of two venues: **Newport Music Hall** or **PromoWest Pavilion** (www.promowestlive.com). Formerly the Agora Ballroom, the Newport has been operating under that name since 1984 but underwent a renovation in 2003 that replaced corroded ceiling tiles and widened the entryway. Located near campus on Columbus' main drag—High Street—the club seats 1,700 people, and it is not unusual for shows to sell out weeks in advance. On a given night, the line to get into a show will stretch out the door and for several blocks down the street. O.A.R. got their start here when they were still students at OSU, and local bands such as Ekoostik Hookah and Red Wanting Blue seem to play here on a monthly basis. But there's no shortage of touring acts gracing the Newport's stage: the Strokes, Ben Folds, Counting Crows, Red Hot Chili Peppers, Badly Drawn Boy, the Shins and Mos Def have all played here in recent years.

Consider Promowest a step up from the Newport. The venue is less than half a decade old, and is owned by the same management as the Newport. Often if a band sells out the Newport quickly, the show will be relocated to Promowest and its larger seating capacity of 3,000. The most striking feature of Promowest Pavilion is its versatility. During the colder months of the year, concerts are held indoors. But during the spring and summer, the stage is moved outdoors, where concertgoers lounge on the lawn. Either way, there is not a bad seat in the house when you come to artists including 311, Muse, Marilyn Manson, Ani DiFranco, LL Cool J and They Might be Giants.

Likewise, you'll spend most of your time—and money—at a pair of Columbus record stores that cater to the true music obsessive. Either **Johnny Go's House O' Music** or **Used Kids Records** will likely carry any disc you're craving. Johnny Go's, whose namesake owner can more often than not be found behind the counter, stocks everything from indie to mainstream rock. Like most mom-and-pop stores, this one has a healthy disrespect for Top 40 pop, and even stocks a limited selection of artists like N Sync under the heading "boy-band crap." If you deign to buy something from that section, be prepared for Go himself to mock you on your way out. If you are looking for a specific album, this is your best bet near campus. The majority of the store contains new music, with prices slightly higher than you can expect to find at Best Buy. Used CDs (and bootlegs) are stored in the back for reasonable prices, and Johnny Go's boasts the best poster selection in town. But the best aspect of the store is the owner himself. If you get on his good side, Johnny Go will share with you a wealth of knowledge about music that will blow your mind. If you earn his ire by purchasing a Lenny Kravitz poster, be prepared to hear about it. (Local legend has it that Go caught a shoplifter in the act and verbally berated him so badly the shoplifter eventually sued Go for intense emotional abuse. He was acquitted.)

Used Kids, meanwhile, is a top-notch used record store whose easy-to-miss entrance is lodged between two restaurants. The store itself is on the second floor, and even when it's open, it looks like it's closed. There are rows of new CDs right across from stacks and stacks of vinyl—new and used. But the real treasures here are the bins of used and promo CDs. If you look carefully, you can find at least one treasure hidden in these stacks, or at least kill some time between classes.

Of course, the monster of all between-class time-killers, the **Virgin MegaStore**, also has an outlet in Columbus. Not only can you find virtually any major new release here, they also stock a remarkably varied array of indie records, DVDs, videogames, and other music-oriented merch. And their listening stations allow you to sample pretty much any CD before you slap down your lunch money.

## *HONORABLE MENTION:*

# ANTIOCH COLLEGE

795 Livermore St.
Yellow Springs, OH 45387
www.antioch-college.edu

Located fifty-five miles west of Columbus, OH, Antioch is one of the nation's most unconventional schools and the kind of environment where creative types can thrive. Founded by the Christian Church, Antioch College's first president, Horace Mann, shaped educational policy by charging students to "[win] some victory for humanity." This lofty goal is achieved through the school's humanistic curriculum and, its most unique and salient feature, the co-operative work-study program: a series of internships that promise practical life experience. The school also preaches moderation and consideration of others' feelings, mutual respect and community. Students can earn a bachelor of arts or a bachelor of science and can take eight interdisciplinary majors. Among the offerings, you can design your own curriculum by focusing on three elements: classroom study, the co-op work experiences and participation in on-campus governance. Music majors will love the arts concentration, which lets you design your own major.

# Dallas, TX

## SOUTHERN METHODIST UNIVERSITY
6425 Boaz Ln.
Dallas, TX 75205
www.smu.edu

**D**espite its name, and its founding in 1911 by the United Methodist Church, this private college is nonsectarian in its teaching and offers students academic freedom and "open inquiry" by stressing research and a broad, liberal arts curriculum. The school offers a bachelor of music degree in performance, composition, music education and music therapy. Students can also earn a bachelor of arts degree in music and a minor in music. Performance majors are invited to specialize in one of many instruments—from harpsichord to guitar—and hone their skills through private lessons as well as performing in one of the university's ensembles. Music therapy contains elements of psychology and a rigorous clinical training to complement the music program. But classes are not limited to stuffy canonical subjects. The music department offers one course called Women and Music, "Like a Virgin": From Hildegard to Madonna, which promises a study of contemporary female singers and their social impact (the course also weaves in elements of gender studies, according to its description). There's also Music for Contemporary Audiences, which studies blues, folk, rock, and, everyone's favorite, Muzak.

## UNIVERSITY OF NORTH TEXAS
PO Box 311367
Denton, TX 76203-1367
www.unt.edu

**T**his Texas school lets students earn either a bachelor of arts—a liberal arts degree with a concentration in music—or a bachelor of music with concentrations in everything from composition studies to composing to jazz studies and music education. You can also study all types of performance, music history, music theory, and ethnomusicology. But the school's unique offerings are its variety of facilities that house the degree programs. Check out the Center for Experimental Music and Intermedia (CEMI) where you can study electroacoustic music and take advantage of technology for collaborative research based projects to composing and recording electronic music. On campus, there's also the Texas Center for Music and Medicine, another interdisciplinary laboratory where you will learn alongside musicians, clinicians and music educators. UNT also offers the Mountain Music Institute, a summer workshop where students can practice and perform in a bucolic, mountain setting.

## VENUES:

### The Gypsy Tea Room, 2548 Elm St., www.gypsytearoom.com

Located in the mostly defunct entertainment district Deep Ellum, the Gypsy Tea Room is now one of the sole reasons to venture down Good Latimer. Interpol, the Killers, Badly Drawn Boy, Coheed and Cambria, and Taking Back Sunday have played in the largest room of the venue, the ballroom, in the past year. But the best part of the Gypsy Tea Room is the actual tea room: a tiny room with a miniscule stage that has seen Sondre Lerche and the Moving Units play to a rapt cache of fans.

### Trees, 2709 Elm St., www.treeslive.com

Trees is a bit like Gypsy Tea Room's little sister. Located a few blocks down Elm Street, it boasts the same kind of high-profile performances, but in a much vaster locale. Trees has two levels, which accommodates both those who like to stand while watching the band and those who'd prefer sitting at a table and on couches to chitchat while listening to the live music. The one trick to master is avoiding getting stuck behind one of the large wood pillars, the venue's namesake, which tend to be quite obstructive at times.

### The Granada, 3524 Greenville Ave., www.granadatheater.com

The renovated Granada Theater recently reopened and its marquee is once again lit up with the names of underground punk bands such as Mae and Relient K, as well as more straight-rockin' fare including the Derek Trucks Band, Supersuckers and Nineties "It" girl Aimee Mann. The Granada is a bit more upscale than your average Dallas rock club, but it's still affordable—even if you want to sample something from the new menu of snacks with musical names such as the Widespread Panic and the Cure Taco.

### Rubber Gloves Rehearsal Studios, 411 East Sycamore, Denton, www.rubberglovesdentontx.com

Less than forty miles north of Dallas, Denton has a nice lil' rock scene of its own. Its preeminent venue is Rubber Gloves. Legend has it the Ataris' "Teenage Riot" was written about a show they played here years ago that was busted by Denton PD. But that was back when the place was small and dingy. Now Rubber Gloves is a little more polished, a little bigger and has noticeably lost some of its spirit. Nonetheless, it remains one of the area's best places to see little-known bands for a tiny price with an ultra cheap bar ($2.50 for 32-ounce beers on Tuesday nights have been a staple at RGRS for many years.) And you can be sure you won't have to worry about anyone having a cooler haircut than you, because you won't find a place less pretentious than Rubber Gloves nowadays.

### Hailey's, 122 Mulberry St., Denton, www.haileysclub.com

Denton music fans either love Hailey's or hate it, but none of them can deny that this new venue is a force to be reckoned with. Opened in 2003, it's squeaky clean, has an amazing sound system, offers plenty of comfy seating, lots of room in front of the enormous stage and a side room with café-style tables and pool tables for patrons coming to relax while enjoying the band. Hailey's also has a beer selection to drool over, and since it's in Denton, prices are pretty low here too (two dollars a pint). If the Walkmen or the French Kicks are in town, this is where they will stop.

### Dan's Silver Leaf, 103 Industrial, Denton, www.danssilverleaf.com

They don't make 'em like this anymore. Dan's has a center stage set in front of a few rows of tables and chairs and one of the coziest patios in Denton, for those long Texas nights. For laid-back evenings with some of Denton's best country, blues, rock, and even hip-hop, Dan's is definitely the place to be.

### Brickhaus, 219 W. Oak St., Denton

Brickhaus is the quintessential arty college student hangout. Listening to aspiring poets and musicians during one of the open mic nights or coming to see a friend play for the first time always feels chill in this ultra-cozy coffee house. The staff is super friendly and the atmosphere always welcoming—which is why both Denton high schoolers and University of North Texas students converge here nightly.

### J&J's Pizza Basement, 118 W. Oak St., Denton

Pizza and rock & roll? Yes, please! J&J's basement is tiny, badly ventilated and slightly stinky, but it's still one of the best settings for a good dose of loud music by local and traveling bands. J&J's also has a kick ass jukebox, where selections range from De La Soul to Hank Williams. The cover charge is donation-only most of the time, so whether you have $2 or $10 dollars in your pocket, you can still get in.

## RECORD STORES:

### Good Records, 617 N. Good Latimer,
### www.goodrecords.com

Located in what looks like a bicycle repair shop/mini junk yard/old gas station, this unassuming shop sells everything from the obscure to the mainstream, and hosts regular in-store performances with complimentary hot dogs and beer.

### Bill's Records, 8118 Spring Valley Rd.,
### www.billsrecords.com

Bill's is the kind of place that inexplicably endures despite many major flaws. Owner Bill Wisener is unabashedly eccentric, and records aren't priced, which leaves a lot of room for getting ripped off. However, there are some good treasures to be found including odd items like MC Hammer toothpaste. (Can't brush this!). There's also a poetry open mic worth checking out every Saturday night.

## HONORABLE MENTION:

In neighboring Denton, **Seasick Records** (www.seasickrecords. com) is similar to Dallas' Good Records, but with a slightly bigger selection. Seasick stocks CD and vinyl releases in a variety of genres, but that's not all: The store includes a few rare juicy imports, which make it an ideal pit stop in Denton for serious record collectors. It's also worth digging around at **Recycled Books and Records** (www. recycledbooks.com), where a careful comb through the ample supply of used platters just might yield you something delightfully weird and kitschy.

# Denver, CO

## UNIVERSITY OF DENVER
2344 E. Iliff Ave.
Denver, CO 80208
www.du.edu

The University of Denver's School of Music splits its curriculum into four divisions: the conservatory program, the community program, the jazz and commercial music program, and the university program. Conservatory students are performance majors, so they earn either a bachelor of music or performance certificate. The curriculum allows students to study a variety of instruments, and also offers opportunities to write and compose original music. The community program is more extracurricular but still offers certificate programs. Meanwhile, the jazz and commercial music program lets students master performance, but also stresses writing and technology—so music engineers, take note, this is the curriculum for you. Finally, the program gives students a bachelor of arts with a music concentration. And for business-minded musicians, take the '3/2 program' approach, a course of study that allows students to earn a bachelor degree AND a masters in business administration in only five years.

# VENUES:

### Bluebird Theater, 3317 E. Colfax Ave.,
### www.nipp.com

This is the place to see small theater shows in Denver—in an adorable 500-seat theater set in a newly hot neighborhood. (More specifically, for the ideal aural/alcoholic experience, stand between the bar and the soundboard, where cheap beer and killer sound are all within easy reach.) Multi-tiered and with a comfortable balcony, the Bluebird has impeccable sound and is the home to touring acts (Pretty Girls Make Graves and Death Cab for Cutie) and some of the larger, more experienced local acts (the Format, Dressy Bessy, DeVotchKa and Slim Cessna's Auto Club). It's also in EaCo, the hot neighborhood along East Colfax Ave., which is lined with countless new bars and restaurants that reside raucously alongside their older and more dive-oriented neighbors. EaCo is always jumping regardless of the Bluebird's schedule, but it's definitely at its best when the theater is open and indie rock kids are out for plenty of post-show action.

### Larimer Lounge, 2721 Larimer St.,
### www.larimerlounge.com

At roughly half the size of the Bluebird, Denver's indie/punk mega-club is the ideal spot for small- to mid-size touring bands in Colorado. It hosts the expected buzz shows with the Arcade Fire, Zeke, Crooked Fingers, the Wrens, Gogol Bordello, and Nebula. But then it surprises you by bringing in bigger acts such as Black Rebel Motorcycle Club, the Rapture, Fu Manchu, the Libertines and the Dirtbombs. Its secret weapon is owner/booker Scott Campbell. Campbell booked the nearby 15th St. Tavern for more than six years before starting his own bar, and has the relentless passion, knowledge and competitive drive to get the right shows for Denver's discerning rock fans.

### Hi Dive, 7 S. Broadway,
### www.hi-dive.com

This local-music Mecca is also making a name for itself with its national talent roster (Har Mar Superstar, Earlimart, and Frog Eyes) and Denver's best impromptu DJ nights (members from the Yeah Yeah Yeahs and Von Bondies have spun there). But first and foremost the Hi-Dive is a bold and vibrant champion of local music—so much so that in March of 2005 it campaigned and assisted multiple local bands (including Matson Jones, the Swayback, Bright Channel and Hot IQs) to hit Austin's annual South by Southwest music festival. It's not often that local clubs take such an active role in the proliferation of the surrounding scene, but the Hi-Dive and its owners Matt and Allison Labarge take pride in the role they play.

**Monkey Mania, 2126 Arapahoe St.,**
**www.monkeymania.net**

This is one of Denver's longest-lasting warehouse scenes, the home to local troubadours Friends Forever (who typically play from their van on the street) and Get Your Going, and also the place where Sonic Youth and Wolf Eyes came together after their show at the Ogden Theater in the summer of 2004 for an experimental, collaborative gig that blew the minds of the few hundred lucky enough to catch it. Monkey Mania has moved a few times already, but it's permanent home is on the web, where it posts its sporadic but thoroughly D.I.Y. schedule.

**Fillmore Auditorium, 1510 Clarkston St.,**
**www.fillmoreauditorium.com**

Yes, the Fillmore is owned by local Clear Channel Entertainment subsidiary Chuck Morris Presents/Bill Graham Presents. But despite its corporate ownership, the venue's size—3,600 seats—and downtown location make it an integral player in the Denver rock market. The Fillmore is home to countless jam bands—this is Colorado, after all—but it's also become an accomplished hip-hop venue, (50 Cent, Jurassic 5, Ludacris, Public Enemy, Lil Jon, Common and the Roots have all played there), and a home for when-big-bands-go-intimate tours (David Bowie, R.E.M. and, yes, even Sting) and indie rockers who have moved to the next level (Interpol, Belle and Sebastian, and the Shins).

## RECORD STORES:

**Twist & Shout, 300 E. Alameda Ave.,**
**www.twistandshout.com**

Bitch about the demise of the physical record store as much as you want, Twist & Shout isn't going anywhere. With its expansive size, its informed, indie-minded staff, and its incredibly supportive owners (Paul and Jill Epstein are ubiquitous throughout the Denver scene), Twist & Shout is one of those record stores that is flat-out inescapable. It presents all the best shows in Denver, and helps stock all the best jukeboxes throughout the metro area. Best of all: Its frequent in-stores with luminaries such as Wayne Coyne and Kristen Hersh are legendary.

**Wax Trax, 638 E. 13th Ave.,**
**www.waxtraxrecords.com**

This is the grittier alternative record store, a venerable institution on Capitol Hill that helped spawn an entire neighborhood of music paraphernalia shops, clothing outlets (new and vintage), nightclubs (the dance-oriented Snake Pit and the rock club Bender's) and indie-minded food pits (the locally owned vegetarian Water Course Foods is excellent). The best thing about Wax Trax is its staff and its local music selection, which tend to overlap: many of the people behind the counter find themselves behind the mic after Wax Trax shuts its doors.

## MISCELLANEOUS EVENTS:

**Westword Music Showcase,**
**www.westword.com**

Every summer, the city's *New Times*-owned alternative weekly throws a big party all in the name of local music. And no matter your tastes, you'll find something that owns you at the Westword Music Showcase, which coincides with the paper's annual local music reader's poll. The categories are varied—rock electronic and eclectic—and the gigs are all within walking distance in one of the city's entertainment districts, such as the Golden Triangle or LoDo (Lower Downtown.) All-inclusive wristband prices are cheap, and with entertainment all day long, it's the ideal opportunity to better acquaint yourself with the surrounding music scene, which seems as if it's on the brink of busting out of the Mile High City.

**Denver Post Underground Band Showcase,**
**www.denverpost.com**

Now in its fifth year, the *Denver Post* Underground Band Showcase and the coinciding survey continue to be on-point indicators of what local music experts are obsessing over. Whereas the Westword poll is a reader effort, complete with bands stuffing ballot boxes and begging for votes via their websites, the *Post*'s effort taps approximately 100 local music experts (including Westword and *Post* writers, Radio 1190 staffers and major players involved with Twist & Shout, Wax Trax and any number of the Denver-based record labels) and rewards veterans and newcomers alike in a more pointed, selective manner. Past winners include 16 Horsepower, DeVotchKa, Planes Mistaken for Stars and Dressy Bessy—all troubadours of the local scene—but have included Matson Jones and the Hot IQs, both relative newcomers.

—*Ricardo Baca*

# Des Moines, IA

## DRAKE UNIVERSITY
2507 University Ave.
Des Moines, IA 50311-4505
www.drake.edu

To the uninitiated, it might seem like Des Moines is one vast, flat cornfield full of heavy metal bands. After all, it was onstage here, in 1982, that Ozzy Osbourne bit the head off a dead bat. And for the past few years, hometown metal band Slipknot has served as the city's ambassador to the world at large—nine guys in grotesque masks and with a barrage of percussion that can give even avid readers of Stephen King the creeps. Yet Des Moines now courts more musical variety than one might assume, thanks to both grassroots support for the city's blues scene and the presence of Drake University, where a formidable jazz program brings big-name performers to town.

Students at Drake University have the advantage of a small, intimate music program, but with the resources and focus of a large institution. Drake promises students opportunities that will shape future careers—including internships and a program dedicated to business instruction tailored for musicians—and invites guest artists to instruct master classes. As for programs of study, take your pick: performance, music education, music with electives in business, church music, jazz studies, or a bachelor of arts, more of a liberal arts degree with a musical focus. A unique program, the music with electives in business, allows music students to take courses in Drake's business school. That degree—which, of course, features a slew of traditional classes on music history and theory—requires classes like Statistics, Marketing Principles, Management Process and Behavior and a professional internship.

But Drake's jazz program is the crown jewel of the music department, which is no surprise considering that Drake president David Maxwell's late father, Jimmy, was an esteemed jazz trumpeter who heard a teenage Wynton Marsalis perform and predicted that the kid from New Orleans with wicked chops was destined for greatness. In recent years, a series of modern jazz luminaries—Marsalis, Stefon Harris, etc.—have made their way to Drake to perform in the college's acoustically warm and intimate Sheslow Auditorium (which has room for an audience of about 780). The Drake University Jazz Ensemble One has recorded and released CDs, as has the director of the music program, clarinetist Clarence Padilla. Students also can audition for the Des Moines Symphony Orchestra.

## VENUES:

**Hairy Marys, 2307 University Ave.,**
**www.hairymarys.com**
This nightclub near Drake University specializes in rock, metal, and hardcore. Its fabled run began at its previous location in a warehouse downtown in the early Nineties, when the venue hosted a broad array of up-and-coming bands (the Smashing Pumpkins, Afghan Whigs, L7, etc.) that went on to wider fame. The current Hairy Marys site near Drake had been a reggae bar (the Safari Club) and was briefly owned by a member of Des Moines metal band Slipknot. This Hairy Marys, in operation since 1999, has welcomed the likes of Frank Black, Fu Manchu, and 3 Inches of Blood. The décor has an emphasis

in biker themes, with one room containing the stage while the other room houses the bar and tables. Owners Jeff Wright and John Limke also operate several other watering holes in the metro (GT Lounge, Kung Fu Tap & Taco and the Walnut Tap) as well as the late-night pizza joint that is a rite of passage, Big Tomato Pizza Co.

### The House of Bricks, 3839 Merle Hay Rd., www.thehouseofbricks.com

Located across the street from Merle Hay Mall, this music bar grounds itself in local rock bands, nationally touring punk bands for crowd and a dash of eclectic variety that might include the occasional open mic night, campy tribute act (in honor of Kiss, Slipknot, Ozzy, etc.) or even a screening of a classic rock & roll film. You enter the club around the back of a strip mall. It's a single room that contains a low stage along the east wall, the bar along the south wall, and a few pool tables at the back of the room.

### Vaudeville Mews, 212 Fourth St., www.vaudevillemews.com

Before this live theater and nightclub opened in December 2002, the nation's crop of indie rock bands was relegated to makeshift venues around Des Moines, if they didn't bypass the city altogether. Happily, today the Mews is home to everything from Matt Pond PA and Joanna Newsome to Jay Farrar and Bill Frisell. Part of the charm of the Mews is its location on Fourth Street, the heart of downtown Des Moines' street life. The nightclub is situated between an independent coffee shop (Java Joe's Coffeehouse) that stages live folk music and the Royal Mile, a British pub that's usually packed full of twentysomethings and thick clouds of smoke on weekends. Fourth Street is the downtown block most likely to be closed off for street parties and festivals throughout the year.

### Blues on Grand, 1501 Grand Ave., www.bluesongrand.com

Unless you're B.B. King or Buddy Guy, this is where you perform in Des Moines if you're a blues musician touring through town. The steady traffic of living legends that this downtown spot books onto its tiny stage is an education in itself, with a curriculum that embraces the deep gospel soul of the Holmes Brothers, bawdy showmanship of Bobby Rush and the star-making pedigree of John Mayall. One wall of the club is devoted to the Iowa Blues Hall off Fame—an array of color photos that feature local legends, many of whom are still performing. If you're looking for an instant introduction to a corner of the Des Moines music scene with deep roots, look no further than BOG.

## RECORD STORES:

### Eastown Music, 1242 E. 14th St.

Opened in 1999 by Cleon George and Albert Smith, this hip-hop specialty shop, not surprisingly, is located on the city's east side. If you're looking for either that obscure mix tape by DJ Green Lantern or just the latest mainstream joint from 50 Cent's posse, Eastown will fit the bill.

### Peeples Music, 4201 University Ave.

After nearly thirty years in the game, Peeples is the last longstanding survivor in independent music retail in Des Moines. Owner Mike Enloe was a business student at Drake University, a new father and ready to risk a $16,000 investment when he opened his store and the Rolling Stones' *Black & Blue* began flying off the shelves. Five different Des Moines locations later, this friendly local shop has served successive generations of punk rockers, MTV brats, and Phishheads—and lived to bemoan the era of digital downloading. Today the store focuses on a basic stock of new rock CDs and DVDs, with some space also given to jazz, blues, reggae, and a variety of used stock.

### Zzz Records, 424 E. Locust St.,
### www.zzzrecords.com

For those still faithful to the warm, crackling sounds and pure romance of vinyl, Zzz is your music retail Mecca in Des Moines. Owner Nate Niceswanger originally opened his shop in 2000 on the west side of downtown, but it's a better fit at its current site, the funkier East Village neighborhood that stands in the shadow of the golden-domed Iowa State Capitol. The East Village boasts everything from great restaurants (Basil Prosperi Bakery, Noodle Zoo) to gay bars and high-end furniture stores. It does lack a live music venue, and sadly, Zzz's campaign to stage in-store concerts was cut short by a hassle over building codes. But Niceswanger serves up racks upon racks of used LPs, as well as a range of new and used CDs.

## *RADIO STATIONS:*

### KDPS 88.1 FM,
### www.kdpsradio.com

Remember when FM radio used to surprise listeners with bold playlists that helped discover and promote a progressive batch of artists? Me neither. But rabid variety still is the daily diet for this modest signal in Des Moines that's operated by a staff of high school students from studios downtown. Considering the station's educational bent, professional polish is of course lacking from most of the banter and public service announcements between songs. But it's worth the stilted promos and inside jokes to be shocked awake in the morning by old-school punk or to lock down the dial for "Hip-Hop Fridays."

### KDRB "the Beat" 106.3 FM,
### www.1063thebeat.com

Clear Channel's newest spot on the dial in Des Moines is the city's first, long-overdue commercial station devoted to the booming anthems of crunk, with the occasional slinky R&B love ballad mixed in for good measure. What launched in October 2003 as a continuous mix of music with no DJs gradually has added local staff and flavor.

## *MISCELLANEOUS ATTRACTIONS:*

### Iowa State Fair

There's no shortage of corn and pigs in this agriculturally rich state, as proven by the annual fair in August that draws about one million residents and tourists in search of fried foods and famous country singers. Believe it or not, the fair also imports a world-class lineup of live music acts that come free with paid gate admission.

### 515 Alive

This is the State Fair's polar opposite, an annual electronic music festival held on the streets and in the nightclubs downtown each July. It's like the Winter Music Conference without the idyllic beach setting or all the velvet ropes.

—*Kyle Munson*

# Detroit, MI

## WAYNE STATE UNIVERSITY
5050 Anthony Wayne Dr.
Detroit, Michigan 48202
www.wayne.edu

**W**ayne State University offers a range of unconventional majors within the school's music program, making it a great choice for anyone interested in music but uncertain about what aspects, in particular, he or she would like to study. Undergraduates pursue either a bachelor of music in one of several majors including jazz studies, music education, music management, and music technology, as well as performance, and theory/composition, or they receive a bachelor of arts, which is designed for students interested in studying music from a broader, more liberal arts-oriented perspective.

All majors must take several departmental core requirements that include ear training, theory, and music history and literature. With these basics in place, students can go on to explore one of the school's less typical areas of study. The music management program, for example, introduces students to the expected theoretical study of marketing and promotion, but also includes course work in independent record production, management, contracts, copyright issues, technology, and wholesale/retail music supply. The major allows students access to professionals in the industry through guest lectures and internships and students supplement courses in recording techniques and music business with hard-core business classes like accounting and macroeconomics. (High-powered music attorney Howard Hertz—who reps Marilyn Manson and Eminem—graduated from Wayne State.)

Wayne State's music technology major is intended for those students who know they want to pursue a career as a record producer or engineer. These students take private instrumental or vocal lessons, on top of their studies of recording techniques, electronic music, and music business. In addition, students investigate computer languages, programming, and digital design to gain familiarity with the practical techniques they will need to employ in the working world. All technology majors are required to take internships either within the department or with an independent recording studio.

## COLLEGE FOR CREATIVE STUDIES
201 E. Kirby
Detroit, MI 48202-4034
www.dev.ccscad.edu/flashHomepage.cfm

**W**here do you think the White Stripes' Jack White boned up on the De Stijl art movement that gave his band's second album its name? Yup, the Detroit native studied at the College for Creative Studies for a spell, though he never graduated. CCS doesn't have a music program, but its interest in merging serious artistic pursuits with innovative courses could appeal to any student interested in looking at pop culture from an academic standpoint. Students concentrate in one of the following eight areas: animation and digital media, communication design, crafts, fine arts, illustration, industrial design, interior design, or photography. Plus, the news section of the CCS website informs visitors that the school's two largest annual fundraising events are the Student Exhibition Opening and the Detroit International Wine Auction. Only good things can come from a school funded by the proceeds of wine and student art.

## VENUES:

**Magic Stick & Majestic Theater, 4120-4140 Woodward Ave., www.majesticdetroit.com**

Undisputedly the epicenter of Motor City rock & roll, this complex occupies an entire city block near the Wayne State University campus and houses a theater, rock club, bowling alley, bar, restaurant, pizzeria, art gallery, and record store. With a capacity of 1,000, the art deco-era Majestic Theater features larger touring acts and numerous all-ages shows. Next door, the Magic Stick is the place to catch that hot new indie band on tour and all the local bands—if they're not onstage, you'll likely see them in the audience. Many of Detroit's best got their start playing this stage, including the White Stripes, Detroit Cobras, the Go and the Dirtbombs. In a city as cold and lacking in adequate public transportation as Detroit, it's good to go somewhere and stay there for the evening. Before the show, you can knock over a few pins at the oldest operating bowling alley in the United States, the Garden Bowl. Afterward, when the time rolls around for that late night slice, Sgt. Pepperoni's is ready to serve one up.

### Alvin's, 5756 Cass Ave.

If you're more comfortable hanging with the heavily tattooed and pierced crowd, Alvin's is a great place to check out. Located adjacent to Wayne State University in Detroit's Cass Corridor, Alvin's has great sound and tends to feature heavier bands as well as the occasional rap show. Admittance is typically 21+ and the cover ranges from five to ten dollars.

### Small's, 10339 Conant St., Hamtramck, www.smallsbardetroit.com

Though a bit of a hike from the Wayne State University area (ten minutes by car), Small's is well worth the trip to Hamtramck. Both geographically and culturally, Hamtramck is a little out of the ordinary—a largely immigrant city within a city. (It's a separate city, but surrounded by Detroit on all sides.) With the best sound of any of Detroit's smaller venues, Small's books both up and coming indie bands as well as local bands. The noir feel era front lounge is a great place for a pre- or post-show drink.

### Leland City Club, 400 Bagley St., www.lelandcityclub.com

Detroit's headquarters for the goth crowd and industrial music, Leland City Club is located behind an unmarked door in the heart of downtown Detroit. An amazing sound system and great DJs keep hundreds of people on the dance floor until 4:30 A.M., though they stop serving alcohol at 2 A.M., per Michigan law. Your alternative lifestyle is welcome here, and it's an 18+ club.

### State Theater, 2115 Woodward, www.statetheaterdetroit.com

Found in the center of Detroit's newly revitalized theater district, the 1920s era State Theater is one of the largest concert venues in

Metro Detroit and is a great place to catch some tours ranging from Widespread Panic to Interpol to Bob Dylan. One of the few theaters in Detroit to boast continuous operation, its opulent lobby with a double marble staircase and Corinthian columns offers a glimpse into to the grandeur of the city's past.

### St. Andrews Hall, 431 E. Congress St.

This 1,000-capacity venue—built in 1907—has been pulling in a diverse array of national acts since 1980, focusing primarily on bands that are on the cusp of breaking into the big time. Before they were popular, bands such as the Red Hot Chili Peppers, Jane's Addiction and Green Day made appearances here. These days, punk-pop acts like Bowling for Soup and New Found Glory are the venue's bread and butter. Downstairs, The Shelter offers a more intimate space that brings in smaller touring acts. Plus, St. Andrew's Hall is located adjacent to the lively Greektown district in downtown Detroit, which affords access to the Greektown casino for your late night gambling needs.

### Elbow Room, 6 South Washington St., Ypsilanti,
### www.ypsirocks.com/elbowroom.html

The rock underground bubbles to the surface at this classic dive in the city of Ypsilanti, near Eastern Michigan University. Originally a biker bar, the Elbow Room books everything from experimental electronica to folk rock. With a packed schedule of both local and indie bands, the Elbow Room is one of the area's best sources for unpretentious underground rock at an affordable price.

## RECORD STORES:

### Young Soul Rebels, 4152 Woodward Ave.,
### www.youngsoulrebels.net

There has been no contesting the street cred of this store ever since Jack White made a surprise appearance on stage for its grand opening in 2003. Located near Wayne State University in downtown Detroit's Majestic Theater complex, Young Soul Rebels stocks the hippest of the hip. That's because its owners are longtime Detroit scenesters Dave Buick and Dion Fischer. Both are former members of Detroit garage revival pioneers The Go, and Buick also owns Italy Records, the small label that launched the career of the White Stripes. Walk up the stairs to Young Soul Rebels and one of them, frequently both of them, will be there to guide you to the hottest new indie releases.

### Record Graveyard, 11303 Joseph Campau, Hamtramck, www.recordgraveyard.com

When you've had enough of the campus indie store and need a break from the same old scenery, Record Graveyard is a great excuse for a short trek to Hamtramck. The place where "great records never go out of style," Record Graveyard stocks more than 100,000 pieces of vinyl, including a remarkable collection of soul 45s, and just about everything else as well. You're likely to spot both famous and obscure garagesters seeking out that rare gem to add to the record collection. On your way out, make a stop for an authentic pirogie from Hamtramck's famous Polish Village Café, located within walking distance.

### Record Time, 262 W. 9 Mile, Ferndale
### www.recordtime.com

Another reason for a field trip is Record Time, located just across the Detroit city limit in trendy Ferndale. With a large, comprehensive stock of both CDs and vinyl, Record Time is a particularly great source for a genre born and bred in Detroit: techno. For house, soul and DJ mixes, Record Time is the best source in the Motor City.

## RADIO STATIONS:

### WDET 101.9 FM,
### www.detfm.org

The highlight of Detroit radio is undoubtedly Wayne State University's NPR station, WDET. Now, I know what you're thinking… "NPR? Come on, dude!" Well, you're right, it's not often the rockers get down with the mad jams on NPR, but Detroit is that kind of city. The remarkably cool mix of music coming from this station leans on rock, techno, and blues. For the late night owls, the Liz Copeland Show gives you four hours of ultra hip new music every weeknight, and will undoubtedly reveal the best music you've never heard.

### 89X 88.7 FM,
### www.89xradio.com

In Detroit, like most other cities, the corporate clutch has a tight hold on the airwaves, but a few gems slip through the cracks. The Motor City has an interesting loophole that assures that the alternative station won't get mowed over by the canned crap cluttering most of the dial. Since a foreign country is only a stone's throw across the murky Detroit River, the city shares alternative rock station 89X with its Canadian counterpart—the city of Windsor, Ontario.

### Radio Fever on Live 97.1 FM WKRK,
### www.live971.com

Having recently bred a number of major label international successes from the White Stripes and Von Bondies to Kid Rock and Eminem, it's not surprising that the local scene is well represented on quite a few stations. The best place to get a taste of Motor City rock & roll is Radio Fever. Longtime Detroit scene experts Sassy and the Wolf mix music from Detroit's phenomenal past (Iggy & the Stooges, MC5, Parliament/Funkadelic) with the best of the current scene (White Stripes, Electric Six, Detroit Cobras). Sassy and the Wolf also fill the studio with some of the Motor City scene's most colorful personalities like Ben Blackwell (the Dirtbombs, Cass Records owner) and Dick Valentine (Electric Six frontman) and clog the phone lines with interestingly named people like (hmmm… who was that really?) who seem to know too much to not be in the band.

### WJLB , 98.1 FM,
### www.fm98wjlb.com

As you might recall from Eminem's film *8 Mile*, JLB is the best source on the dial for Detroit rap and hip-hop. WJLB's DJ "the Bushman" was one of the first to play young Slim Shady's jams and you'll catch lots of other up and coming Detroit talent on this station.

## MISCELLANEOUS ATTRACTIONS:

### Hamtramck Labor Day Festival,
### www.hamtramckfestival.com

Hamtramck is a city that feels like a place where time has stood still for twenty or thirty years. Initially a Polish immigrant community, its makeup is now extremely diverse and reminiscent of working-class, first-generation immigrant communities such as Queens, New York. For an experience that is colorful, local and genuine, check out the Hamtramck Labor Day Festival. The city's main drag is blocked off and two large stages are set up. Interspersed among them are beer tents sponsored by the local fire department and food booths filled with local specialties (read: best cheese pirogies you will ever find). The stages are filled with all of Detroit's best up-and-coming bands. With affordable food and brew, plenty of rock and a laidback atmosphere, it's bound to be a fun time.

**Movement Festival,**
**www.movementfestival.com**

The debate over whether techno was birthed in Detroit or Chicago is for another day, but while the Movement Festival is blasting beats on the shore of the Detroit River, there's no question that Detroit feels like the genre's home. One of the largest free music festivals in the world, Movement brings in over a million people and seventy of the world's best electronic artists over a period of three days on Memorial Day weekend. Movement was co-founded by techno legend Carl Craig in 2000, and is organized by pioneers of the genre, Derrick May and Kevin Saunderson. If you're stocked up on energy drinks and feel like keeping it going until sun up, you shouldn't have any problem finding a pumping after-party at one of Detroit's many electronic clubs.

**Dally in the Alley,**
**www.dallyinthealley.com**

Dally in the Alley is the event that epitomizes the downtown Detroit music and art scene more than any other. The festival is interspersed between Wayne State University buildings and spread out among the streets and alleys of the Cass Corridor. The sometimes-seedy district has been the center of Detroit art since the early Sixties when it was home to the MC5, White Panther Party and influential rock mag *Creem*. Best described as eclectic, the festival is devoutly anti-corporate (no co-branding or product placement here!). What you will find is good food, plenty of original art, fashion and rock & roll on four stages.

**Rock City Festival,**
**www.rockcityfestival.com**

Founded in 2004, Rock City Festival is a newer addition to Detroit's summer music festivals, but has already received a nod from *USA Today* as one of ten best summer music festivals. Staged in June behind the Majestic Theater complex in downtown Detroit, two side-by-side stages trade off featuring the best of the downtown garage scene. Headlined by the Dirtbombs in 2004, the free event drew 3-4,000 people.

**Comerica Tastefest,**
**www.newcenter.com/tastefest/info.htm**

As the name might imply, this five-day festival—which coincides with July 4th—mixes to two vitals of life: food and music. Held on West Grand Blvd between Woodward Ave and the Lodge Freeway, the event packs in booths by local restaurants offering passers-by a taste of their best dishes. Three stages are set up and acts range from rock to jazz to techno. Both local and national acts are on the bill and recent highlights include Jet, Cake and Wilco. There's no charge to walk around and check out the music, but you may want to purchase some food tickets for a taste of Detroit.

*—Ryan Sult*

# Evanston, IL

Only twelve miles north of Chicago, **Northwestern University** (www.northwestern.edu) has one of the country's most renowned journalism programs. Take note if you want to be the next Lester Bangs: Northwestern students interested in pursuing a career as a rock scribe can complete a cross-school certificate program between the School of Music and the Medill School of Journalism. On-campus music resources also include the music library, which includes both an extensive library of recorded music and printed music, rare books and periodicals (including full back issues of rock & roll publications such as *Creem* and *Crawdaddy*). And history professor Jeff Rice has offered seminar classes in the social history of punk rock and included guests such as Jon Langford of the Mekons.

In general, the strength of the university's theater, film, and music programs make for a vibrant creative scene on and around campus. The School of Music requires applicants to audition but also closely examines and values academic work as much as musical ability. While at Northwestern, students in the School of Music follow a rigorous coursework that includes weekly private lessons with instructors, classes in composition, conducting, ethnomusicology, music theory, and music history. Classes in the music school are open to non-music majors, but spots are usually limited. For non-classically inclined students, popular courses include the history of jazz and a Beatles class that is offered every two years.

If you end up at Northwestern, chances are you'll also end up at **Pete Miller's** (www.petemillers.com/evanston). The place is mainly a top quality (and expensive) steakhouse, but for poor college students, it has even more value. Most jazz clubs in Chicago are far away, require you to be twenty-one or older, and charge a steep cover, which can be upwards of twenty-five dollars. Pete Miller's, on the other hand, is only four blocks from campus, has no age minimum, and has no cover charge. They don't even make you buy anything on their menu, so you can literally walk in there and have a front row seat for some of Chicago's best jazz musicians. Every fall, Pete Miller's hosts a jazz festival, which usually draws some of their more prominent acts.

A recent addition to the Evanston music scene, the laidback **Bill's Blues** (www.billsbluesbar.com) offers live music every night of the week, including some of Chicago's best blues acts. They just recently started a Thursday hip-hop night that showcases rappers on Evanston label Gravel Records. Bill's is also great place for musicians looking to jam. Assuming that you've got decent chops and won't embarrass yourself, you can get onstage with other amateurs and rock out. And if you show up after midnight, you get in for free.

Northwestern's **Pick-Staiger Concert Hall** hosts nearly all jazz and classical performances by groups on campus. Just because they're your fellow students, don't think that it's not worth checking out. In addition, Pick books guest artists throughout the year, with past performers including Beck and Rufus Wainwright. Shows here are almost always discounted for NU students, rarely requiring you to spend over ten dollars for a show.

Every year in late May, a couple weeks before finals, Northwestern holds Dillo Day, which is basically a campus-wide party. In addition to house parties, frat parties, and general inebriation, there are consecutive concerts held on the Lakefill from the early afternoon to the late evening. Seeing a show on Dillo Day is one of the most serene experiences one can have. Standing in a vast area right next to the lake while listening to music will probably be one of your best experiences at Northwestern. Last year there were fireworks and a light show during the final act, and one can only expect better things in the future. Over the past few years, artists such as Robert Randolph and the Family Band, Bela Fleck and the Flecktones, and the Wailers have come to NU for the Dillo Day festivities.

## RECORD STORES:

**Dr. Wax** is only three blocks from campus, but that's not the only reason Northwestern students rate it highly: The store offers an impressive selection of CDs by underground, local, and indie rock artists, as well as selling used discs and DVDs. A few blocks farther away, **Second Hand Tunes** (www.2ndhandtunes.com) specializes in used vinyl—for cheap! You can pick up a copy of Bob Dylan's *Highway 61 Revisted* for a mere six bucks, and that's before you factor in the 10 percent discount 2HT offers Northwestern students. They sell CDs, too, and will let you listen to anything you're interested in before you buy it. For the true music geek, hit **Vintage Vinyl** (www.vvmo.com): You won't find blockbuster new releases here, but this is your best bet for hunting down bootlegs and rare recordings by both major and indie artists. Problem is, prices tend to be too rich for the average co-ed, ranging anywhere from thirty to seventy dollars.

## RADIO STATIONS:

**WNUR 89.3FM,**

**www.wnur.org**

Calling itself "Chicago's Sound Experiment," WNUR is North-western's radio station and can be heard across the north side of

Chicago. Its morning free jazz show is internationally renowned via its website, and also has "streetbeat" every evening and freeform all night. It is the largest student-run station in the country.

# Hartford, CT

## UNIVERSITY OF HARTFORD
The Hartt School
200 Bloomfield Ave.
West Hartford, CT 06117
www.hartford.edu/hartt

Locals still see the University of Hartford as something of a commuter campus, but the private school has an increasingly prestigious reputation elsewhere. The Hartt School is a big reason why. With three separate areas of instruction, Hartt students can focus on music, dance, theater for both undergraduate and graduate degrees.

The music program is split into four disciplines: instrumental studies, vocal studies, academic studies and music education. The school is very selective—playing Nickelback covers in your friend's basement probably won't cut it—and most students are required to audition in person. There are typical conservatory offerings in classical music instruction, along with degree programs in composition, music and performing arts management, music production and technology, music theory, and music history. Of particular note, though, is the Jackie McLean Institute of Jazz. Founded by McLean, a saxophone player, the institute gives students the opportunity to learn from—and play with—acclaimed jazz musicians in master classes and workshops. The faculty includes McLean and trombonist Steve Davis, and jazz giants such as Tito Puente and Charles Mingus have been guest instructors. Although most classes at Hartt are restricted to music majors, the school also includes a community division with courses in music and theater open to, well, the community.

# TRINITY COLLEGE
Department of Music
Austin Arts Center
300 Summit St.
Hartford, CT 06106
www.trincoll.edu/depts/musc

**T**rinity's music program doesn't get as much attention as its larger counterpart at the University of Hartford, but it's not a conservatory, either. The department is small, with only four full-time faculty members, but its offerings are surprisingly broad. In addition to overviews on music theory and composition, students can take classes on more specialized topics, including Italian Music of the Renaissance and Baroque, Protests in Music, Women and Music and Current Trends in Black Musical Expression. Trinity offers performance opportunities in its concert choir, musical theater program and instrumental, chamber, Latin and jazz ensembles. There's an emphasis on internships, particularly for music-ed students, and the department helps place students at area arts organizations, in local schools and with media outlets. Trinity is on the small side, with about 2,100 students, and the school takes pride in both its picturesque campus and its urban location in Hartford. The college also has a campus in Rome, where many music majors (and plenty of students pursuing the thirty-six other majors) spend a semester or more.

# UNIVERSITY OF CONNECTICUT
University of Connecticut Department of Music
1295 Storrs Rd.
Unit 1012
Storrs, CT 06269-1012
www.uconn.edu

**T**he University of Connecticut is best known for championship basketball teams. But someone has to staff the pep bands. That's where the music department comes in. It's a huge department, with more than forty faculty members, and it combines the academic discipline of a conservatory with the social opportunities you'd expect to find at a giant state school—fraternities and sororities (including one of each for music students), more than 250 clubs and organizations, annual Spring Weekend keg parties busted up by cops, the usual. Whatever your interests, the UConn music department probably offers a class on it in one of six different programs of study: "applied music" (that is, performance), music history, music theory, music education, jazz, or ensemble.

Outside the classroom, UConn boasts performance groups in sixteen different categories, including pep bands for men's and women's basketball, a marching band (whose members get preference during pep band auditions), a symphonic band, concert band, symphony orchestra, wind ensemble, opera theater, various jazz ensembles, and a whole mess of different choral groups. Students planning to major in music are required to audition. Some classes are open to non-majors, though, and the department promises, "Whether you are preparing for a career as a performer or educator or you simply want to learn more about music, the Music Department has a degree for you." Yup— UConn offers six different bachelor's degrees, five master's degrees and four doctoral programs in music.

There's one drawback, if you're looking for a school in a city— UConn isn't in one. The main campus, where 14,000 undergraduates attend classes, is in Storrs, a small town about twenty-five miles east of Hartford.

# WESLEYAN UNIVERSITY
Music Department
Middletown, CT 06457
www.wesleyan.edu

**W**esleyan was the model for the movie *PCU*, and this small school is certainly a bastion of political correctness. It's also an eccentric, artsy place with a first-rate film program and a music department heavily into world music. Along with a recording studio and a computer and experimental music studio, Wesleyan is home to a prized collection of world-music instruments. Course offerings include histories of various musical forms, including rock, African-American and South-Indian music, and performance study groups for players of everything from cello to gamelan. Wesleyan music students are active outside the classroom, too—one group recently compiled a benefit album of top Afrobeat artists, with proceeds going toward relief efforts in Sudan. The project has raised more than $100,000.

## VENUES:

**Webster Theater, 31 Webster St.,**
**www.webstertheater.com**

Originally an Art Deco movie house in the 1930s, the Webster was a porno theater in the Eighties before reopening in 1996 as Hartford's only full-time rock club. The seats are gone, and the stage is where the screen used to be. There are bars are at the back of the theater in the 21+ section. The club books a mix of rock acts and occasional rap and Americana shows. The Webster has a soft spot for Eighties hair metal, and Bret Michaels is a frequent headliner. The club also operates the Webster Underground next door, a 250-capacity bar for local bands and for budding national acts who aren't quite ready for the 1,250-person theater.

**Real Art Ways, 56 Arbor St.,**
**www.realartways.org**

A renovated warehouse west of downtown, Real Art Ways hosts an eclectic assortment of performers, usually with an avant-garde edge. Music isn't the primary function, though. RAW also has an art gallery and a small movie theater for independent films. The third Thursday of every month is reserved for Creative Cocktail Hour, where local arts types sip drinks and wander through the latest gallery installment.

**Sully's Pub, 2071 Park St.,**
**www.sullyspub.com**

This is the only place in Hartford that offers original live music seven nights a week, including open-mic nights: electric on Sunday, acoustic on Monday and Tuesday. Wednesday through Saturday feature local and regional bands, with occasional stops by smaller national touring acts like Mofro. Sully's is tiny—the horseshoe-shaped bar is just a few steps from stage—but shows don't get much more intimate. The pizza at Lena's, next door, isn't bad either.

**Black-Eyed Sally's, 350 Asylum St.,**
**www.blackeyedsallys.com**

Sally's serves up barbecue and live blues, and it's hard to say which is the bigger attraction. There's a bar in the middle, and tables in open rooms on either side, one of which contains the stage. The crowd is middle-aged and the food's not cheap for college kids on a tight budget, but it's worth splurging for the occasional rack of ribs or a set of stinging blues.

**Municipal Café, 485 Main St.,**
**www.spiritualemporium.com**

The antidote to the Top 40 emphasis at most area nightclubs, the Muni hosts an underground dance party every Friday night. Hip DJs come from all over the East Coast to spin, and the party lasts until 4 A.M., long after the bars have closed. The Muni's future is uncertain— ownership of the building recently changed hands, but club nights are expected to continue, if only in the basement under the record store next door.

**Hawk's Nest, 200 Bloomfield Ave.,**
**www.uhaweb.hartford.edu/hawksnest.**

The quality of this student-run venue at the University of Hartford varies with the dedication of the staff. Sometimes the booking is imaginative, other times not so much. More than a few national bands got started here, though—the Starting Line, Taking Back Sunday and Finch all played here before MTV had ever heard of them. Band or no, the place is open from 4:30 P.M. to midnight every day. Food is available, and there are pool, foosball and air hockey tables.

## RECORD STORES:

**Spiritual Emporium Records, 493 Main St.,**
**www.spirtualemporium.com**

Tucked away on a seemingly empty block south of downtown, Spiritual Emporium has an incredible selection of house, trance and jungle on vinyl. The store is ideal for DJs searching for hard-to-find stuff from overseas, and owner JJ Blades runs the underground club in the Municipal Café next door, where he spins records on Friday nights.

### Brass City Records, 489 Meadow St., Waterbury

Make friends with someone who has a car—Brass City Records is about thirty miles west of Hartford, but it's worth the trip. With thousands of new and used independent-label and import CDs and rooms full of vinyl, much of it rare or out of print, this is probably the best record store between Boston and New York.

### Aquarius Record Shop, 858 Albany Ave.

It's a small storefront, but Aquarius has a whole wall full of hip-hop on vinyl, and a display case loaded with mix tapes. The store also sells CDs and, for some reason, snow brushes.

### Heartbeat Sounds & Communications, 1156 Albany Ave.

Heartbeat features the best selection of rap CDs and vinyl in Hartford, with new releases, a section for old-school artists and an eclectic array of 12-inch singles.

### Ishi Records, 1442 Albany Ave.

Serving all your reggae needs, Ishi sells records, CDs, mix tapes, t-shirts bearing the likeness of Bob Marley, and Clarks-brand shoes.

## RADIO STATIONS:

### WRTC, 89.3,
### www.wrtcfm.com

Trinity College's station is one of a few bright spots in the rigidly formatted corporate wasteland of local radio. Staffed by students and community volunteers, WRTC has shows devoted to rock, fu jazz, Latin, Caribbean, and even polka.

### WWUH, 91.3,
### www.wwuh.org

The other bright spot, the University of Hartford's station has a heavier emphasis on folk and roots music (which correspond to folk and Celtic concert series at the college), with heavy doses of jazz and classical.

—*Eric R. Danton*

# Indianapolis, IN

## BUTLER UNIVERSITY
4600 Sunset Ave.
Indianapolis, IN 46208
www.butler.edu

## INDIANA UNIVERSITY
535 W. Michigan St.
Indianapolis, IN 46202
www.iupui.edu

It could be said that Indianapolis is a place where the undercurrents of American music meet. Nicknamed the Crossroads of America— several interstates join within its borders—the city has for decades produced a flavorful mix of jazz, blues, rock & roll and classical musicians. Sure John Mellencamp grew up in nearby Seymour and is a hometown favorite played in heavy rotation on at least one radio station, but he isn't the only legend Indy calls its own. From the tidbits of trivia (the now-demolished Hoosier Dome was the last venue Elvis played before he died) to the word-of-mouth lore about the city's legendary musicians (jazz guitarist Wes Montgomery and trombonist J.J. Johnson learned their licks while kicking around the Circle City), Indianapolis has held its music history in a modest embrace. You would think Hoosiers favor their basketball—and surely they do—but Butler University and a combined campus of Indiana University and Purdue University have both quietly maintained the city's musical roots. For decades, Butler's Jordan School of Fine Arts has produced classical musicians who have gone on to greatness. The school is small, but its century-old tradition and international reputation have deep roots in the city's musical community, which give students work opportunities with the Indianapolis Children's Choir and the Indianapolis Opera. The school's undergraduate degrees range from theory to practice, where vocalists study German or French diction, gobs of music theory, as well as less common studies in the digital arts and music in literature.

Alumni include Pulitzer Prize finalists, vocalists who have won Tony honors, played on Broadway, and composers whose works have been featured by some of Europe's most esteemed orchestras.

Nearby IUPUI—pronounced "Ooey-Pooey"—is no less notable. Jazz luminary David Baker is a professor at IU's Bloomington campus, and the coursework through the program in Indianapolis includes titles such as The Music of the Beatles, Music for Film, and The History of Jazz. That's right. Indy once was a major hub for traveling jazz musicians. In fact, if St. Louis was the gateway to the West, Indianapolis could be regarded as the jump-off point. The city became a surrogate home to round-bound musicians when jazz left New Orleans in the early 1900s en route to New York, Chicago, and St. Louis. The old Gennett Studios in nearby Richmond, IN, was one of the first recording stops legends such as Louis Armstrong and Jelly Roll Morton made on the long road out of Louisiana. And even now, artists crisscrossing the nation on tour generally find time for Indy.

## VENUES:

### Slippery Noodle, 372 S. Meridian St., www.slipperynoodle.com

Don't let the bouncers who park their Harleys outside the front door scare you off. Founded in 1850 as the Tremont House and listed in the National Register of Historic Places, the Slippery Noodle prides itself on being Indiana's oldest bar. In past lives, the building has been a bordello and a stop on the Underground Railroad. Today it is a nationally recognized blues venue, ranked tops by several publications, including *Rolling Stone* in 1998. With two stages and endless rooms, the Noodle has unparalleled ambiance, which might be what attracts giants such as Luther Allison, Matt "Guitar" Murphy, Country Joe McDonald, and Jay Giles to jam on its stages. Celebrity sightings are also frequent. Robert DeNiro, Harrison Ford, and Vince Neil have all popped in to the bar, likely drawn to Indy by the abundance of the city's national sporting events.

### The Murat Centre, 502 N. New Jersey St., www.murat.com

Since a multi-million dollar renovation in the mid-nineties, the Murat Centre has become one of the best venues to see national tours in Indianapolis. The nearly 100-year-old building in the shadow of downtown serves as a stage for everything from punk to pop artists. Wilco and Sting, Elvis Costello and Jeff Beck have all played the former Masonic Temple. The centre has two rooms– the larger and more opulent Murat Theater and the intimate Egyptian Room, which is decorated with hieroglyphics to carry the motif—that allow the centre to accommodate head-banging Slayer fans as well as bohemian ruffians dancing wildly to Ani DiFranco.

### Chatterbox Tavern, 425 Massachusetts Ave., www.chatterboxjazz.com

Tucked into a sliver of a building in the heart of Indianapolis' arts district, the Chatterbox Tavern enjoys a nearly constant lineup of musicians who stroll onto its tiny stage. The Chatterbox is small in size alone. While aging local favorites still prop in front of the piano with cigarettes dangling from their lips to hammer out the jazz they love, top bills such as Wynton Marsalis and Mick Jagger have both popped into the bar for late-night, impromptu jam sessions.

### Vogue, 6259 N. College Ave., www.thevogue.ws

The name may conjure fantastic images of lingerie clad Madonna clones or Duran Duran diehards, but the Vogue has evolved in recent years into a premiere concert venue. When it's not providing the chest-thumping beats that have earned it accolades as one of Indy's best dance clubs, variety carries this bar on the edge of the city's Broad Ripple neighborhood a long way. In the last twenty-five years, punk cowboy Hank Williams III, country surf guitarist Junior Brown, Johnny Cash, the White Stripes, and the Dave Matthews Band have all played the Vogue.

## RECORD STORES:

### Indy CD and Vinyl, 808 Broad Ripple Ave., www.indycdandvinyl.com

With shuttered storefronts still advertising records and tapes, Indy CD and Vinyl is perfect for those whose tastes aren't directed by "Nice Price" stickers. And it doesn't hurt that the store is located in one of the city's artsy Broad Ripple neighborhood. With a heavy emphasis on the kinds of acts who have yet to break through on MTV and on mainstream radio, Indy CD and Vinyl is an old school shop for new school tastes.

**Luna Music, 1315 W. 86th St.,**
**www.lunamusic.net**

Luna is the kind of place where you can ask a question about a song you've heard but don't know the name of, and chances are the employees will know exactly what you're talking about, B-sides included. That's exactly what Todd Robinson had in mind when he opened the store with his brother on the city's north side in 1994: a kick-ass place where the help shared the same passions as the customers because they once rifled through the same racks.

## RADIO STATIONS:

**WFBQ "Q95" 94.7 FM,**
**www.wfbq.com**

Rock & roll is dead, you say? Not on Q95, home to nationally syndicated shock jocks Bob and Tom. Led Zeppelin, Bad Company, John Mellencamp, and more appear frequently on this Clear Channel station. Its jocks are avid rock fans, the kind who discovered music in the aftermath of Woodstock and before pop production took over. The station's playlists might as well be a checklist of Hall of Fame musicians, even the more obscure recordings that give continued listening a bit of a myopic feel. But if you're going all rock, better leave no stone unturned.

**WRZX 103.3 FM,**
**www.wrzx.com**

You'll know you've found "Indy's New Rock Alternative" on the dial when the music seems a little harder than the other stations. Home of the Friday Hour of Power, an all request metal show, WRZX has a honed niche on the dial in Indianapolis. You won't find Bob Seger popping into the mix—and its jocks would probably run Mellencamp out of town—but the station provides Indy with a complement to its other stations. Also, WRZX hosts a summer festival called X-Fest, which has brought the likes of Korn and Linkin Park to town.

## *MISCELLANEOUS ATTRACTIONS:*

### Indy Jazz Fest

The brainchild of jazz enthusiasts who wanted to celebrate the city's place in the annals of jazz history, the Indy Jazz Fest has had a tumultuous run. Twice the summer festival has struggled to return after years that saw headliners such as B.B. King and Arturo Sandoval. But even in smaller versions, the event provides an opportunity to broaden musical horizons on those long summer days.

—*Ryan Lenz*

## *HONORABLE MENTION:*

# INDIANA UNIVERSITY, BLOOMINGTON
300 N. Jordan Ave.
Bloomington, IN 47405-1106
www.iub.edu

**T**wo hours south of Indianapolis, Indiana University's Bloomington campus houses a majority of the school's arts and communications programs, including a renowned journalism school and a highly acclaimed music program. The large university, with thirteen undergraduate schools, offers more than 130 majors, but most freshmen begin by taking courses in the "university division," where they take a general liberal arts curriculum. Music majors are admitted directly into the program once they pass an audition. The school offers a comprehensive music curriculum and promises the intensity and focus of a conservatory with the academic resources of a major research institution. Once you're in the program, your degree options include a bachelor of music (in composition, early music, jazz studies or performance), a bachelor of music education, a bachelor of science (in recording arts, for example), a bachelor of science in music and an outside field or an associate in science. Apart from the traditional classes, IU Bloomington has a remarkable array of unconventional, rock & roll-oriented classes and even gives students the chance to participate in a study-abroad program in London that considers the Beatles' music. The best part? You needn't be a music major to take these classes. Some of the offerings include a two-part, comprehensive history of rock & roll and Rock Music in the Seventies and Eighties, and more specialized ones include: The Music of Jimi Hendrix or Beach Boys, Beefheart and the Residents. And there is a bevy of music courses that are not exclusively rock related, including The Art of the Live Performance, Special Topics in Popular Music and Contemporary Jazz and Soul Music. Plus, in addition to Indianapolis, the Bloomington campus is a reasonable distance from three other thriving rock scenes: Louisville, KY (105 miles), Cincinnati, OH (127 miles); and Columbus, OH (225 miles).

# Iowa City, IA

Iowa City is home to the state's largest university (with nearly 30,000 students) and therefore also boasts the most international flair of any college community in Iowa. The prestigious Iowa Writers Workshop alone has been a magnet for talent and recognition from around the globe.

The **University of Iowa**'s School of Music (www.uiowa. edu/~music/) offers both a bachelor of arts (with concentrations in composition, music history and performance) and a bachelor of music (with concentrations in composition, jazz studies, music therapy and performance). Ensembles run the gamut, from marching and pep bands to Afro-Cuban and steel drum. Degrees in music education also require admission to the Teaching Education Program, in the College of Education. The university's core music curriculum is fleshed out by some popular unorthodox offerings, such as the Elvis as Anthology course taught by Peter Nazareth, professor of African-American studies. At the center of Nazareth's teaching is the notion that Elvis Presley's enduring iconic status results from how he channeled the musical/performance styles of no fewer than 130 other artists—Jackie Wilson, Hank Williams, Mahalia Jackson, etc. Nazareth says that Presley had the knack for "twinning" his musical contemporaries. IU faculty and students also have been at the forefront of debating copyright law and fair use in the age of digital downloads.

The Student Committee on Producing Entertainment (SCOPE Productions) helps import rock bands into the student union (Modest Mouse, G. Love, Umphrey's McGee) and stages the occasional major concert in Carver-Hawkeye Arena. The classy Hancher Auditorium (with room for audiences of about 2,500) is where students go for a dose of the seasoned performers revered by their parents—Tony Bennett, Aretha Franklin, James Taylor, etc.

For music fans, the epicenter of college life is downtown Iowa City, where the campus intertwines with the Pedestrian Mall—a street lined with bars, live music venues, and record shops. **Gabe's Oasis** (www.gabesoasis.com) books the steadiest diet of indie rock into a long, narrow room on its second floor. **The Mill** (www.icmill. com) has been a home for local folk, bluegrass and roots musicians since 1962. It's also a worthwhile restaurant, where a pub quiz takes place every Sunday night, as well as acoustic brunches on Saturday and Sunday mornings. **The Yacht Club**, is a basement venue where the first Saturday night of the month features local guitar legend Dennis McMurrin and his Demolition Band—a ritual performance in which the band sets up in the middle of the room and the audience surrounds them. The stately **Englert Theater** (www.englert.org) was built in 1912, eventually converted to a movie theater, and then shuttered in 1999. A community group refurbished and reopened the Englert at the end of 2004, and today it programs a full range of live entertainment including concerts.

There's really only one record shop in town worthy of your time: **Record Collector** (www.recordcollectorinc.com) on Washington St. carries a mixture of vinyl and CDs in genres including indie rock, drum n' bass and jazz, as well as an impressive variety of more obscure sub-genres such as Sixties psych pop.

—*Kyle Munson*

# Ithaca, NY

Surrounded by miles of farmland, the small town of Ithaca is dominated by students from both **Cornell University** (www.cornell. edu) and **Ithaca College** (www.ithaca.edu). For a sleepy town, Ithaca has a strong grassroots music scene with an earthy-crunchy appeal. Local folk and reggae musicians routinely congregate at the pedestrian mall downtown to play steel guitar and sing for their supper, and a small stage in the middle of the walkway occasionally hosts weekend shows.

The music departments at both universities are fairly traditional, though each includes some noteworthy course offerings: Cornell has classes on rock history, the psychology of music, and how to write film scores; Ithaca—founded in 1892 as a music conservatory—prides itself on a highly selective program focusing on music theory and performance. Ithaca College's conservatory teaches 500 students total, with around 120 freshmen admitted out of 1,000 auditions. The four-story James J. Whalen Center for Music contains recital halls, more than ninety practice rooms and four chamber music rehearsal rooms. The facility is also equipped with various recording rooms, electroacoustic music studios, and several labs.

Ithaca may have a reputation for jam bands and bluegrass, but some college students have been working to boost the town's rock scene. The Cornell-based Fanclub Collective, for instance, formed in 2001 by Chris Adams and Jessica Wolkoff to encourage the development of a stronger indie rock scene in Ithaca. Previously, the Cornell Concert Commission was the only group dealing with the campus' entertainment, drawing in acts such as Guster, O.A.R. and Rufus Wainwright. But the collective worked to bring in more obscure acts, and has succeeded in booking bands including Interpol, the Arcade Fire, the Walkmen, Broken Social Scene, and Ted Leo and the Pharmacists.

Off campus, several coffee shops put on shows by local acts, as does the pirate-themed **Castaways** (www.castawaysithaca.com), which occasionally books national indie acts such as The New Deal. **The State Theatre** (www.statetheatreofithaca.com), Ithaca's biggest performance center, is currently renovating its 1,626-seat auditorium. The "Save America's Treasures" program has awarded the theater $150,000 in a dollar-for-dollar matching grant for restoration costs. This venue plays an important role as a cultural and social center for the town, drawing large acts such as Ani DiFranco, David Byrne, Herbie Hancock, and Joan Baez.

There is a Sam Goody on the Cornell campus, but you can find a more eclectic selection at **Autumn Leaves**—a used bookstore downtown that sells records in its basement—and **Sounds Fine**.

Cornell radio station **WVBR** 93.5 (www.wvbr.com) hosts DJ and producer Phil Shapiro's nearly forty-years-running folk show "Bound For Glory," which features live performances from artists including Utah Phillips, Dave Carter and Tracy Grammer and Mike Seeger—Pete Seeger's brother. You can either catch the show on your hi-fi, or attend the Sunday gigs live in a wood-paneled room on the Cornell campus that fills with around seventy-five people eager to clap and sing along.

Ithaca College also runs a successful non-commercial radio station, **WICB** (www.ithaca.edu/radio/wicb/), which airs genre-specific shows such as "Modern Rock,' "Acoustic Café," "Jazz Impressions," "Hobo's Lullaby" ("two hours of everything from the spoken word to folk, world and other homeless music"), the "Punk Rock Show," and "Breakfast with the Beatles." WICB is student-operated and provides a unique opportunity for Ithacan collegiates to receive pre-professional experience in deejaying, programming, public relations, sports writing, news reporting, production technology and much more. WICB reaches a quarter of a million listeners and there is no previous experience required to join the staff.

# Lawrence, KS

## THE UNIVERSITY OF KANSAS, LAWRENCE
Lawrence, KS 66045
www.ku.edu

The **University of Kansas, Lawrence**, is a strong choice if you want to study architecture, nursing or journalism. Its music program, however, is nothing to write home about. But that doesn't mean Larryville hasn't earned its rock cred. In fact, this is one of the country's most underrated college towns, where a thriving music scene has churned out successful indie bands including The Get Up Kids, Butterglory, The New Amsterdams, Appleseed Cast, Ultimate Fakebook and The Anniversary. The university itself gets props for its radio station, **KJHK**, where the playlist reflects the town's emo-leaning aesthetic.

# VENUES:

### The Bottleneck, 737 New Hampshire

THE place for live music in Lawrence; if you like 'em, they played here. Radiohead, the Flaming Lips, the Pixies, Wilco, Trip Shakespeare ... the list goes on and on. With a 350-capacity, the 'Neck is big enough to get lost in the crowd but small enough to feel like you can hang out with the band.

### The Replay Lounge, 946 Massachusetts

The loveliest little hole in Larryville, The Replay Lounge is home to pinball, rock & roll and a host of townies. The sound system ain't much to brag on (a couple small PA speakers hanging from the ceiling), but it was good enough for The White Stripes and gaggles of other I-can't-believe-they-played-there bands. The heated beer garden makes the bar a big draw in winter, and the bathroom artwork from Lawrence expatriate Travis Millard is the stuff of legend.

### The Jackpot Saloon, 943 Massachusetts

Lawrence's newest venue has filled a much-needed niche by splitting the difference between the top-flight sound of the Bottleneck and the spit-in-your-face stage of The Replay Lounge. Since opening in the summer of 2003, the club has hosted a diverse roster including the Arcade Fire, the Decemberists, the Walkmen, Clearlake and local favorites the Appleseed Cast.

### Liberty Hall, 644 Massachusetts

As a meeting house, an opera house, a movie theatre and a music hall, Liberty Hall has hosted countless events throughout its rich 142-year history. Bands from Iggy Pop to Interpol to local emo legends the Get Up Kids have chosen the venue for its sparkling atmosphere, theater-style seating and giant stage.

### The Granada, 1020 Massachusetts,

"The Granasty" is no longer a fitting moniker for this recently renovated nightclub. Less of a hangout than a place to see bands, The Granada hosts big ballers like Ben Folds and Weezer in addition to a bevy of weekly dance nights.

# RECORD STORES:

### Love Garden, 936 Massachusetts St.

As much a Lawrence institution as any venue, Love Garden is tops for vinyl and used CDs. The friendly staff is snobbish in the best way, meaning the selection is stocked with hip new indie rock, obscure foreign imports, beaucoup hip-hop and even a solid selection of bluegrass and old-time. The friendly staff won't give you any attitude if you come in looking for a 50 Cent record, but one of the half-dozen cats might send a snide glance your way.

### Kief's Downtown Music
### www.kiefs.com

Kief's only does a few things but it does them well. Limited floor space means vinyl is a luxury, but new releases are often sold at bargain-basement prices when the store's staff takes a liking to them. The listening stations keep a healthy selection of new music available, and the store also goes out of its way to host ambitious in-store performances like Super Furry Animals and British Sea Power.

# RADIO STATIONS:

### KJHK-FM 90.7
### www.kjhk.org

The only station for the truly enlightened, KJHK is a college radio powerhouse with a solid 50-mile reach and diverse programming that rarely leaves any stone unturned. Independent rock and hip-hop are the station's bread and butter, but there's a specialty show for just about everything else. The station also goes out of its way to promote local music and host live performances, and leaves the door open to just about anyone who wants to be involved.

### KZPL-FM 97.3
### www.973theplanet.com

An upstart big-market station with the rare distinction of being privately owned, "The Planet" showcases an adventurous play list that runs the gamut from Wilco to Folk Implosion to Rooney. Specialty shows include "Jam Planet" and "The Unplugged Planet."

**KPR-FM 91.5**
**www.kpr.ku.edu**

Don't overlook Kansas Public Radio just because it caters to a more "sophisticated" audience. The University of Kansas-based station features primo left-of-center programming like "The Retro Cocktail Hour" (Space-Age Pop, Lounge and Exotica) and "Trail Mix" (bluegrass, old-time and new folk). Fans of syndicated variety shows like "This American Life" and "A Prairie Home Companion" can also get their fix here.

## MISCELLANEOUS EVENTS:

### Wakarusa Music and Camping Festival
### (Clinton Lake State Park)

Lawrence had been host to a variety of huge summer festivals throughout the Nineties but a void developed in recent years. That changed with the arrival of Wakarusa 2004, a four-day festival featuring more than seventy bands including Robert Randolph, Galactic, Spoon, Guided By Voices, Drive-By Truckers, North Mississippi All Stars and local favorites Split Lip Rayfield. The festival will return in 2005 with another jam-heavy yet diverse lineup and looks to be a fixture in the area.

### Farmer's Ball

This KJHK-sponsored annual event pits eight of the best up-and-coming local bands against each other in a battle-of-the-bands format. Less a competition than a celebration of local music, the Farmer's Ball has spawned past winners including Chebella! (an early incarnation of Mates of State), Ghosty and The Capsules.

### Wax Clash / Mic Mechanics MC Battle

Hip-hop in Kansas? Hell yes. Lawrence is a veritable magnet for some of the Midwest's most off-the-chain talent, from SoundsGood to Approach to Archetype. The hip-hop community rallies around these biannual events, which attract the cream of the local DJs and MCs.

—*Richard Gintowt*

# Los Angeles, CA

## UNIVERSITY OF SOUTHERN CALIFORNIA
Los Angeles, CA, 90089
www.usc.edu

I t's difficult to know where to start when it comes to the University of Southern California. USC's Thornton School of Music is a flagship institution at one of southern California's most esteemed universities. Though the academics at the Thornton School are extremely strong, there are plenty of non-academic reasons to come to USC if you love music. Of course, the school's location in Los Angeles is a perk, but it also has one of the most famous and entertaining marching bands in the country! The Trojan Marching Band, which is comprised of students from a huge range of majors, is known as "The Spirit of Troy" and has played for seven presidents, appeared in movies such as *Forrest Gump* and *Grease 2*, and has performed at the Academy Awards and at the 2004 Grammys with Andre 3000 from Outkast. The band has also released platinum albums thanks in part to its famous collaborations with Fleetwood Mac, including hits "Tusk" and "The Dance." The band covers, among other tunes, Offspring's "The Kids Aren't All Right" in honor of Offspring lead singer and USC alumni Dexter Holland. Holland even has an official UNC cheer aptly known as "Dexter Holland's Cheer" which goes as follows: "Ohhhhhhhhhhhh Vic-tor-y!!! We will never lose to you!"

As for the academic stuff, undergraduates at USC can pursue several music degrees. The bachelor of music is offered in one of the following concentrations: Composition, composition with special emphasis on film scoring, electroacoustic media, jazz studies, jazz studies with special emphasis on vocals, music education, the music industry, and performance (in a dizzying array of instruments). Also offered is the bachelor of science in jazz studies, the music industry, music recording, and bachelor of arts degrees in music and humanities. For aspiring film score composers, the bachelor of music in composition with an emphasis in scoring for motion pictures and television arms students with the skills they'll need to create music that's marketable for Los Angeles' biggest industries. The music industry program is also well-suited to those whose interests extend beyond performance: Students are exposed to a huge range of courses including The Business and Economics of the Recording Industry, The Mixing Console, Introduction to Music Law, Radio in the Music Industry, and Artist Management and Development.

# UNIVERSITY OF CALIFORNIA, LOS ANGELES
Department of Music
1642 Schoenberg Music Building
Box 951616
Los Angeles, CA 90095-1616
www.music.ucla.edu

**T**he UCLA department of music proclaims its focus to be on the "musical traditions of Europe, and the international and American musical styles of the last century." Considering that the school is located in the heart of Los Angeles, an ethnically and culturally diverse city jam-packed with musicians, pop-culture enthusiasts, and trend-setters—it's not surprising that UCLA has at least the American side of things totally covered.

UCLA offers bachelor of arts degrees in the following music-related subjects: music (with concentrations in performance, music education, or composition,) music history (also referred to as musicology,) and ethnomusicology. The academic requirements for each of these degrees (and their different concentrations) vary but are consistently demanding. All music majors, regardless of concentration, participate in at least one of more than twenty departmental ensembles, and all students who concentrate in performance present junior and senior year recitals. Music history students focus more on the use of music as a part of cultural identity throughout history and ethnomusicology students become familiar with a myriad of musical traditions and the cultures that create them.

Though UCLA's different music programs vary greatly in accordance with their declared focus, one thing they all have in common is the extent to which they are influenced by Los Angeles. The course offerings in all of UCLA's music programs are as contemporary and innovative as any in the country. A UCLA music major interested in the sounds of Hollywood might take Understanding Movie Music, Hollywood Musical and the American Dream, Film and Music, Music Now, or Composition for Motion Pictures and Television, and someone interested in music education has Music Literature for Children and Historical and Philosophical Foundations of Music Education to delve into. If you are drawn to the history of music try Development of Latin Jazz, History of Rock and Roll, History of Electronic Dance Music, or The Beatles—all offered to UCLA music majors. Students looking for the rare course on gender issues in music can take Music and Gender, or Gay and Lesbian Perspectives in Pop Music. Even wannabe rock critics have a course specially designed for them at UCLA: Writing About Music exposes students to the skills and "stylistic conventions" necessary to be a music journalist. And extra special bonus: This class even satisfies a writing requirement!

# LOYOLA MARYMOUNT UNIVERSITY
1 LMU Dr.
Los Angeles, CA 90045-2659
www.lmu.edu

**T**rue to its Jesuit and Catholic principles, LMU promises to educate the full person, and encourages students to participate in enriching co-curricular activities that augment the liberal arts program the school offers. Musicians will take courses in the College of Fine Arts and Communication and earn a bachelor of arts degree in music. As for concentrations, you have your pick: performance (study vocal or a variety of instruments), theory/composition, music history/literature, world music, instrumental studies, vocal studies, instrumental conducting and choral conducting. Students don't declare a concentration until junior year, so there's plenty of time to figure out which facet of the program is especially intriguing. But one of the school's most distinguished features is a program in its School of Film and Television: a B.A. with a recording arts concentration. Always dreamt of becoming a master engineer? You'll study and master the theoretical and practical aspects of sound engineering, and focus on everything from live performances to music for film or television. The curriculum comprises classes from the school's general liberal arts division as well as music theory courses. Then, take it to the lab setting where you'll work with engineering equipment and familiarize yourself with the intricacies of a working studio.

## VENUES:

### Henry Fonda Music Box Theater, 6126 Hollywood Blvd., www.henryfondatheater.com

This theater is a key venue for fast-rising underground acts (the Hives, Distillers, Mars Volta, etc.) and fans fueled on adrenaline, booze and canned energy drinks. Now booked by the same astute crew behind the influential indie haven Spaceland (see below), the Fonda is also expanding into cutting edge dance music. A roomy patio on the roof offers a quick escape outdoors for serious smoking addicts.

### Avalon, 1735 N. Vine St., www.avalonhollywood.com

Formerly known as the Hollywood Palace (and site of the last-ever Ramones performance), this refurbished art deco castle now claims one of the city's most advanced sound systems, ready for either high-decibel rock or all-night DJ parties by the likes of Junkie XL and the Crystal Method. As a result, the Avalon attracts the top touring acts in dance music, with the occasional awards show (the Shortlist Prize) or a wildcard like bluegrass revivalist Gillian Welch. Weekend nights are otherwise devoted to turntables, house beats. But the vibe is less about glow sticks than an elegant early morning out on a modern dance floor in the heart of old Hollywood, with comfortable booths and balconies, plus an upstairs lounge called the Spider Club, decorated in a plush Moroccan theme for your immediate post-party chill-out needs.

### Spaceland, 1717 Silver Lake Blvd., www.clubspaceland.com

This most adventurous rock club began its first decade in 1995 with an opening night show headlined by Beck and the Foo Fighters. There have been many memorable shows since, introducing fans to fresh new acts from the indie, alternative, underground nation. Established bands and unknowns pass through, with new sounds and visions, beneath a lonely disco ball. The raw, boho décor is fittingly barebones, though it has two full bars and an old videogame machine for twenty-five-cent rounds of intergalactic warfare between acts. Pool tables are in the back room. Parking is increasingly difficult on neighborhood streets, but well worth the struggle if the club's tiny valet parking lot is full. Big nights with buzz bands can mean sold-out shows and long, frustrating waits in line outside.

### Troubadour, 9081 Santa Monica Blvd., www.troubadour.com

This is the birthplace of southern California folk rock, where Linda Rondstadt, Jackson Browne and the Eagles first perfected that peaceful, easy feeling. But in the decades since, it's been home to hair metal, punk rock, drum 'n' bass and lo-fi folk, while showcasing the likes of Radiohead and Queens of the Stone Age on their way to the stratosphere. The fading rustic décor hasn't changed much since the Seventies, and the kitchen menu is only for the truly desperate, but the Troub hosts some of the most essential music in town. A VIP area upstairs may be annoying to the unconnected, but the stage is where the important action happens, continuing the local rock history that is part of the club's special cache. John Lennon was once ejected for heckling the Smothers Brothers and wearing a tampon on his head. Which is all some fans will need to know.

### Viper Room, 8852 Sunset Blvd., www.viperroom.com

This tiny room is a venue both for emerging bands and for major acts looking for a cozy showcase setting, which explains how the likes of Johnny Cash, PJ Harvey, and Bruce Springsteen have landed on its triangular stage for a nightly capacity crowd of only 250 people. Allen Ginsberg and Hunter S. Thompson have performed readings here, and this is where actor River Phoenix spent his final moments collapsed on the sidewalk from a drug overdose. Co-founded by Johnny Depp, the Viper Room is a dimly lit club with its art deco walls painted black and deep purple. A downstairs lounge bar offers escape or another round.

### Whisky a Go Go, 8901 Sunset Blvd., www.whiskyagogo.com

A good share of rock & roll history has passed through this corner club on the Sunset Strip since 1964, from Led Zeppelin to Radiohead. It is also the last surviving club in a two-block radius on the Strip where Jim Morrison first horrified promoters and A&R men alike by singing of killing his father and raping his mother in his infamous Oedipus Complex epic, "The End." His picture now hangs behind the downstairs bar, Jimbo apparently forgiven. The cages and go-go dancers from the early days are long gone, leaving a barren room, well suited to the bruising hard rock and punk that appears there now. T-shirts are sold at the bar, complete with the ancient original club logo of a smoking hipster chick in heels and beret.

### The Derby, 4500 Los Feliz Blvd., www.the-derby.com

Beneath this thirty-foot-high curved wooden ceiling is where the Nineties swing revival once flourished, as twentysomethings and nostalgic eighty-year-olds found common purpose in the desire to dance to sounds rooted in the Forties and Fifties. The Derby, founded in another century by director Cecil B. De Mille, still hosts high-octane jazz, blues and swing, creating an atmosphere not unlike the climactic romantic scene from *Swingers* that took place right beside the same ancient oval-shaped bar. Drinking is encouraged. And the club offers swing dance lessons on Sundays for the hopelessly out of step.

### Hollywood Palladium, 6215 Sunset Blvd., www.hollywoodpalladium.com

This big, streamlined ballroom claims the title of longest-running music venue in the city, opening with a 1940 dance party led by skinny teen heartthrob Frank Sinatra and the Tommy Dorsey Orchestra. The hardwood dancefloor has seen several decades of music history since, from the Rolling Stones and Black Flag to Public Enemy and the Strokes. There are drawbacks, beginning with security measures that strip fans of lighters, cigarettes, aspirin, pencils, eye drops, and much more. Long, slow lines for drink bracelets mean you will have missed the headliner's opening song by the time of your first sip. The sound can often be great in the center of the dance floor, but pretty dicey everywhere else. And yet, the Palladium remains a vital setting for rising acts one step removed from the club scene.

### House of Blues Sunset Strip, 8430 Sunset Blvd.,
### www.hob.com

Founded in 1994, this is just one of eight high-concept clubs in the House of Blues chain offering musical diversity with a spiritual bent and a roster crowded with rock, blues, plus a gospel brunch every Sunday. But its location on the Sunset Strip also makes it an important showcase for breakout bands and arena rockers (Eric Clapton, Metallica) in occasional need of closer contact with fans, as crowds literally rub against Southern folk art nailed to every wall. Upstairs is the Foundation Room, a velvety lounge decorated with couches and Indian décor. Though reserved mostly for club members and special guests, it's often open to the public for performances by solo artists and DJs. It was there that Phil Spector met the woman who wound up dead in his foyer only hours later. Most fans escape unharmed.

### Roxy Theater, 9009 W. Sunset Blvd.,
### www.theroxyonsunset.com

Since 1972, the Roxy has been an essential, intimate rock venue, hosting the original stage version of *The Rocky Horror Show*, career-making club shows by Bruce Springsteen and the first wave of punk. A kitchen serves pizza, tacos, and burgers. Monday nights are reserved for National Lampoon's Metal Skool, a ridiculous and loving comedy tribute to the Eighties hair metal bands that once dominated the Strip.

### Wiltern Theater, 3790 Wilshire Blvd.,
### www.thewiltern.com

This sophisticated former movie palace, built in 1931 as part of an aqua-colored art deco landmark office building, draws a 2,300 capacity crowd to what is now Koreatown. It's where touring prestige acts (Tom Waits, Elvis Costello, Jane's Addiction, Paul Oakenfold, etc.) in search of a big, elegant theater tend to land.

### Greek Theater, Griffith Park, 2700 N. Vermont Ave.,
### www.greektheaterla.com

Neil Diamond once outdid himself in this grand outdoor venue, where he transformed into a denim-clad shouter on a hot August night in 1973 for about 6,000 fans, and for a rare moment was more rock star than easy-listening crooner. Clearly, the man was inspired. Nestled in the hills of Griffith Park, the Greek books top acts in a spectacular setting with excellent sound. The seats up front are highly coveted, but the view from the back rows provides a fittingly epic visual to your musical nirvana. Stacked parking lots can mean being trapped between cars long after the final song. But fans unwilling or unable to buy tickets sometimes watch or listen from the forest just beyond the cheap seats.

### Hollywood Bowl, 2301 N. Highland Ave., www.hollywoodbowl.com

This massive open-air amphitheater set in the hills overlooking Hollywood remains one of the most famous music venues in the world. Originally designed in 1922 for classical music, the Bowl calendar is now also shared by pop music acts that have hit and want to make a grand statement. Not everyone is up to the task of making music big enough to fill its wide open spaces, but Sting, Elton John, Radiohead, and others still managed to find the right mix of energy and inspiration for nearly 18,000 fans a night.

### Universal Amphitheater, Universal City Dr., www.hob.com/venues/concerts/universal/

This 6,000-seat room is a favorite stop for major acts: a big indoor amphitheater with excellent sound and comfortable surroundings, as fitting for Ludacris as for Yanni. The event calendar, booked by House of Blues Concerts, is hard to beat, though parking is too damn expensive.

## RECORD STORES:

### Amoeba Records, 6400 Sunset Blvd., www.amoebamusic.com

Amoeba calls itself the world's largest independent record store, and it's hard to disagree with an inventory of almost a million CDs, vinyl LPs, singles, and ancient 78s. It's an almost overwhelming warehouse of musical pop culture, with walls covered in new and vintage rock posters for sale, and an upstairs section mostly devoted to new, used and rare DVDs, laser discs and videotapes. A big rear room is reserved for jazz, blues, and classical recordings, while other racks are loaded with 12-inch dance singles and reggae discs. More than 300,000 new and used albums are bought and sold each month at this outsize trading post. And it's a place for surprising musical discoveries, like spotting Fred Durst in line with an armload of My Bloody Valentine discs. There's also a small stage where major acts (White Stripes, PJ Harvey, etc.) perform short but worthwhile sets before sitting down for autographs. Obsessive music lovers will find no better selection anywhere.

### Aron's Records, 1150 N. Highland Ave., www.aronsrecords.com

Since 1965, Aron's has been an essential dealer in new and used vinyl and CDs for hardcore collectors and music obsessives desperate for fresh young sounds and overground classics. Customers can sell CDs and vinyl for beer money and the rent, or make a pilgrimage to the store's twice-yearly parking lot sale in search of forgotten treasures, where prices range from twenty-five cents to three dollars.

### Tower Sunset, 8801 Sunset Blvd., www.towerrecords.com.

While it's a given that Los Angeles would have a big Tower outlet, this particular record shop is the true, cultural flagship of the forty-five-year-old store chain, a great big supermarket of a room located right at the heart of the Sunset Strip, just steps away from such historic clubs as the Roxy, Viper Room and the Whisky a Go Go. That makes the store a dependable pit stop during a rock & roll night out, with listening stations in every row beneath the fluorescent tubes, and a magazine rack filled with international pop culture titles and obscure fanzines. Tower Sunset is also the most likely spot for autograph signings by the likes of KISS or N.E.R.D. But most important is the selection. If a CD is still in print, it's probably here.

### Vinyl Fetish, 1614 Cahuenga Blvd., www.vinylfetishrecords.com

This monument to punk, goth, and industrial rock was founded in 1979 by a pair of Ramones fanatics at the peak of the original punk explosion, and hosted early in-store appearances by U2, Iggy Pop, Duran Duran, and the Misfits when almost no one else would have them. With claims of about a million pieces in stock or storage, from low-end junk at $1.99 to a $250 autographed Madonna disc, the store draws a devoted clientele to its racks of CDs, rare LPs and 7-inch singles.

Also between its purple-colored walls are medallions, buttons, fishnet stockings, and a wide selection of punk-rock t-shirts. Morrissey, Alice Cooper, Brody Armstrong of the Distillers, and even Michael J. Fox have been spotted searching the aisles or plugging into the row of turntables and headphones. The guys behind the counter share in the obsession, proudly "polluting the mainstream for twenty-five years," says manager Andy Franzle.

**Virgin Megastore, 8000 Sunset Blvd.,**
**www.virginmega.com**

Hardly anything here can be found in any Virgin Megastore anywhere in the world, but even in the mighty L.A. metropolis it's an important supermarket for music, movies, and books just the same. Built on the former location of Hollywood's infamous Schwab's Drug Store and Pandora's Box (site of the true-life Sixties "riot on the Sunset Strip"), this Megastore also features a special room upstairs for dance fanatics devoted to hot 12-inch singles.

# *RADIO STATIONS:*

**Indie 103, 103.1 FM,**
**www.indie1031.fm**

This is rock radio that matters. Clearly designed to take on the profoundly influential but too often stagnant KROQ (see below), Indie 103's eclectic playlist mixes challenging new sounds with rarely aired classic punk and alternative tunes from the Seventies, Eighties, and Nineties. It has also been home to a startling lineup of vet rockers (Henry Rollins, Rob Zombie, Courtney Love) as sometime DJs. Sex Pistol guitarist Steve Jones is the star of this station, his daily afternoon "Jonesy's Jukebox" show riding his slacker cockney vibe and a playlist with no rules and no disappointments, while the Crystal Method hosts a dance music show on Friday nights. Radio like this is not meant to last. Listen while you can.

**KCRW 89.9 FM,**
**www.kcrw.com**

This station of split personalities devotes half its airtime to NPR News and public affairs talk. What's left amounts to one of the most influential stations for new music in the United States, offering grown-up alternative sounds for the musically enlightened. Broadcast from a basement at Santa Monica College, KCRW enjoys a full lineup of music programming that includes the daily Morning Becomes Eclectic and other shows devoted to rock, dance, world music, and more.

### KROQ 106.7 FM,
### www.kroq.com

One of the most influential stations in the country for nearly two decades, KROQ helped establish the soundtrack for the new wave Eighties and alternative Nineties, but has too often strayed from a genuine sense of fun into the corporate imperative of new metal and never much in the way of hip-hop (except the Beastie Boys). Even with its shortcomings, the station still breaks important new bands, finding common ground in the likes of Queens of the Stone Age, Green Day, and System of a Down, and remaining an acceptable and still-needed alternative to most commercial radio. Longtime Hollywood scenemaker and station mascot Rodney Bingenheimer (the "Mayor of the Sunset Strip") is sadly banished to Sundays at midnight, but is still usually the first to introduce exciting new bands to the airwaves, often months before they are officially added to the KROQ playlist.

### KXLU 88.9 FM,
### www.kxlu.com

This is L.A.'s version of college radio in the classic mode, uncovering the newest punk, indie and lo-fi bands around. Sloppy, unpredictable, and essential uneasy listening, it's where locals can first discover the next new thing, as young DJs champion music that is either destined for greatness or total oblivion.

## MISCELLANEOUS EVENTS:

### Coachella Music and Arts Festival

Though the Coachella festival is staged in Indio—a Palm Desert town more than 100 miles from LA—it is rightfully considered one of southern California's best rock & roll offerings—a two-day concert held on the gorgeous green fields of the Indio Polo Grounds, where acts ranging from Queens of the Stone Age, Radiohead, the White Stripes, Weezer and Coldplay have performed before the sunburned masses for four years running. In the great tradition of U.K. rock fests like

Reading and Glastonbury, Coachella books the coolest alternative and indie rock acts and presents them to a friendly crowd of true music lovers. This is, hands down, the best American rock festival going and well worth the two-hour drive inland.

—*Steve Appleford*

## HONORABLE MENTION:

# POMONA COLLEGE

340 N. College Ave.
Claremont, CA 91711-6324
www.pomona.edu

L ocated thirty-two miles east of Los Angeles in Claremont, Pomona makes it a priority to provide music courses appropriate for students of different musical backgrounds and interests. Pomona kids who want to sample an interesting course or two in the Music Department will find plenty to choose from here, as will those who come looking to devote four years to the pursuit of a serious pre-professional musical education. Music majors at Pomona take several required courses including Twentieth-Century Music History and Theory, at least one ethnomusicology course, and must participate in four semesters of music ensemble, and four semesters of music performance. In addition to these central requirements, music majors at Pomona select from one of five concentrations, which include composition, history, performance, ethnomusicology, and special research. The course offerings at the Pomona Music Department are expansive, and include some pretty original inclusions like Music and Cultural Currents in Paris, Nationalism and Music, Words and Music: Song, Musical Theater in America, Survey of American Music, Emotion in Music, Gendering Performance, and Music, Gender, and Ritual in Latin America. Private music lessons are offered at Pomona on more than twenty different instruments such as piano, voice, harpsichord, harp, and most orchestral and band instruments, a series that draws students from all of the Claremont Colleges to Pomona for personalized instruction.

The town of Claremont is also home to one of southern California's best rock venues, **Glasshouse** (www.glasshouse.us), which regularly showcases punk, indie, and emo acts such as the Ataris, From Autumn to Ashes, Bloc Party, the Honorary Title and the Kills on its main-stage and regional and local acts in the brick-walled adjacent room. And a few short blocks away from the Pomona campus, the thirty-year-old **Rhino Records** (www.rhinorecords.cc) occupies 6,000 square feet packed with CDs and new and used vinyl covering genres from the mainstream to the obscure. Rhino stages a fair share of in-stores (past performers have included Soul Coughing, MXPX, and Jimmy Eat World) and peddles an assortment of toys, stickers and other miscellany.

Also of note: The historic **Folk Music Center** (www. folkmusiccenter.com), owned by roots rocker Ben Harper, has been located in Claremont since the late 1950s. In its early years, the Center's "Golden Ring" venue brought in such legends as Doc Watson, Gary Davis, and John Fahey. In addition to selling rare instruments—guitars, banjos, dulcimers, and autoharps—the center offers music lessons and includes a museum stocked with antiquarian six strings from the late nineteenth century as well as artifacts from around the world.

# CALIFORNIA INSTITUTE OF THE ARTS
24700 McBean Pkwy.
Valencia, CA 91355
www.calarts.edu

**C**alArts is the inspiration for LacArts—the college attended by all the freaky cool kids in *Six Feet Under,* but there are actually many reasons, other than that (very good) one to check this place out! This laidback arts school thirty-seven miles north of LA has the reputation for attracting creative and talented students, many of whom have gone on to work as filmmakers, performers, and musicians. The school was established in the early sixties by Walt and Roy Disney and now offers degree programs in six main areas: art, critical studies, dance, film/video, music, and theater. CalArts allows its students a lot of freedom to merge one area of study with another, but within the school's official music program, degrees are offered in composition, performance, musical arts, music technology, and integrated media. All undergrads at CalArts are required to take a series of critical studies requirements, which ensure that analytical, quantitative, and writing skills are not neglected as the student's work on the specialized art they've come here to study.

# Madison, WI

## UNIVERSITY OF WISCONSIN, MADISON
140 Peterson Bldg.
750 University Ave.
Madison, WI 53706
www.wisc.edu

In spite of its massive size—30,000 undergrads enrolled—the University of Wisconsin maintains a noble set of goals for its music majors. The mission is twofold: to provide a comprehensive approach to music education by "fostering critical thinking" and inspiring students to perform, as well to involve students in community outreach, public education, and public service. Majors have a few options in terms of degrees. There's either a bachelor of music, with concentrations in performance, music education, jazz, composition, and string pedagogy, or a bachelor of arts/bachelor of science with concentrations in music history, performance, and music theory. There's also a Digital Music Studio that allows students exploring electronic-based composition ample room to experiment. And non-majors who want to brush up on a particular instrument can arrange for private lessons from School of Music students (the best, naturally) for a small fee. Best of all, UW Madison has an extremely active student music committee that programs a variety of events at four on-campus venues (see below).

The University also publishes its own student-run magazine, *Emmie*, which features extensive music coverage including features, reviews and interviews with the likes of Yo La Tengo, the Hives, Death Cab for Cutie, Sleater-Kinney, and AFI. "It's a great opportunity for the staff to learn about the music industry, to get work published, to learn about layout and design, and to be a part of the Madison music scene," says UW student April Williamson. Budding rock critics should check it out at www.emmiemagazine.com

## VENUES:

### Der Rathskeller and the Terrace (Memorial Union) and Club 770 (Union South), on campus

The Wisconsin Union Directorate Music Committee, a student committee, books an array of free (!) jazz, rock, and folk shows into these three all-ages venues. Club 770 is the hippest of the three spots, and depending on which night you show up, you might get to see national punk and indie rock acts such as Secret Machines and Moving Units before they become too big for such an intimate club. The Terrace— an outdoor area packed with colorful tables and metal chairs—is the largest of the three, with a capacity close to 3,000. When the weather gets bad, shows are held in Der Rathskeller—a 600-capacity, smoke free club with archways and wooden furniture adding to the room's Teutonic vibe. The Memorial Union holds a Friday evening jazz and singer/songwriter series called Behind the Beat, and amateur performers show up every Thursday to participate in the venue's open mic series.

### Catacombs Coffee House, 731 State St., on campus, www.catacombscoffeehouse.com

This volunteer-run, non-profit venue usually has a few shows a week in the basement of Pres House (home to the Presbyterian Student Center Foundation) on the UW Madison campus. If you can get past the fact that it bills itself as a "faith-based" venue, you'll find that Catacombs hosts many of the best indie rock shows passing through Madison. Recent acts onstage at this welcoming little café include such left-of-center critical faves as TV On The Radio, John Vanderslice, CEX, and Earlimart. The venue maintains no strict religious affiliation, but they definitely are committed to doing the right thing: Catacombs supports fair-trade coffee and sustainable agriculture by purchasing organic food from local and regional farms. They do not make any money off the shows and often serve a homemade dinner to the bands that play there.

### High Noon Saloon, 701 E. Washington Ave., www.high-noon.com

The High Noon Saloon is a mid-size 21+ venue opened last May by Cathy Dethmers, who ran a popular venue called O'Cayz Corral ("the CBGB's of the Midwest"), before it burned down. The best recent addition to the Madison scene, the Saloon offers live music seven nights a week, mostly of the folk and country variety. Recent headliners have included Irish ensemble Carbon Leaf and singer-songwriter Ray LaMontagne. And if that's not your cup of tea, consider stopping by on the nights the Saloon hosts rock & roll karaoke (sing with a live band!) or pull up a chair for the Boggle tournament.

### Luther's Blues, 1401 University Ave., www.luthersblues.com

Once a band gets too big for the Catacombs, it tends to move its act over to Luther's. Drawing its inspiration from old blues clubs, Luther's Blues is one of Madison's more upscale venues. Though a mural of blues legend—and the club's namesake—Luther Allison dominates the wall behind the stage, the variety of performers here is certainly not limited to one genre: Shows at Luther's have run the gamut from indie (the Decemberists, Blonde Redhead) to alt-country (Rhett Miller) to jazz (the University Jazz Band.)

### The Barrymore Theater, 2090 Atwood Ave., www.barrymorelive.com

If jam bands, blues, folk, world music or funk is your thing, you can bet your bottom dollar you will find yourself at the Barrymore when Umphrey's Magee or Patty Larkin roll through town. The venue, which is decorated with an assortment of African masks and twinkling lights, has the perfect setup for chilled-out performances: a sizable area with seats, slanted toward the stage, and an open area down front where you can do the noodle dance to your heart's content.

### Café Montmartre, 127 E. Mifflin St., www.themomo.com

A fancy wine bar and jazz café located near the Capitol, Café Montmartre hosts jazz trios, hip-hop flamenco guitarists, local bands, national acts such as Freedy Johnston and April March, AIDS benefits, film screenings, urban poetry slams, open mics and CD release parties.

**The Overture Center, 201 State St.,**
**www.overturecenter.com**

The Overture Center, the newest addition to State Street, was made possible by a $205 million contribution from a private donor. The massive center, designed by Cesar Pelli, is actually not completed yet. The main concert hall (capacity 2,251 hosts classical music as well as acts such as Brian Wilson, is breathtakingly beautiful and has great acoustics, but manages to maintain an intimate vibe. It was designed with a lot of subtle curves, including a huge organ behind the stage. When it is completed, the Center will have the Capitol Theater, the Playhouse, Promenade Hall, Rotunda Stage, Rotunda Studio, Wisconsin Studio, and galleries.

## RECORD STORES:

**B-Side, 436 State St.,**
**www.b-sidemadison.com**

A quaint, independent store on State St., B-Side lives up to its motto: "Supplying music connoisseurs since 1982." The store has a great selection of rare and hard-to-find indie and rock and small sections of jazz, world, electronic, vinyl, and oldies. Check out the imports stocked behind the counter, and don't miss an entire wall full of noteworthy new releases not found in the Top 40. Plus, anything they don't have they will special order.

**Mad City Music Exchange, 600 Williamson St.,**
**www.madcitymusic.com**

This vinyl haven—at its current memorabilia-plastered location for fifteen years—caters to everyone from college hipsters to DJs to ex-hippies. Most of the vinyl is cheap, but the store does carry, for instance, a rare edition of the Crystals' "He's a Rebel," valued at $250. It's almost too easy to lose track of time in this narrow shop, which also carries CDs—and lots of 'em.

**Trim Records, 212 W. Gorham,**
**www.trimtunes.com**

Trim specializes in reggae and dancehall vinyl and CDs, and the store's laidback vibe matches the ganja-smoking fare it sells.

**MC Audio, 515 University Ave.,**
**www.mc-audio.com**

A counterpart to Trim, MC Audio attracts local DJs looking to stock up on new and used house and electronica platters. They carry both domestic and import releases, plenty of white-label singles, and you can even rent lighting and sound equipment for your upcoming house party.

**Strictly Discs, 1900 Monroe St.,**
**www.strictlydiscs.com**

Strictly Discs' small size is deceptive. A quality independent record seller since 1988, it packs in new and used CDs and vinyl that will appeal to budding DJs. They also have a room dedicated solely to rare and import albums and reward regulars with a buy twelve, get one free policy.

**CD Exchange, 521 State St.**

A half-price used record store on State St, CD Exchange carries the typical resale staples—just in case you never got around to buying Oasis' *What's the Story Morning Glory* or Green Day's *Dookie*. Once in awhile, if you can spare the time to look through it all, you'll find an unexpected gem. And, remarkably, considering its moniker, you can also nab some used vinyl, though the selection is kind of paltry.

**Earwax, 254 W. Gilman,**
**www.earwaxwisconsin.com**

Walk up a flight of stairs to find this hidden metal and punk supplier, where the selection ranges from über-underground to mainstream.

# RADIO STATIONS:

**WSUM 91.7 FM,**
**www.wsum.org**

WSUM is a relatively new, commercial-free independent station in Madison funded mostly by University of Wisconsin segregated fees. The amateur student DJs range in talent, but don't lack passion. The station plays a lot of hardcore, metal, punk, indie, and rock, but jazz, hip hop, experimental, electronic, jam, blues, and classical programming is becoming more frequent. Talk programming ranges from sex to sports to film to university events. Although the signal used to be hard to pick up, WSUM has started webcasting at www.wsum.org.

## MISCELLANEOUS EVENTS:

### Party in the Park

An annual festival hosted by WSUM, Party in the Park features local and national acts on four stages in James Madison Park, near campus. The fest has been running since 1999, and previous performers include Andrew W.K. and indie rock act Califone.

### Hip Hop Generation,
### www.hiphopgeneration.org

Hip Hop Generation is a University of Wisconsin, Madison student organization centered on cultural education and social justice. The group's main goal is to sponsor the three-day Hip Hop as a Movement conference each spring with performances, discussion panels, film screenings, exhibitions, dance demonstrations, and workshops.

# Milwaukee, WI

## UNIVERSITY OF WISCONSIN, MILWAUKEE
Peck School of the Arts
P.O. Box 413
2200 E. Kenwood Blvd.
Milwaukee, WI 53201-0413

The state school's Milwaukee branch offers students an urban campus and an educational philosophy that promises an "inclusive, multidisciplinary [curriculum] ... marked by excellent research and outstanding teaching." Musicians will enroll in classes in the Peck School of the Arts. Students earn either a bachelor of fine arts, or a bachelor of arts in music. The school prides itself on a close-knit community and strong relationships between professors and students. Curriculum-wise, students seeking the B.F.A. must complete music courses—including music theory, history and music performance— and an assortment of liberal arts classes. Additionally, all majors must fulfill performance requirements, including holding recitals. Non-majors can also seek private lessons with music faculty if they are qualified. In addition to the traditional music curriculum, U of W, Milwaukee, offers classes such as American Popular Music (a class that requires no prerequisites) that examines music from 1900 on. Another course, American Folk and Popular Music, takes the discussion back a few hundred years, studying music and social history from 1750 through today.

## VENUES:

### Cactus Club, 2496 S. Wentworth Ave., www.cactusclubmilwaukee.com

Established in the increasingly hip Southside neighborhood of Bay View long before the area's first signs of nascent hipness, the club does an outstanding job year after year of bringing in of-the-moment acts before their moment on the national radar even arrives. It was here that the White Stripes made their Milwaukee debut, and it's here in this tiny club nestled between modest bungalows that indie, punk, noise rock and alt-country stars show up ahead of their own hype.

### Art Bar, 722 E. Burleigh St., www.artbar-riverwest.com

Art is seen and heard in this eclectic Eastside spot—the walls and furniture are covered with bold creative statements and the bar even hosts "open canvas" nights. Live music bookings range from neo-folkies to kitsch-tastic DJs.

### BBC Bar & Grill, 2022 E. North Ave.

The last gritty live music-lovin' holdout on a block that once housed a number of such venues—overeager attempts at gentrification pushed them out—the BBC's small and murky upstairs bar is a good place to catch local and regional rock acts. The downstairs has your standard sports bar/meat market vibe, especially popular with the nearby UWM crowd.

**Bremen Cafe, 901 E. Clarke St.,**
**www.bremencafe.com.**

The folksy Eastside hangout sometimes brings in rising national names in the singer-songwriter genre but is best known for encouraging local talent, including those among the UWM student body, with frequent open mic nights. Surf the Net, too, with WiFi and dial-up connections.

**Cage, 801 S. Second St.**

The grand dame of Milwaukee's gay nightlife scene, this long-running club now brings in patrons of all persuasions with its ultrachic basement bar and various rooms upstairs where DJs spin the full spectrum of dance music.

**Hi-Hat Lounge, 1701 N. Arlington Pl.,**
**www.hi-hat.com**

Hire out the adjacent, swanky "garage" for your next party, enjoy a luxurious Sunday brunch in the restaurant or check out local alt-rock and DJ acts in the bar, which features frequent quirky promotions such as Pod Squad nights, when customers each get a turn at controlling the tunes by plugging their iPods or MP3 players into the sound system.

**Mad Planet, 533 E. Center St.,**
**www.mad-planet.net**

Resident promoter Marc Solheim frequently brings in rising names in punk, emo, and other alt-rock genres, and fans will tell you the friendly club is a more conducive place to enjoy the tunes, compared with some larger venues staffed with overzealous security. Another plus: weekly Eighties dance parties are 2 legit 2 quit.

**Mecca Niteclub and Lounge, 3801 W. Hampton Ave.**

Located on Milwaukee's near North Side, this is the epicenter of a thriving spoken word community that has been attracting national notice thanks to talented acts such as Black Elephant. When the rhymesmiths aren't throwing down, the club books a mix of local hip-hop and DJs who favor smooth R&B grooves.

### Milwaukee Ale House, 233 N. Water St.,
### www.ale-house.com

Water St., the main social drag through downtown, is lined with bars and clubs, but the ale house earned its rightful place as a locals' favorite by offering a mix of its own hand-crafted brews, which change seasonally, and a fun but eclectic offering of live music that ranges from alt-country to Western Swing. The juicy burgers ain't bad, either.

### The Pabst Theater, 144 E. Wells St.,
### www.pabsttheater.org

Though it shares a name with beer, you won't find a classier music venue in the city—the nineteenth-century landmark was designed in the opulent style of Europe's great opera houses. For a long time, the bulk of its schedule was devoted to fine arts programming and the theeea-tah. In the last few years, however, eager in-house promotions have brought in acts such as Bright Eyes and Gavin DeGraw. This is also a great place to catch world music stars—actually, with pristine acoustics and a posh marble and velvet setting, it's a great place to catch any show.

### The Rave, 2401 W. Wisconsin Ave.,
### www.therave.com

Milwaukee music fans have had a love-hate relationship with this cavernous, multi-room venue for decades. On the plus side, the venue—just-and-a-jump from Marquette University—hosts tons of music in every conceivable genre. On a busy night, it's not unusual for world-class DJs to be spinning in the basement while a promising local metal band thrashes around the ground-level bar and the act du jour plays to the upstairs ballroom. Everyone from Modest Mouse and Scissor Sisters to 50 Cent and Wilco have spent time on The Rave's stage. The venue has earned its share of detractors, however, for often-muddy acoustics—bands that don't perform a thorough soundcheck are doomed—and sometimes employing douchebag security guards. A policy of often "papering" shows—handing out coupons good for free admission if you buy two drinks—also robs hard-working bands of door profits.

**Shank Hall, 1434 N. Farwell Ave.,**
**www.shankhall.com**

Fans of the movie *This is Spinal Tap* will appreciate the Eastside venue's in-house shrine to the flick (owner Peter Jest named his place after a fictional Milwaukee club referenced in the cult classic). Come for the mini-Stonehenge motif, but stay for the music, a mix of jam bands, babyboomer favorites, roots rockers and neo-folkies.

**Up & Under Pub, 1216 E. Brady St.**

Located on the East Side bar and eatery row of Brady St., the dark, nicotine-stained walls of this landmark club could tell a thousand tales. Don't let its modest facade fool you—when world-class blues and jazz acts play Milwaukee, they usually play here.

**Vnuk's Lounge, 5036 S. Packard Ave., Cudahy,**
**www.vnuks.com**

Yes, it's on the south fringe of Milwaukee, in the working-class town of Cudahy, close to the airport, but Vnuk's is also on a convenient bus line from downtown for those without wheels. And it's worth the extra distance. The venue is both an old-school neighborhood bar—the kind where everybody knows your name, for real—and showcase for acts that range from cutting edge (this is where the Raveonettes made their Brewtown debut) to quirky (Tito Jackson, anyone?). A favorite with local acts, particularly in the metal and alt-country genres, Vnuk's is known for its friendly, unfussy and unpretentious atmosphere.

## RECORD STORES:

**Atomic Records, 1813 E. Locust St.,**
**www.atomic-records.com**

This Eastside establishment, popular with the UWM crowd and hipster types, excels at stocking under-the-radar acts. Owner Rich Menning also lures a number stars for in-house acoustic sets and CD signings, and frequently packages freebies such as posters or 7-inch discs with new releases. Its famously snarky staff is just part of its allure.

### Rush-Mor, 2660 S. Kinnickinnic Ave., www.my.execpc.com/~rushmor/main.htm

Located on the main shopping street of Bay View—call it KK for short to sound like a local—Rush-Mor is a tiny haven for listeners of every genre that you don't hear on Top 40 radio, especially alt-country, prog and the weirder subgenres of rock. Super-helpful co-owner Dan Duchaine, usually behind the counter, can turn special orders around in sometimes less than twenty-four hours.

### The Exclusive Company, 1669 N. Farwell Ave.

With four locations around the greater Milwaukee area (the Farwell store is the closest to downtown and the UWM and Marquette campuses), this local chain is probably the first place to turn if you're looking for something of the blues, jazz, classical, or world beat variety. Their rock and metal collections also are impressive and, best of all, you get a discount if you pay in cash instead of plastic.

### Trounce Records, 422 N. 15th St., second floor, www.trouncerecords.com

DJs and those of us who just like to collect massive amounts of expensive equipment and obscure vinyl flock to this emporium of electronica, just south of the Marquette campus.

## RADIO STATIONS:

### WMSE, 91.7 FM,
### www.wmse.org

The home station for the Milwaukee School of Engineering, WMSE is arguably the lone bright light of radio programming in a market dominated by cookie-cutter formats. The playlist bounces between punk, world beat and jazz, and—increasingly rare in radio—the on-air talent is passionate about the music they play.

### WLUM, 102.1 FM,
### www.rock102one.com

Rock 102.1 has made continual tweaks to its format over the years, trying to lure listeners from the heavier Lazer 103 without selling out completely. That's why, in any given hour, you might hear Taking Back Sunday sandwiched between Limp Bizkit and vintage Green Day. It's not always pretty, but the playlists are often more broad than those of the station's competition.

**WLZR, 102.9 FM,**
**www.lazer103.com**

The biggest rock gorilla in the room, at least ratings-wise, Lazer plays commercial metal, neo-grunge and a lot of what its programmers call "heritage rock." Music for old guys in denial that it's time to cut the ponytail? Well, that's one way to put it. But if you like your Finger 11 and Seether tempered with Queensryche, Sabbath and Nirvana, well then, look no further.

## MISCELLANEOUS ATTRACTIONS:

**Summerfest,**
**www.summerfest.org**

Is it the world's biggest music festival or the Midwest's best-kept secret? It's both. The eleven-day celebration, kicking off the last Thursday in June annually for more than thirty years, is Milwaukee's biggest party as well as its biggest target for whining. It all depends on your perspective. With more than a dozen stages lined up along Lake Michigan and live music cranking noon till midnight, most people would say paying twelve dollars to get in for the whole day was a steal. Performers range from Black Eyed Peas and the Darkness to bigger mainstream names such as Kenny Chesney and Prince, who fill up the festival's crown jewel, the 20,000 seat Marcus Amphitheater (an additional ticket is required for Marcus shows). A sizeable segment of Milwaukee remains unimpressed with the fest, however—the most frequent complaints are too-pricey plastic cups of beer and too few cutting edge acts. With roughly one million people passing through the turnstiles each year, however, critics are in the minority.

—*Gemma Tarlach*

# Minneapolis/St. Paul, MN

## UNIVERSITY OF MINNESOTA, TWIN CITIES
2106 Fourth St. South
Minneapolis, MN 55455
www.umn.edu

The state's largest public university has four separate campuses, including one convenient to the Twin Cities of Minneapolis and St. Paul. Fortunately for you, the cities offer not only a great rock & roll scene—the same one that spawned Prince, the Replacements and Soul Asylum—but also a strong music department within the university's College of Liberal Arts. The school offers not only the traditional bachelor of music in performance and music education, but also a noteworthy music therapy program that will train you in how to treat patients by using the healing power of song. Whereas performance majors should expect to take about 70 to 80 percent of their classes in music, therapy students will also be required to study psychology and sociology.

Alternately, you can get a bachelor of arts, with 50 percent of your classes comprising musical study, and the other half drawn from a liberal arts program. The school also offers flexible students the ability to double major by completing two majors within the music school (for instance, music therapy and harp performance; think how soothing that would be!) or to create a major of your choosing, a specialized degree combining music and another disciplines.

Like some type of music-major dating service, the university's Website boasts that, "Regardless of your major, schedule or ability level, there is an ensemble for you." That means: take advantage of the school's diverse performing groups and put your skills and interest into practice.

The university also offers the annual Spark Festival of Electronic Music and Art. Held in February, Spark brings esteemed academic and musical guests to campus, but also welcomes compositions and work by contributors. As a final perk, cruise over to the school's website and check out the feature called "Listening Room," where you can sample streaming audio from recent university performances.

## VENUES:

### 400 Bar, 400 Cedar Ave. S., www.400bar.com

Locals love to complain about the 400: the cover charges are high, the beer prices are high, sometimes it seems like the guitar-strumming folkies on stage are high. But Minneapolitans continue to frequent this friendly rock-postered hangout because of its scene-vet cred and savvy booking. Co-owner Bill Sullivan spent years on the road with Minnesota legends the Replacements and Soul Asylum (he currently tours with Bright Eyes), and his brother Tom oversees performances by alt-country and indie rock groups destined for bigger stardom: Iron and Wine, Broken Social Scene, the Shins. Plus, when you consider that just a few dollars a day helps the Sullivans battle bad juju from its Clear Channel-kissed competitors, those extra bucks at the door feel like they're worth something.

### Fine Line Music Café, 318 First Ave. N., www.finelinemusic.com

Barflies, beware the wrath of Bob Stinson. The Replacements guitarist was supposed to play here on February 17, 2005—the night he died. When a pyrotechnics accident set the Fine Line ablaze on the same night eight years later, some believed that Stinson's ghost had a hand in the disaster. (A C-list Replacements tribute had been scheduled for the next day.) It's easy to see why the co-author of *Stink* might wish ill will on this sterile venue, which reopened a few months after the fire: The elegant spiral staircases, the unscuffed floors, perfume-scented bathroom—everything here seems designed to offend your average blue-collar rocker. Yet, the floorgasm-inducing sound system overwhelms any urge to heckle the VH-1 crowd who may block your view. The Pixies' drummer once sneezed three feet away from the main micro and the wet trickle of individual snot molecules reverberated throughout the room. If a band ever covers Black Sabbath on stage, they'll need to pass out extra-strength earplugs in Omaha.

### First Ave./7th St. Entry, 701 First Ave. N.,
### www.first-ave.com

For many Minnesotans, this is where it all began: your first concert, your first ecstatic stage-dive attempt at your first concert, your first time getting thrown out of your first concert by a tattooed bouncer, your thousandth time trying to relive your first time. Even those who don't have personal memories of First Ave. know that *Purple Rain*'s finale was filmed here, and most everyone agrees that the converted Greyhound bus station has become a beloved historical landmark over the past quarter-century. When filled to its 1,400 capacity, the main room still maintains the best sightlines in town, with a glassed-off mezzanine that allows a clear view of headliners from Wilco to De La Soul to Rammstein. Upstairs in the V.I.P. Lounge, DJs spin house, electro, and dancehall reggae while clubbers practice their best NC-17 dance moves, and next door in the 7th St. Entry, fledgling indie bands and black-paint décor pay tribute to the spirit of punk rock.

### The Quest, 110 5th St. N.,
### www.thequestculb.com

When dance nights cater to the barely legal crowd, this disco inferno should have a sign above its door: Abandon all hope, ye who purchase beer. Still, even when 18 + admission prevents the bartender from lighting up your liver, the Quest's expansive hardwood floor and Disneyland-worthy audio-visual equipment makes it the ideal place to hear DJs play house, salsa, hip-hop, and any other genre anchored by a good beat. On other occasions, 21 + crowds gather for electronic and rock acts alike: Both Basement Jaxx and Franz Ferdinand have filled all 24,000 square feet with pogoing fans. For anyone who still misses the outdoorsy vibe of a classic rave, the upstairs Ascot Room provides tree-lined walls and a sparkling fountain fit to cleanse the feet of the gods—or at least the sweaty necks of concertgoers.

### Triple Rock Social Club, 629 Cedar Ave,
### www.triplerocksocialclub.com

Three times the rock... and a zillion times the hangover. On Tuesday nights, when two-for-one specials give way to ten-for-five, the only unhappy hour at this West Bank lair is the sixty minutes hipsters often spend hugging the porcelain bowl. Still, a wide range of tasty anti-Atkins menu items (vegan pancakes, vegan chili cheese fries) help soak up the vodka, and those who have come to partake of liquid or solid sustenance happily empty the change from their duct-tape wallets for the relatively inexpensive shows. (All-ages performances take place in the early evening, with 21+ shows later at night.) Cutting-edge punk bands most often grace the silver, Chipotle-style main room, but T-Rock owner and Dillinger Four guitarist Erik Funk showcases a variety of genres, both onstage and in the adjoining bar's jukebox. Though the machine offers eighteen songs for five dollars, rumor says it will let you have 20 as long as you choose the angstiest selections. And the playlist options—Bikini Kill, Public Enemy, Agnostic Front—would make the devil himself sell his soul for two more tracks.

**Turf Club, 1601 University Ave. W., St. Paul,**
**www.turfclub.net**

The Christmas lights that drip from the ceiling like raindrops from eyelashes. The photo booth that immortalizes grinning patrons in black and white. The slightly creepy velvet paintings that turn the downstairs Clown Lounge into a pervy den. There are many reasons to love this former country two-step haven, a relic from the 1940s in St. Paul—or as Minneapolitans call the city, "whatsitcalled, across the river." But aside from its long-term loyalty to carpetbaggers like Jonathan Richman and Handsome Family, the Turf Club's best attribute may be its commitment to local music. When Minnesota's own gonzo balladeer Mark Mallman broke a world record by performing a 52.4-hour song, he chose to do it here, paying tribute to the bar's—and his fans'—endurance. What other venue can make the local music scene's fifteen minutes of fame last that long?

## IF YOU DON'T TRUST ANYONE OVER TWENTY-ONE...

When you're too young to drink and too old to hold "private solo concerts" in your bedroom, Minnesota can seem like an unwelcoming place. Luckily, local music scribe and blogger Peter S. Scholtes compiles an encyclopedia of resources and calendars for the overwhelmed and underaged: www.complicatedfun.com/allages

## *RECORD STORES:*

### Cheapo, 1300 W. Lake St., and 80 N. Snelling Ave.

The moniker is a bit of a misnomer—you'll likely shell out a few too many Washingtons for new releases. But the tactile delights of the vast used CD stacks, and the hypnotic click click click sound of the masses sorting through plastic give this chain store a value all its own.

### Electric Fetus, 2000 4th Ave. S.,
### www.efetus.com

You can take the hippie out of the head shop, but you can't take the Nag Champa scent out of the hippie's head. Which is why this music retailer always reeks of incense—the sticks are stored alongside a fine selection of "water pipes"—and free-spirited clientele. In 1972, the Fetus offered gratis records to customers who agreed to disrobe in the back of the store and walk naked to the front counter. These days, album-hunters keep their shirts on, but the staff maintains its old brother-and-sisterly vibe: This is probably the only place in town where, if you bring a new CD up to register, the clerk will alert you of a used copy that costs less. And the in-store performances have an even better price: free.

### Fifth Element, 2411 Hennepin Ave. S.

This graffiti-graced shop carries a kitchen-sink array of hip-hop releases, from Billboard-charting beats to the rare backpacker seven-inch, and often opens its doors to freestyle battles where the champs cheer on the novices. Co-owned by local MC Slug of Atmosphere, home to the Rhyme Sayers label, and frequented by a number of the imprint's demi-celebs, Fifth Element also stocks a vinyl selection that's custom-made for your favorite local DJ—which is, of course, you.

### Let It Be, 1001 Nicollet Mall,
### www.letitbe.com

At this record collector joint, the assortment of cuts from more uncommon subgenres would make audiophiles' heads spin at 78 rpm: gabber, blip-hop, instru-metal, Goa trance, illbient, cowboytronica… okay, we made that last one up, but if the category doesn't exist, the vinyl junkies who work here will surely find a way to create it. Though its hand-picked albums come with price tags, Let It Be is less a profit-driven business than a resource library where you can purchase an education—a place to school yourself on little-known releases while thumbing through foreign music rags, self-produced zines, and the type of avant-garde collectible vinyl that would make readers of the *Wire* feel bourgeois. But even among those dusty platters, retrophobes can rest assured: In this brave new world, Let it Be also issues new music on little silver discs.

## RADIO STATIONS:

### KUOM 770 AM,
### www.radiok.org

Despite the fact that the fuzzy AM broadcast sometimes makes the music sound like it was recorded in a bucket at the bottom of a garbage can that someone kicked into the river, this is the only radio station in town that matters. Greil Marcus once noted that the University of Minnesota broadcast bunker is "the best college radio station imaginable," and even the post-graduation set agrees with him. The weekly K-but (rhymes with debut) unearths gems like the Fiery Furnaces and Brother Ali before Pitchfork picks them up. The specialty shows span genres from plunderphonics ("Some Assembly Required") to world music ("Radio K International") to old-school ska ("Rude Radio"). And the student DJs, whose real-person voices raise the standard baritone by two octaves, introduce their favorite tracks with a passion that defies pretension.

### KFAI (90.3 FM Minneapolis, 106.7 FM St. Paul),
### www.kfai.org

Finally, airwaves that service all your Hmong rock, East African pop, and transgendered cabaret needs. This diverse community radio station—where the slogan is "one world, two frequencies"—takes on volunteer DJs in a grassroots format that's as democratically-inclined as its leftist soapbox programs. Replacing traditional pop singles with forays into blues, jazz, Latino music, and more obscure flotsam and jetsam for your ears, KFAI underscores the reason why its antenna has withstood a beating from satellites for all these years: In a state that once confounded CNN by electing a wrestler for governor, we're not necessarily fans of what's popular. But we certainly love what's populist.

*—Melissa Maerz*

# Nashville, TN

## VANDERBILT UNIVERSITY
Blair School of Music
2400 Blakemore Ave.
Nashville, TN 37212-3499
www.vanderbilt.edu

The Blair School of Music is one of a group of Vanderbilt University affiliated colleges and schools that includes the Peabody School of Education, the School of Engineering, and the College of Arts and Sciences, among others. Within the music school, students can concentrate their studies in the usual variety of theory and composition-focused majors. The Blair School's bachelor of music degree program offers majors in composition/theory and in musical arts. The composition/theory major involves studying the literal art of composing and performing music. The musical arts concentration supplements the basic components of music study with courses in, for example, music literature or history. One of the Blair School's more exceptional assets is the dual degree program it offers in conjunction with the Peabody College. The program allows students to graduate in five years with a bachelor of music degree (with a concentration in musical arts/teacher education) as well as a master of education degree.

While the basics of the Blair School's most fundamental programs are relatively standard, the program's commitment to interdisciplinary study is not. For starters, non-majors enrolled in Vanderbilt's other colleges and schools are eligible for enrollment in any of the Blair School's courses providing that they are qualified, and this is not just for show: The Blair School has ensured that many of its courses not only fill requirements for non-music majors or minors but are also interesting to those who've not been studying violin since the age of five.

The music school has a range of totally atypical courses that require little to no musical background. American Popular Music, for example, invites students to study the "ways the culture of a nation is reflected and sometimes shaped by the chosen musics of the group comprising the American 'salad bowl,'" while the History of Rock Music focuses on the "history and development of rock and roll music and its performance from the 1950s to the present" and includes study of both rock's subgenres and major, representative artists from each decade. Other notable classes include The Business of Music, Tai Chi for Musicians, which applies principles of Tai Chi to performance, Musical Theater in America, which looks at melodrama, vaudeville and the history of the American musical, and, of course, Country Music, which provides students with insight into the history of the industry that defines Nashville.

In addition to Vanderbilt's academic offerings, the university's student organization pulls together some top-notch shows on campus, luring artists such as Modest Mouse and Toby Lightman to perform for students on an almost monthly basis.

# BELMONT UNIVERSITY
1900 Belmont Blvd.
Nashville, TN 37212
www.belmont.edu

You won't find courses on the history of the lute or the role of the folk singer at Belmont's Mike Curb College of Entertainment and Music Business, but the program is perfect for those seeking a business degree tailored to the music industry. Students who graduate from Mike Curb College receive a B.B.A. (bachelor of business administration) with a concentration in entertainment and music business. The degree is comprised of three major areas of study: a general education core, a business core, and courses emphasizing business and production, two areas the college views as particularly important. Typical courses taken by those enrolled in the program include basics of business administration like micro and macro economics and accounting, and others even more specific to the music industry such as intellectual properties, history of the recording business and legal issues in music business.

The program takes advantage of its location in Nashville, exposing students to the inner workings of a music industry town using extensive internship placement programs and the integration of adjunct faculty primarily employed in the music industry. In addition, all students are encouraged to apply for internships within the business in Los Angles, New York, and Melbourne, Australia. Internships are extremely important in an industry where job placement is a catch-as-catch-can enterprise, and the Mike Curb College Website claims that 85 to 100 percent of all their music business students who take advantage of these internships end up employed in the industry upon graduation. And there's evidence to back up that claim: The highly regarded institution has churned a string of Cinderella success stories including Trisha Yearwood, Lee Ann Womack, Brad Paisley, Josh Turner, Bobby Bare, Jr., and *American Idol* contestant Kimberly Locke.

Another Belmont perk is the Curb Café, a performance venue perched on the outskirts of campus. The café brings in burgeoning country stars/college students like moths to the flame. Of course, there's the mundane open-mic/writer's nights, where future songwriters warble through their latest attempt at Music Row mastery. Every now and then, the loosely Southern Baptist affiliated Belmont finds the next guitar-stroking John Mayer in their midst, and rewards them with the respected Curb Cafe gig.

# MIDDLE TENNESSEE STATE UNIVERSITY
Department of Recording Industry
1301 East Main St.
Murfreesboro, TN 37132
www.mtsu.edu

**M**iddle Tennessee State University—located in the surprisingly hip Murfreesboro, Tennessee—boasts one of the preeminent music business programs in the country. With about 1,300 students currently enrolled, the Recording Industry Management program is the largest in existence, but attendance is not recommended for those wishing to casually explore the tech side of the music industry: Studying here is intense.

Students pursue a bachelor of science degree in what the school calls "Recording Industry," which includes "General Studies" course work in classic liberal arts disciplines like mathematics and English, in addition to the school's specialized courses. Recording Industry students must concentrate in either Music Business or Production and Technology, and from there they choose from an even more detailed and highly specialized group of classes. For example, all RIM students take core courses like Understanding Mass Media and History of the Recording Industry, but those concentrating in Music Business will then go on to take Artist Management or Music as Popular Culture while Production and Technology concentrators might study Techniques of Recording or Critical Listening.

It gets more complicated. Each Recording Industry student is also required to minor in an area related to their concentration within the program. So, a Music Business concentrator can minor in Management or Business Administration, but not in, for example, Computer Science or Entertainment Technology like a RIM student concentrating in Production and Technology might. The Recording Industry Management program also uses something called "candidacy" to assess their student's status after completion of the RIM core courses and the math requirement (which is part of the general studies requirements— you don't get out of taking math just because you're studying the music business!) Essentially what this means is that the department will only open up a limited number of spots in each of the two concentrations per year. Candidacy is granted twice a year—at the end of both fall and spring semesters—to sixty music business concentrators and fifty production and technology concentrators. Those who are not granted candidacy can reapply the following semester.

The school offers an excellent internship program, which serves both to place students in existing positions and to talk up its graduates to potential employers and intern-seekers. The facilities at the school are completely state of the art, largely open twenty-four-hours a day, available almost exclusively to RIM students, and include two recording studios, a post-production laboratory, and a mastering studio among other assets.

It's also worth mentioning that MTSU is home to the Robert W. McLean School of Music, an excellent if more traditional music program which offers a classic bachelor of music degree with a concentration in one of seven areas including instrumental music education, voice performance, and music industry among others. The music industry concentration includes course work in Commercial Songwriting and Principles and Practice of Electronic Music but is overall a less involved look at the music industry than the university's Recording Industry Management program.

## *HONORABLE MENTION:*

# FISK UNIVERSITY
Department of Music
1000 Seventeenth Ave. North
Nashville, Tennessee 37208
www.fisk.edu

**F**isk University was founded in 1866 to provide educational opportunities for recently freed slaves. The university's paramount claim to musical fame is its affiliation with the Jubilee Singers, a renowned vocal group that began in 1871. The Jubilee singers specialize in performing "slave songs" and have been credited with helping to keep traditional African-American music alive throughout the last century by performing around the world. Students from all academic areas are eligible to audition for the group.

## *VENUES:*

**The Belcourt, 2102 Belcourt Ave.,**
**www.belcourt.org**
This historic theater doubles as Nashville's reigning independent movie house and a pseudo-intellectual music venue. The Mexican-style adobe design scheme meshes well with the district's overall bohemian feel, and shrewd booking agent James Pitt (who also books musical guests on *Late Night with Conan O' Brien*) brings in highbrow bluegrass acts (Maura O' Connell), critically acclaimed up-and-coming songwriters such as Jamie Cullum, Damien Rice, Bright Eyes, and Badly Drawn Boy, and old-school troubadours including Nick Lowe and Sam Phillips. The Belcourt Theater also hosts foreign films, local documentaries, and a slew of film festivals including the Nashville Gay and Lesbian Film Festival and the Nashville Jewish Film Festival.

**Ryman Auditorium, 116 Fifth Ave. North,**
**www.ryman.com**
Home to the Grand Ole Opry—which puts on shows at the Ryman every Friday and Saturday night—the more than one-hundred-year-old venue has hosted concerts by everyone from Dolly Parton and

Patsy Cline to James Brown and Bob Dylan. These days, you can still catch country legends like George Jones on its stage, as well as pop acts from Ashlee Simpson to Jill Scott.

### Exit/In, 2208 Elliston Pl., www.exitin.com

In the face of numberless closings and reopenings over the past thirty years, the venerable Exit/In has staggered onward, gradually becoming Nashville's premier nightclub. The club first found a level of fame with Robert Altman's *Nashville*, and the resulting éclat brought big-budget rock bands into the Nashville music scene, as well as abrasive experimental shows featuring a young Steve Martin. These days, the Exit/In books trendsetting indie acts (the Mosquitos, Mates of State), well-known rock and country acts (The Donnas, Emmylou Harris) and the occasional local band. In fact, local bands view The Exit/In as a regional litmus test. Chances are, if The Exit/In books your band, then you've finally "made it."

### Cafe Coco, 210 Louise Ave., www.cafecoco.com

Located directly behind the Exit/In, Nashville's Cafe Coco is a who's who of preppy college students, soy-loving vegetarians, and indie rock hipsters. Erroneously denoted by some as "a gay bar," Cafe Coco is actually the heart of Nashville's vibrant arts community. During the sweltering summer months, CC's adjoining patio gives way to a gaggle of spoken-word poets and Jack Kerouac-reading beatniks. The petite patio has also played host to benefits for local anti-Clear Channel radio station, WRFN-FM 98.9, better known as Radio Free Nashville.

### The End, 2219 Elliston Place

Aside from its flamboyant purplish décor and glittery carnival lights, The End is a by-the-numbers rock venue that has long been a standard in the rough-hewn Elliston Place district. The nightclub has played host to a wide range of brand-name rock groups including pre-MTV versions of R.E.M. and the White Stripes. The weekly schedule boasts cutting-edge local acts including some from Middle Tennessee State University, Belmont and Vanderbilt.

### The Muse 835 4th Ave. South,
### www.themusenashville.com

Located directly across from the supposed "World's Largest Adult Bookstore," The Muse is housed in a neglected cinderblock-of-a-building tagged with graffiti and illuminated by the glaring neon sign from its porn shop neighbor. The alternative-rock club (whose name is actually is a goofy acronym for Mixed Urban Sound Equipment) caters to the skater-punk set by booking acts such as Anadivine and Say Anything.

### Rocketown, 401 6th Ave. South,
### www.rocketown.com

Technically a "safe haven" for white bread, suburban teenagers, this masked nightclub of Christian values began at the behest of Christian recording artist, Michael W. Smith. And despite Rocketown's desperate attempts to shed its squeaky-clean image, most chain-smoking college students won't touch this club with a ten-foot pole. (Rocketown employees strictly enforce no-smoking signs.) Unfortunately for the chain smokers, Rocketown's acoustics and spacious setting makes the club one of the best music venues in Nashville. 50 Cent recently threw a post-concert party there, but the regular shows are mostly of the indie rock variety: Past performers include Death Cab for Cutie, Ben Kweller, and Finger Eleven.

### Springwater, 115 27th Ave. North,
### www.springwatersupperclub.com

This Twenties-era speakeasy was an alleged stomping ground for infamous gamblers including Jimmy Hoffa. In contemporary times, however, the dingy dive bar shabbily serves beer at a reasonable price. In the adjoining playroom, beer-stained pool tables abound, with the occasional boisterous arcade game to boot. Musically, the Springwater books underground local bands nightly.

### Kijiji's Coffeehouse & Deli 1207 Jefferson St.,
### www.kijijicoffee.com

A regular haunt for students at Tennessee State University, Kijiji's is adorned with vintage, indigo-blue posters of jazz greats Billie Holiday, Duke Ellington and Ella Fitzgerald. Each Friday night, Kijiji's provides an open-mic night for local spoken-word poets, freestylers, and jazz musicians.

## RECORD STORES:

### The Great Escape, 1925 Broadway,
### www.thegreatescapeonline.com

Geeky comic-book aficionados and vinyl rabble-rousers flock to the moth-eaten aisles of this downtown record store. As far as bargains go, the Great Escape is one of the best bets in town. Coupled with the cutting-edge Grimey's Record Shop, The Great Escape is one of the few record stores in town with a worthwhile selection of vinyl. And since it's across from the infamous Music Row, the Great Escape attracts a suit-and-tie music exec crowd as well. It's the place where penniless wannabe musicians rub elbows with the corporate bigwigs while browsing through Nina Simone LPs.

### Grimey's Record Shop, 1604 8th Ave. South,
### www.grimeys.com

Grimey's Record Shop is Nashville's paradigm of indie sensibility and vintage goodness. The shop's namesake/owner, Mike Grimes recently moved his reputable record store from its constrictive Bransford Ave. location to the posh, twenties-era Sophia building. The store has already aligned itself with Eighth Avenue nightclub the Basement, a nearby neighbor that routinely partners with Grimey's to put on acoustic gigs by artists such as Sondre Lerche, Pedro the Lion, Joseph Arthur, Ambulance Ltd., Bobby Bare, Jr., Tift Merritt and Butterfly Boucher.

### Tower Records, 2400 West End Ave.,
### www.towerrecords.com

Nestled among the second-rung fast food restaurants and gaudy tanning beds of Vanderbilt University's collegiate haunts, West End's Tower Records stocks mainstream Top 40 releases alongside obscure works from local artists and bygone musicians of the bebop jazz era. The downside to this faceless corporate branch is, of course, capitalism run amok: Tower Records haggles customers with an outrageous $25 asking price for the latest Wilco album; a release that Grimey's Record

Shop offers with Jeff Tweedy's book of poetry thrown in as well. Tower Records also attracts national touring acts for in-store performances before their higher profile gigs at the Gaylord Entertainment Center or Starwood Amphitheater.

# New Brunswick, NJ

## RUTGERS UNIVERSITY, NEW BRUNSWICK
33 Livingston Ave.
New Brunswick, NJ 08901-1959
www.rutgers.edu

**R**utgers is one of the largest state universities in the country—with major campuses located throughout New Jersey in Camden, Newark, and New Brunswick/Piscataway. At Camden College, which is located just across the Delaware River from downtown Philadelphia, the study of music is integrated with the study of related arts, like literature and musical theater. Particularly interesting courses offered by the department include Masterpieces of Music, Computer Applications in Music, American Music, Opera, and Gender in Music. The college also hosts the Mozart Orchestra of Philadelphia, making it the only Department of Fine Arts in the country blessed with a resident professional orchestra.

Rutgers' Newark campus offers a music program adaptable to both the most serious and the most casual music student. Basic courses include Music and Film, Opera and Music Drama, Creative Musicianship, Rock, and Women in Music, among others. The school ensures that any Rutgers student can earn course credit for singing in the chorus, playing in the jazz, percussion, or chamber music ensembles, and by taking private lessons.

Rutgers' New Brunswick campus is home to the Mason Gross School of the Arts music degree program. This department offers undergraduate music education in classical performance, jazz, and music education. Students enrolled in the performance or jazz programs train for careers as professional performers or performer educators. All music students must satisfy university-wide core requirements, music department requirements, (like four years of solo and ensemble work) and enjoy a relatively low faculty to student ratio. Best of all, the New Brunswick campus is close to a number of cool venues and record stores, and the city itself is home to a long-running punk rock scene that continues to churn out promising young bands.

## VENUES:

### Court Tavern, 124 Church St., www.courttavern.net

With a jukebox that includes the Clash and Johnny Cash, cans of the working man's Pabst Blue Ribbon, and tattoos up-and-down the arms of every bartender, this 21+ bar and venue upholds the punk rock traditions of New Brunswick. Upstairs you can drink, listen to indie and punk tunes blaring from the stereo, and talk to the friendliest group of working-class stiffs, while the bands play downstairs. New Brunswick legends Bouncing Souls and Stick and Stones hit their power chords and danced all night during their early days, along with New Brunswick emo greats Lifetime and Midtown. Today, bands like the Killing Gift, Chris Batton and the Woods and more make regular appearances. Music festivals are common (like the annual Diomandpalooza), local and touring bands play every weekend, and though it sometimes gets too loud and too smoky, the Court Tavern is the closest thing to a punk rock version of Cheers you could possibly hope for.

### Starland Ballroom, 570 Jernee Mill Rd. Sayreville, www.starlandballroom.com

Considering that the Continental Airlines Arena is about an hour north of campus—and not to mention pretty expensive for those on a shoe-string collegiate budget—The Starland Ballroom is the place to go if you want to catch popular acts in concert. The year-old venue isn't huge: a few thousand fans can fill the general admission dancefloor located in front of the stage and a seated bar area is located along the back of the venue for those twenty-one and older (shows are usually open to anyone 18+.) Performers tend to be of the classical variety, with headliners ranging from David Lee Roth and the Allman Bros. to Guster, Ben Folds, and Taking Back Sunday.

**Hamilton St. Café, 22 Hamilton St., Bound Brook,
www.hamiltonstcafe.com**

Ten minutes down the road from Rutgers University's New
Brunswick and Piscataway campuses, Hamilton St. Café books tiny
local bands as well as full-time underground headliners such as
Bane, Ensign, Pansy Division, and more. The space is rented out to
independent promoters, so the variety of events includes not only gigs,
but also political education forums where you might find Ted Leo doing
a solo performance. Its walls are covered with the works of local artists,
its café has vegan grilled cheese—tasty, but a bit overpriced—and the
lounge area is filled with beat up old couches where lusty teenagers are
wont to make out before, during and after the shows.

**Red Lion Café, 126 College Ave.**

Located in the basement of the Rutgers Student Center, the Red
Lion Café is one of the most popular student hangouts on campus—and
one of the best places at Rutgers to catch a free show. Even as students
study, play pool, or watch TV, it's common to find some sort of musical
performance going on at the venue's small stage. Tuesday afternoons
typically feature hour-long lunchtime sets from local rock and acoustic
acts, while Wednesday nights offer anyone a chance to take the stage
during a four-hour open mic. WRSU, the student radio station, also
presents special live music events throughout the semester, such as
jazz nights and mini-concerts featuring well-known New Brunswick
bands. All shows are free of charge and open to anyone.

# THE NEW BRUNSWICK BASEMENT SCENE:

All over New Brunswick, virtually every day of the week, shows are
put on in the basements of the beat-up old houses in the neighborhoods
surrounding Rutgers. Emo powerhouses Midtown and Thursday both
got their start playing these kinds of gigs, and today underground
touring bands and local projects set up under floorboards, wires, and
leaky fifty-year-old pipes. Look for fliers throughout New Brunswick
or eavesdrop on the trendy indie and punk kids in your poli-sci class for
when and where, as the locations frequently change. Some basements
may not be best suited for shows, with piles of laundry, and boxes of
old stuff left for storage in the way of the audience. But many houses set

up their basement with a powerful PA system, ad hoc lighting (usually strings of white Christmas lights), couches and plenty of space cleared out for a small audience. These basements make small crowds seems huge. Many shows have a no alcohol policy (who wants some drunk dude smashing up their house?) and most of them only cost about five bucks a head.

## RECORD STORES:

**Vintage Vinyl, 51 Lafayette Rd., Fords,**
**www.vvinyl.com**

Since it opened its doors in 1979, Vintage Vinyl in nearby Fords, N.J., has evolved into one of the country's best independent record stores, drawing raves from fans and press alike. A huge 10,000 square-foot space about seven miles away from Rutgers, Vintage Vinyl lives up to its slogan, "From the Obvious to the Obscure." The store carries new and used CDs, vinyl, DVDs, VHS, books, magazines, and wide selection of toys and collectibles. Hundreds of small New Jersey bands consign their recordings over to Vintage, so almost anything can be found here. Don't let the indie rock décor push you away if that stuff isn't your bag: Jazz, blues, classic soul, R&B, and all other sub-genres can be found here, too. Plus, national acts often stop at Vintage Vinyl to play for audiences and sign copies of their records.

**Curmudgeon Records, 256 US Highway 206, Hillsborough**

Though it's a bit of a trek from Rutgers (nineteen miles), Curmudgeon is still a popular destination for music lovers throughout the Rutgers community and all of central New Jersey. The store specializes in punk, indie rock, hardcore, and metal, and carries an extensive collection of 7-inch vinyl. Its stock is highly selective and fairly genre-specific, but—in spite of its name—Curmudgeon employs non-intimidating clerks who won't make you feel goofy for asking about the new Green Day album. And if they don't have what you are looking for, they will happily order it for you. Prices tend to be low—from $10 to $13, on average—and bands play free in-stores here on a semi-regular basis: Look for fliers in the store to see what's coming up, or put on your own show. Seriously. Just talk to the owner: He charges nothing to stage a gig.

# RADIO STATIONS:

## WRSU, 88.7 FM,
## www.rsu.org

For more than fifty years, WRSU has operated as the official college radio station of Rutgers University. Run almost entirely by students—with the help of a few faculty and professional advisors and on-air personalities—the station features your typical college radio blend of indie rock, hip-hop, talk shows, news, and sports, but also broadcasts reggae, Latin music, jazz, and gospel-inspired programs. Funded by the university itself with grants from local record shops and underwriting by local businesses, RSU also airs a number of live events around campus, many of which are held at the Red Lion Café in the basement of the Rutgers Student Center.

## THE CORE, 90.3 FM,
## www.thecore.rutgers.edu

The university's independent source for news and entertainment, the Core is a joint venture between Rutgers' Livingston College and Piscataway High School. The Core plays a variety of indie and alternative acts, ranging from U2 and R.E.M. to NOFX and The Zutons. It also plays metal, urban, jazz, and blues music. In 1999, RLC pooled its resources with Piscataway High to make the Core the high school's official station, WVPH, which broadcasts Piscataway-related programming from 6 to 8 A.M. and 2 to 4 P.M. Monday through Friday.

# MISCELLANEOUS EVENTS:

## RCPC Events

Throughout the year, the Rutgers College Programming Council provides students with oodles of entertainment, from comedians to dance and dating nights and even a reunion between *Saved by the Bell's* Mr. Belding and Screech Powers. The group's bread and butter, however, is the music acts it brings to Rutgers each year. Recently, RCPC presented the RU student body with concerts from Talib Kweli, Gavin DeGraw, and the Bouncing Souls. The shows are usually held in either the Rutgers College or Busch Campus multi-purpose rooms (which hold anywhere from 400 to 1,000 students). Though some concerts are free, others are available to students for five dollars and guests for seven dollars. (Non-RCPC events this year also featured lectures from *Apprentice* alum Kwame Jackson and famed author Nicholas Sparks and a Rutgers Idol competition—a parody of *American Idol* featuring Rutgers students and guest judge Max Weinberg.)

RCPC also sponsors the biggest music event on campus each year: an outdoor festival known as Rutgersfest. The mini-Woodstock-like event is held every May adjacent to the Rutgers soccer complex. Usually two to three popular music acts perform hour-long sets on a giant stage, and food vendors form an outline around the audience. In 2004, Kanye West and Sugar Ray performed in front of thousands of students the area in front of the stage.

—*Brent Johnson and James Caverly*

## HONORABLE MENTION:

# PRINCETON UNIVERSITY
Department of Music
Woolworth Center of Musical Studies
Princeton, NJ 08544-1007
www.princeton.edu

Seventeen short miles from New Brunswick's bustling punk scene, Princeton University has the right attitude about music, which it treats as "a wonderful aspect of what it means to be human." Music majors have two distinct goals in Princeton's program: the first, to master and gain a solid foundation in the study of Western music and, second, to engage in a project of special interest—whether it be a student's major passion or something unknown and intriguing. Expect hefty doses of history, theory, and performance. To augment that curriculum, Princeton's campus promotes independent research by allowing students to pen a senior thesis or take advantage of the school's performance opportunities. Classes range from theory-based coursework like Music in Antiquity and the Middle Ages to composer-based classes such as The Symphony from Haydn to Stravinsky. Modern music fans might enjoy Urban Blues and the Golden Age of Rock or Music Since 1945. There's also Evolution of Jazz Styles or culturally based courses such as Music of India or Music of Africa, which will appeal to fans of ethnomusicology.

Princeton's student union puts together a semi-annual **Lawn Party Festival** each fall and spring that brings some alt.rock heavy-hitters to campus for a day's worth of performances. In recent years, headliners have included O.A.R., Maroon 5, and Presidents of the United States of America.

One of the Northeast's best record stores, the **Princeton Record Exchange** (www.prex.com/nj/links.html), is just a few blocks away from the Princeton U campus. This huge retailer deals in new and used CDs, but the majority of its comprehensive stock is devoted to used vinyl at remarkably reasonable prices. Plus, the university houses the expansive Mendel Music Library, packed with books, CDs and videos that ought to appeal to music obsessives. And you can use the library even if you're not a student: No ID required!

# New Haven, CT

## UNIVERSITY OF NEW HAVEN
300 Boston Post Rd.
West Haven, CT 06516
www.newhaven.edu

**T**he University of New Haven offers bachelor of arts degrees in three separate areas: music, music industry, and music and sound recording. The straight music degree allows students to concentrate in either performance or musicology, and prides itself on offering exposure to music from all over the world via required course work in world music and History of European Art Music, for example. The bachelor of arts in music industry prepares its students for careers in music management, arts administration, record production, promotion and sales, artist management, marketing, and music publishing among others. Topics studied in this program include music theory, musicianship, history, marketing, accounting, and performance. Music industry students in this program will spend a lot of time in the school's recording studios and enjoy courses specifically designed for the music industry program such as the History of Rock,

Recording Fundamentals, Art Music, and Production, Promotion, and Distribution.

The UNH bachelor of arts in music and sound recording is, like the music industry program, designed for any student drawn to the technical side of today's music industry. This four-year degree program is founded upon the philosophy that "musicians should have a working knowledge of the media through which their art is...heard and that sound recordists should have a working knowledge of the art form they are recording," according to the school's website. As such, the program focuses on three interrelated areas: music history, theory, and aesthetics; musicianship; and sound recording methodology and technique. Intriguing courses music and sound recording students might take include Film Music, The Physics of Music, and Sound with Laboratory. Additionally, the music and sound recording program offers a bachelor of science degree that provides its students with much of the same course work as its partner B.A. program, but includes stronger emphasis on science and technology, which is represented by courses in seemingly un-rock related disciplines like calculus, physics, and electrical engineering.

# YALE UNIVERSITY DEPARTMENT OF MUSIC
Department of Music at Yale University
P. O. Box 208310
New Haven CT 06520-8310
www.yale.edu/yalemus

The Department of Music at Yale serves two kinds of students: those looking to become music scholars by studying music as part of a comprehensive liberal arts education, and those looking to pursue careers as performers or composers. In keeping with Yale's reputation as one of the best academic institutions in America, the music program is excellent all around. The department offers introductory instruction in all the fundamental areas: history of music, composition, theory, music technology, and performance, and there are many introductory courses offered in these subjects that require no prerequisites.

Music majors at Yale are subject to many requirements including the completion of a broad music history survey course, a course in theory sequence, plus a major seminar during the student's junior year, and a senior seminar during his or her senior year. Since this is Yale, of course there is an even more intensive course of study offered for the super-ambitious. The aptly titled "intensive major" is actually a great opportunity for truly innovating students to do what the school calls "independent and original work" in music history, theory, or composition.

## VENUES:

### Toad's Place, 300 York St., www.toadsplace.com

Toad's Place is on the Yale campus and the only spot in New Haven that regularly gets big-name acts. The club has an illustrious history: Since it opened in 1975, it has featured the likes of Bob Dylan, the Rolling Stones, and U2. Some of the bigger names that have played Toad's recently include Phantom Planet, Talib Kweli, De La Soul, and Medeski, Martin & Wood. Yet somehow, the club occasionally falters in separating the wheat from the chaff, and bookings include a lot more cover bands and shitty local acts than you'd expect. Toad's also hosts Yale's annual Battle of the Bands, where student artists compete for the chance to play at the school's Spring Fling.

When there isn't live music, the dance parties at Toad's—usually on Wednesday and Saturday nights—are crowded with Yale and Quinnipiac students shaking their stuff for the "booty cam," which projects images of the partygoers on screens around the club. And no matter what's going on in the area downstairs where the concerts and dancing take place, the recently opened upstairs bar, Lilly's Pad, is slightly classier thanks to its freshly carpeted floors, new furniture and flat-panel TVs.

### BAR, 254 Crown St.

Before it closed in 2001, Tune Inn was a dirty rock venue that sometimes hosted larger acts like Nirvana and was adored by most of the local musicians who play the tiny New Haven circuit. Since then, BAR—a microbrewery, gourmet pizza joint, and hipster lounge—has tried to take up some of the slack. Most nights feature DJs and dancing, but on Sundays BAR hosts live music from bands that are too indie for Toad's and too big for the smaller New Haven venues. Owner Rick Omante, a member of now-defunct ska outfit Spring Heeled Jack, takes music very seriously and is doing his best to attract more bands to play BAR. For now, most of the shows are national indie acts such as Enon, the Thermals, Saturday Looks Good to Me, the Detachment Kit, and the Wrens.

### The Space, 295 Treadwell St., Hamden,
### www.thespace.tk

Aside from a few recognizable names (Ben Lee, Mates of State), the calendar at The Space is heavy on local rock groups, acoustic singer/songwriters, open mic performers, aspiring rappers, or some combination of the above. A short cab ride from New Haven in the town of Hamden, the Space is a "multi cultural arts venue" located in a converted redbrick house; it includes a medium-sized performance area, a small recording studio, practice space, and a gift shop. Perhaps because of the building, the Space makes you feel at home—unless you like to drink or smoke in your home. The owner, Steve Rodgers, is a born-again Christian who takes the promotion of local talent and the goal of attracting a clientele of all ages so seriously that he prohibits alcohol. While this fact is a turn-off for many music fans, the Space's lack of alcohol and overall cleanliness create a feeling of community and encourage a real focus on the music. The audience is almost universally attentive. The atmosphere is often so intimate as to disallow talking during sets, with most audience members seated on worn couches, loveseats, and armchairs. This intimacy can make for a painful experience if the band isn't good or if you're in the mood for a wilder time, but at least there's plenty of visual distraction provided by the fabulous decorations behind the stage—strings of Christmas lights are entwined with a clutter of beauty parlor furniture, toy trains, abstract paintings, old records, steering wheels, baby carriages, gnomes, and other assorted goodies.

### Cafe 9, 250 State St.,
### www.cafenine.com

Advertised as "the musicians living room," Café 9 is New Haven proper's coziest venue. With live music every night, Sunday jam sessions, and Monday night open mics attended faithfully by regulars, Cafe 9 tends toward acoustic shows and spoken-word performances of rap and poetry. Nevertheless, this venue provides local music lovers with opportunities to hear pretty much everything—from jazz and blues to punk and hardcore. Because even the rowdier performances are mostly by local groups like punksters Murder Van, Cafe 9 is a great for students looking to learn a bit more about the community and the New Haven music scene.

**Rudy's, 372 Elm St.,**
**www.rudysnewhaven.com**

Rudy's is a true dive bar that, after installing more sound insulation, is hosting live music again after a brief hiatus. Best-known for its cheap drinks and the incredible variety of sauces it offers to accompany its delicious frites, this local watering hole also gets a variety of homegrown groups and national acts like Asobi Seksu and Runner and the Thermodynamics. When there's live music, the cover charge ranges from one to five dollars—a small price to pay considering the laidback vibe and the generally decent rock, jazz, and funk groups that take the stage.

## RECORD STORES:

**Cutler's Compact Discs** (www.cutlers.com) is the one and only record store in New Haven proper. Which is not entirely a bad thing when you consider how remarkably well stocked this family-owned shop is. The inventory covers much of what is available in chains and beyond: all the big new releases, a small but excellent rack of early a decent selection of indie rock, a fair number of used discs, a vast classical section, vinyl, and more. Because it tries to cater to a wide range of customers—true New Havenites, the students around the corner, and serious Connecticut-area music fans alike—Cutler's maintains a nice balance of new and old, popular and obscure. Perhaps more importantly, the atmosphere in Cutler's is conducive to browsing. Located right in the heart of the city on the Yale campus, Cutler's is the perfect spot to drop in on a cold New Haven winter day and spend an hour or two scrounging around. At the back of the store, there are even old-school arcade games, including Asteroids, which you can still play for old-school prices. The store itself is a lynchpin in the New Haven music scene and most local band members either work here or shop here.

## RADIO STATIONS:

**WYBC 1340-AM,**
**www.wybc.com**

The Yale student radio station dishes out a smorgasbord of shows that vary widely in content and quality, but it is easy to get involved with. The station has been improving in recent years and now has a redesigned website, Internet streaming, and broadcasts twenty-four hours a day, seven days a week. The other station funded by the Yale Corporation, **94.3 WYBC-FM**, is more traditional, serving up mild R&B and oldies. Though not directly connected with the student body, it also has opportunities for interested students to get involved.

Recently, an internet radio station, **Ultra Radio** (www.ultraradio. com), began broadcasting out of a downtown storefront in New Haven right across the street from central campus. You can watch the DJs as they choose from among songs by a wide range of local Connecticut bands as well as the Top 40 modern rock regulars, and from home you can tune in and vote for songs on their website. Ultra Radio also sponsors concerts at nearby clubs to showcase the local talent it plays.

# New Orleans, LA

## LOYOLA UNIVERSITY
6363 St. Charles Ave., Box 8
New Orleans, LA 70118
www.music.loyno.edu

The stated goal of the Loyola College of Music is to combine basic professional music courses with the study of fundamental liberal arts subjects such as philosophy, history, and foreign language. To this end, all students enrolled in the College of Music are required to supplement their Recital Hour and Music Theory courses with, for example, History of Western Art, Music, Bibliography and Research Methods, or Italian Diction and Repertoire. The college offers bachelor's degrees in a variety of music disciplines, from the traditional (music composition, education, and theory,) to the unusual (music therapy, music industry studies, piano pedagogy, and ballet) and master's degrees in performance, music education, and music therapy.

Students enrolled in the music industry studies program pursue one of two tracks: the bachelor of music degree with music industry studies, which emphasizes performance, or the bachelor of science degree in music industry studies, which emphasizes the legal and business aspects of the industry. The bachelor of science in music industry studies is the only degree the college offers that does not require an audition. Even those students seeking a minor in music must audition for admission to the college.

The Loyola University College of Music is the most distinguished academic music institution in the New Orleans area. Its facilities (which include a recording studio and a music library) are expansive, its student orchestras and choruses travel all over the world, and it offers exposure to rare programs like the Texaco-sponsored preschool music curriculum training program, which coordinates the efforts of the college's faculty and the New Orleans Public Schools to bring music into the classrooms of the city's elementary schools.

## VENUES:

### TwiRoPa, 1544 Tchoupitoulas,
### www.twiropa.com

TwiRoPa has been operating out of this renovated twine, rope and paper mill since 2001. Today, it is one of the city's largest clubs, with five rooms and a combined capacity of more than 8,000. The variety of room sizes—the Mill room holds 350, Godzilla! can pack in almost 5,000—allows the club to book both underground and on-the-rise acts. Recent performers include TV On The Radio, Black Keys, the Bad Plus, Duran Duran, O.A.R., Air and Chris Robinson. And, if there's a Thursday night when you just can't handle seeing another band, stop by TwiRoPa's "Leighties Night," where gals drink free until 1 o'clock while DJs spin classic new wave tracks.

### House of Blues, 225 Decatur St.,
### www.hob.com

Corporate or not, House of Blues knows how to put on a great show in an environment equally inviting for bands and fans. The New Orleans HOB is no exception: With two separate rooms—the Music

Hall and the Parish—the club has a surprisingly cool atmosphere for a corporate venue. In the larger space, the Music Hall, two bars frame the room, and the main floor is close enough that you won't miss a thing if you need to grab a drink. A diverse array of artists including B.R.M.C., the Vines, Jet, Gavin DeGraw, Howie Day, Scissor Sisters, Buddy Guy, the Killers, and George Clinton has graced the stage in recent years. The Parish is a 250-capacity space with portraits illustrating the seven deadly sins lining the walls. Another cool thing about HOB is that artists can only exit the main exit, which comes out on Decatur St. So line up behind the barricades and you'll have a decent shot at meeting your favorite band—or at least getting to see them run to the bus before motoring out of town.

### Tipitina's, 501 Napoleon Ave., www.tipitinas.com

Though a giant picture of New Orleans legend Professor Longhair still occupies the wall behind the stage, that doesn't mean this thirty-seven year-old venue—named for a Longhair song—is stuck in the past. The 1,000-capacity Tipitina brings in plenty of modern roots rockers (North Mississippi All-Stars, Drive By Truckers), jam bands (Widespread Panic, Galactic) and indie heavyhitters (Death Cab for Cutie, Wilco).

For a taste of authentic N'Awlins music, check out the club's Sunday night Cajun Fais Do Do with the Bruce Daigrepont Band—a fourteen-year tradition that helps keep the Acadian culture of Louisiana alive. Tips also gets bonus points for supporting local charities and working tirelessly to promote music within New Orleans' most destitute neighborhoods. They also operate a recording studio and a smaller, less traversed downtown venue.

### Howlin' Wolf, 828 S. Peters, www.howlin-wolf.com

This Warehouse District club showcases mostly regional acts, with occasional appearances by touring indie and punk bands such as Rilo Kiley or Murder by Death. Like most New Orleans venues, Howlin' Wolf is 18+, and offers a laid-back atmosphere where you'll be as comfortable watching a show as you will be playing pool, lounging on the couch, or dropping quarters in the videogames in the corner near the bar.

**One Eyed Jacks, 615 Toulouse St.**

In 2004, New Orleans' famous Shim-Sham club was converted to One Eyed Jacks; though locals were sad to see the Shim-Sham 86'ed, fans of punk and indie rock aren't complaining: The 18+ club brings in national noisemakers including Hot Snakes, the Ponys, Holly Golightly, and Bad Wizard for shows that sometimes cost as little as five bucks. And the décor—wallpaper covered with burgundy and gold paisley, a split-level music room, a sleazy 80s glam vibe—make the place at once comfy and cool.

**Saenger Theatre, 143 N. Rampart St.,**
**www.saengertheatre.com**

Saenger is the biggest little club in the city, and when its stage isn't being used for whatever Broadway show is passing through New Orleans, this is where artists such as the Strokes, String Cheese Incident, Ozomatli, and Norah Jones perform. It's got a good vibe: The ceiling is dotted with lights arranged like the constellations, the walls are decorated with fleurs de lis, and the lobby still has the only remaining chandelier of sixteen that were built into the place when it opened in 1911.

## RECORD STORES:

**The Mushroom, 1037 Broadway**

For a full-sensory experience, you might want to load up on some incense, tapestries and, um, "pipes" along with your music purchases. If so, hit the Mushroom—a combination record store/head shop. The store carries most major label releases, along with a few rare imports and loads of indie CDs. The staff consists mainly of stoner kids, so don't expect them to be overly attentive while you're shopping. If you're a student at **Tulane University**, the Mushroom is perfectly situated near campus, on fraternity row, right above a popular Tulane bar, the Boot.

**Virgin Megastore, 620 Decatur St.,**
**www.virginmega.com**

Like all outlets in the Virgin chain, this three-story shop sells so many hundreds of CDs, it will make your head spin. In addition to the usual stuff—mainstream CDs and a decent indie selection, plus DVDs, books, magazines and videogames—you can also find a wide array of regional music here, including zydeco, blues, jazz, and world music from Louisiana artists past and present.

### Rock'n'Roll Collectibles, 1214 Decatur St., www.rockcollectibles.org

Now *this* is your classic messy, tiny record store. It's not always easy to find what you're looking for at Rock & Roll Collectibles, but the disorganization is part of the shop's charm: looking for an album here is like going on a treasure hunt that kicks up a lot of dust along the way. (Beware, allergy sufferers: our friend at Tulane says trips to R&RC always make her eyes water and her nose run.) The store carries rare vintage pressings of vinyl LPs (an advance promo copy of Aerosmith's *Toys in the Attic* for only $65), plus stacks of 45s and old posters. The owner will play any record for you and will even help you decide which vinyl weight—heavy grade or lighter—best suits your needs. Plus, he's somewhat flexible on pricing, so feel free to gently haggle with him.

### Tower Records, 408 N. Peters St., www.towerrecords.com

If you feel like shopping at a giant record store, you're better off at Virgin. But Tower is still a reliable bet for everything from classic rock and alternative music to jazz, soundtracks and classical. Their DVD room lets you rent as well as buy, which is great for those times when you're not sure you'll want to watch *Catwoman* more than once.

## RADIO STATIONS:

### WTUL 91.5, www.tulane.edu/~wtul/

Tulane U's WTUL is the only remaining prog-rock station in New Orleans, and its audience has substantial overlap with the clientele at The Mushroom. That is, if you dig indie-pop or mainstream alterna-rock, the playlist at WTUL will probably be a bit far-out for your tastes. Aside from spinning bands such as TV On The Radio, Sigur Ros and The Faint, the station gives plenty of airtime to local bands. Best of all, WTUL has proven to be a great launching pad for aspiring DJs; many of the student jocks at the station have scored real jobs at commercial stations after they graduate.

**WRNO 99.5**

**www.wrno.com**

"The Rock of New Orleans" plays typical mainstream classic cuts, but they do have a few cool shows to set them apart from the rest of the city's crappy stations. Sunday nights, WRNO broadcasts Little Steven's Underground Garage—two hours of obscure garage rock selected by Bruce Springsteen sideman Little Steven Van Zandt. And every day at 4:30 p.m., check out "Kat's Lost Classic," during which WRNO DJ Kat lets a listener call in and suggest a great song from a classic rock band that never made it into the Top 40.

# MISCELLANEOUS EVENTS:

### Voodoo Music Experience

Halloween in New Orleans is becoming as popular for tourists as Mardi Gras, prompting the organizers of Voodoo—which used to be held just before Halloween—to move the festival up to early October. The fest is held on five stages and has attracted major national acts including Marilyn Manson, the White Stripes, Jack Johnson, Ben Harper, 50 Cent, Counting Crows, Velvet Revolver, Snoop Dogg, and the Killers. But you can also see plenty of local and underground bands, too.

### New Orleans Jazz and Heritage Festival

This legendary seven-day event has been running for thirty-five years, staging performances by everyone from Bob Dylan and the Steve Miller Band to John Mayer and North Mississippi Allstars. It is hands down the biggest music happening in the city, and remains the longest-running music festival in the entire U.S. Used to be only jazz, blues and soul acts played the event, but in recent years the organizers have added roots-rock artists to the line-up. For only $45, you get a weekend pass, affording you the chance to take in the big acts, plus plenty of zydeco, gospel, African, jazz and folk music; and don't forget to sample the oodles of food and merch on sale in tents stationed throughout the fairgrounds.

# New York, NY

## NEW YORK UNIVERSITY
22 Washington Square North
New York, NY 10011
www.nyu.edu

**M**usic students at NYU study a stone's throw away from where Bob Dylan got his first big break, walking distance from the legendary punk venue CBGB's, and a few blocks across town from where the Strokes recorded "Is This It?" It's no surprise then, that NYU-ers enjoy exposure to aspects of the industry not available at most other universities. There are two main schools of music at NYU: the School of Arts and Sciences' Department of Music, which offers a bachelor of arts degree in music, and Clive Davis Department of Recorded Music, which operates with the Tisch School of the Arts, and offers a bachelor of fine arts degree.

Those pursuing the bachelor of arts degree study theory, history, and criticism of Medieval to contemporary Western music as well as music outside of the western canon like jazz, popular, and world music. Majors take courses like Harmony and Counterpoint and the History of European Music, and are required to demonstrate proficiency in piano and sight reading. Students are encouraged to attend performances, apply for internships, and participate in Harmony, a nonprofit organization affiliated with NYU that supports the study of music in low-income settings such as certain schools and housing projects.

The Clive Davis Department of Recorded Music is named after NYU alum Clive Davis, whose many claims to fame include discovering Janis Joplin, signing Bruce Springsteen and Patti Smith, resurrecting Carlos Santana's career in the Nineties with *Supernatural*, and making Alicia Keys and Maroon 5 superstars in his current position as head of BMG's North American music division. The department seeks to educate students in all aspects of contemporary recorded music, with a special focus on the art of identifying music talent and producing creative material. Students enrolled in this program are expected to develop both the creative and business skills necessary to forge a career as a talentscouting music exec. The program follows a four-year progression of courses that run the gamut, from the history of contemporary musical genres to courses that focus on the legal and business aspects of the music industry. Courses you might take as a student here include History and Culture of Recorded Sound, The Music Producer as Creative Entrepreneur, Techniques of Recording, The "Alternative" in Popular Music, and Artist Development: The Image Makers.

## JUILLIARD SCHOOL
Music Division
60 Lincoln Center Plaza
New York, NY 10023
www.juilliard.edu

Chances are if you're into music and you're interested in Julliard, you already know a bit about why you would want to go here. Julliard's distinguished reputation as one of the preeminent performing arts schools in the country is strongly established and well deserved. Julliard's music division offers a four-year program for undergraduates, which leads to a bachelor of music degree. The school also offers a three-year diploma program available to particularly gifted performance students. The areas of study available to Julliard music students include composition, harpsichord, orchestral instruments, organ, piano, and voice.

All areas of music study at Julliard come complete with the expected individualized attention, accomplished faculty, and ample ensemble participation opportunities you would expect from this venerable institution. In addition, Julliard hosts over 700 drama, dance, and music events each year, ensuring that music students have the opportunity to integrate their studies with the other varieties of performance art taught at the school. Those interested in pop music would likely get the most out of Julliard's Music Technology Center. Students enrolled in this school pursue specialized areas of tech-friendly music study like computers in performance, film scoring, and music production. Courses you would take if studying in Music Technology at Julliard include Interactive Computer Music Performance, Scoring to Picture, and Music Production Workshop among others.

# FIVE TOWNS COLLEGE

305 N. Service Rd.
Dix Hills, New York 11746
www.fivetowns.edu

**G**ranted, Five Towns College is less prestigious and less competitive than Juilliard or NYU, and it is, after all, out in the suburbs of Long Island. Then again, it's more affordable and its music programs offer perks you won't find at other area schools. Five Towns is geared specifically at providing practical knowledge to those looking to work in the entertainment industry, and its curricula aims to prep students for careers as professional composers, recording engineers, music video directors, journalists, and record label executives. The college's degree programs include concentrations in music business, audio recording technology, music education, and jazz and commercial music performance and composition.

Courses in the music business concentration examine legal issues, marketing, and management strategies, while the Jazz/Commercial Music degree program provides a bachelor of music to students interested in writing and performing their own compositions—and actually having a profitable career along the way. But the college's most distinguished offering is the audio recording technology concentration, which rivals similar programs at Orlando's Full Sail Center, among others. Students in this program study engineering procedures, production techniques, recording electronics and theory of sound in a setting equipped with a 48-track studio and individual MIDI workstations. Plus, Five Towns is close enough to Manhattan to allow students to nab internships at some of the biggest music companies—from law firms and management offices to recording studios and radio stations—in the world. And, if those aren't enticing enough reasons to check out Five Towns, consider this: Before his band got its big break, Strokes singer Julian Casablancas used to schlep to Dix Hills on the Long Island Railroad to study here.

## FOR THOSE ALREADY LIVING NEAR NYC...

The **City University of New York** includes a number of strong music programs, most notably the Aaron Copland School of Music at

**Queens College** (www.qc.edu). According to Veronica York, a college advisor at Manhattan's esteemed LaGuardia School of the Performing Arts (a.k.a. the school where *Fame* was set), **Brooklyn College** and **City College** also offer great programs at affordable prices: Tuition to CUNY schools—for those already living in New York State—is still less than $3,000 a semester. And all of these schools are only a subway, bus or car ride away from downtown Manhattan, where all the best rock happens.

## VENUES:

### Bowery Ballroom, 6 Delancey St., www.boweryballroom.com

Just off the once-seedy Bowery on New York's Lower East Side, this mid-sized venue has filled a much-needed gap in the city's rock scene ever since it opened in the late Nineties. The Bowery is just big enough to accommodate rising stars such as Hot Hot Heat and Tegan & Sarah, but small enough to make you feel like you're part of the in crowd. Before they earned whatever mainstream appeal they now have, acts ranging from the Strokes and the Darkness to Death Cab for Cutie and even Coldplay stormed the stage at the Bowery for crowds of about 1,000 fans. In spite of its newness, the Bowery already feels like a place with history: Perhaps that's because the building is a late twenties Beaux Arts construction that was once a three-story theater. They kept the brass-railed balcony and mahogany-accented VIP rooms upstairs, but you'll only get a good look at the latter if you butter up one of the opening bands. There's a big candlelit bar downstairs, which is a great place to retire to when the crowd watching the show gets to shove-y or when the band playing isn't living up to their hype. Even better, the Bowery staff doesn't rush you out as soon as the show's over, giving you plenty of time to finish your beer or give your digits to the boy with the velvet blazer and vintage t-shirt.

### Mercury Lounge, 217 E. Houston, www.mercuryloungenyc.com

You know you've made a good start to your career as a New York band when you graduate to playing your first gig at the Mercury Lounge. Bookings haven't been as consistently strong during the past year or two as they were during the late Nineties, but this is still the coolest little club in the city. Most shows are 21+ and feature the likes of the Bravery, the Dears, and Rainer Maria—though Sleater-Kinney recently did a sold-out stint, old school-style. The Mercury Lounge suffers only from poor architecture: the elongated bar room in front is too narrow to accommodate 250 people as they exit the show, and you're likely to get stuck, pressed up against a stranger for awhile before you land safely on the sidewalk out front. The same people own Bowery Ballroom and recently started booking bigger gigs (Kings of Leon, Jimmy Eat World, Arcade Fire) at an unlikely spot: bridge-and-tunnel dance club Webster Hall.

### Knitting Factory, 74 Leonard St., www.knittingfactory.com

Relocated to Tribeca in the mid-Nineties from its Houston St. location (don't call it Hyoo-ston, or you'll reveal yourself as an out-of-towner), the Knitting Factory has long been downtown's most adventurous venue. With three stages housed in a lair of never-ending basements and sub-basements, the Knitting Factory is eclectic enough to book experimental art-rock from the Swans' Jarboe one night and anthemic emo from Midtown the next. (The Knitting Factory's own label represents its more avant-garde bent, with oodles of progressive jazz and post-everything releases to its name.) The "main space" has great sound, but beware the giant pillar on the right-hand side of the floor: Once you're behind it, you won't see a darn thing.

### Irving Plaza, 17 Irving Pl., www.irvingplaza.com

This 1,800-capacity venue isn't as welcoming as the smaller Bowery Ballroom, but it's hard to find fault with the reliable spate of shows that roll through Irving Plaza. Before your favorite act—whether it's Straylight Run, the Thrills, Vanessa Carlton or Lostprophets—gets big enough to move uptown to the roomier Hammerstein Ballroom or Roseland, its fans will pack into Irving, where your view of the stage hardly worsens at all when you're in the back of the room. One caveat: the sound quality isn't as good if you're standing under the balcony—half of which is usually cordoned off for VIPs, VVIPs, and people who know a guy who knows a guy who works at the label.

### Hammerstein Ballroom, 311 W. 34th St.

The floor at this 3,000-capacity venue (built as an opera house by Oscar Hammerstein I in 1906) gets really crowded when acts such as Switchfoot and Marilyn Manson take the stage, but you can always avoid the mosh pit and secure a good view of the stage if you spring for a seat in one of the balconies. The earlier you get there, the better your seat will be, since the balcony chairs are up for grabs on a first-come, first-served basis.

### Pianos, 158 Ludlow St.,
### www.pianosnyc.com

A recent addition to NYC's rock scene, this bar/venue is housed in a former piano store, but all that remains is the old sign. The front bar serves the usual array of bar food—burgers, fries, sandwiches—all of which are yummy, but the service tends to be at a snail's pace. In the back is a tiny room with a stage: The sound is sucky but the selection of bands is pretty spot-on. You might find an act here before they're esteemed enough to get a booking at the Mercury. The jungle-themed upstairs bar hosts the occasional acoustic show.

### Roseland, 239 West 52nd St.,
### www.roselandballroom.com

In the middle of Midtown's theater district, you can mingle with tourists on their way to *The Producers* on Broadway before you head inside the Roseland Ballroom—an old school concert- and dancehall that still occasionally hosts swing dancing parties. When you're too big for Irving and a ways away from filling an arena (e.g., Snow Patrol, the White Stripes, or Dashboard Confessional) you might end up onstage at the 3,500-capacity Roseland. If you don't plan to mosh and the thought of a mosh-induced fat lip has you nervous, don't get too close to the stage. For some reason, Roseland seems to generate the biggest pits you'll see in the city. Also, expect to have your bag searched and your bod patted down on the way in, so leave your one-hitter in your dorm room.

### Rothko, 116 Suffolk,
### www.rothkonyc.com

In spite of how new and how tiny this red-walled Lower East Side club is, it's already reputed to be one of the city's finest lil' rock clubs.

Even though you probably won't be able to get into the listening parties labels often hold here for artists from You Will Know Us by Our Trail of Dead to the Donnas, it's a good sign, eh? My money's on this place to fill the void left in our city's scene since indie rock stalwart Brownies shut down a few years back. Small touring acts and buzz-worthy locals dominate their calendar, and Rothko also makes room for a recurring hip-hop karaoke night for those interested in showing off just how pasty white they really are.

### Sin-E, 148 Attorney

In its old location on St. Mark's Place, Sin-E hosted gigs by David Gray, the late Jeff Buckley, and an assortment of other noteworthy new school folkies. Today, it books bands slightly better than what you'll see at places like Arlene Grocery, but who aren't yet good enough to get a gig at the Mercury Lounge.

### Northsix, 66 N. 6 St., Williamsburg, www.northsix.com

The Feng Shui in this place sucks. The ceilings are too high, the vibe too industrial, and for some reason, it always smells like unwashed armpit. But if you're in Williamsburg—where all hipsters end up at some point—you'll thank your lucky stars that you don't always have to go into Manhattan to see the Bravery or Ted Leo.

### Southpaw, 125 Fifth Ave., Park Slope, www.spsounds.com

A deceptively spacious 5,000 square-foot lounge with a stage, this place offers those even farther out in Brooklyn—in Park Slope, to be exact—an excuse not to get on the subway. A few times a month, they score a coup by booking the kinds of acts who could easily sell-out a bigger, more conveniently located Manhattan venue (i.e., Sleater-Kinney, TV On The Radio, the Raveonettes.)

## RECORD STORES:

### Other Music, 15 E. 4th St., www.othermusic.com

Since it opened in 1998, Other Music has established itself as New York's quintessential indie record store: The kind of place where, if they've got it, it must be cool. Don't let yourself be scared off by the array of obscure vinyl on the walls of this bright and browse-able East Village shop. The staff is friendly and expert, and they won't laugh if you ask them which sixties French pop record you ought to buy first. That said, a store this hip is bound to seem intimidating, and you're better off if you go in there knowing what you're looking for. They specialize in indie rock and electronica, but also stock psychedelic, no wave, prog rock, soul. First, you'll have to figure out what the heck the section listings—"Then," "Now," "In," "Out"—mean.

### Rockit Scientist, 43 Carmine St., www.carminestreet.com/rockit.html

Serious music aficionados swear by this itty-bitty West Village shop, where the staff is so nice that the clerk once gave my friend a free Television live CD because it had a scratch on it. Free! Turns out the thing played just fine, and when my friend returned to Rockit to pay for the disk, his money was refused nonetheless. The selection favors Nuggets-worthy garage rock, prog, Sixties psych but includes a well-curated assortment of new indie rock, plus some soul, jazz, and blues.

### Academy Records, 12 W.18th, www.academy-records.com

OK, so your first clue to Academy's bent is the plastic dinosaur toys that live in its front window: This is one of Manhattan's best shops for new and used classical music on vinyl and CD. They've got a fantastic jazz section, and unbeatable bargains (some CDs go for as little as $1), but their rock offerings are pretty much limited to whatever they bought used from someone looking to liquidate all their old Eurythmics records. Academy has a chill, friendly vibe in spite of it's high-falutin' stock, and the store tends to be abuzz with activity even on weekdays. Go. Browse. Buy. You can't subsist on rock alone.

### Etherea, 66 Ave. A, www.ethereaonline.com

I wasn't going to include Etherea at first, even though it's better than most of the indie rocktronica shops downtown. But then a friend told me a story about how she went in there to buy her boyfriend a birthday gift, told the clerk she wanted "something like Eric Satie, but not Eric Satie," and was treated to a totally non-condescending list of recommendations. So there you go. Plus, with its bright yellow walls and pane-glass windows, the clean and sparse Etherea won't make you feel compelled to disinfect after you leave.

### Rocks in Your Head, 157 Prince, www.rocksinyourhead.com

Just below street level in SoHo's shopping district, Rocks in Your Head seems impervious to the tide of gentrification that has swept through that neighborhood during the past decade. It's dark, dusty, and packed with new and used vinyl at remarkably reasonable prices. (A new copy of *Bob Dylan's Greatest Hits 2* fetches $10.99; a used one, $7.99.) No one will bother you if you happen to feel like browsing through a stock that's heavy on Sixties and Seventies rock. They've got videos, magazines, books, and used turntables laying out in the open, but if you wanna look at CDs you're going to have to ask the clerk to unlock one of the glass cases lining the walls.

### Mondo Kim's, 6 St. Mark's Place, www.kimsvideo.com

Even though several friends of mine have clerked at Mondo Kim's over the years, I'm not going to lie to you: The staff at this East Village staple tend to be on the somewhat snooty side. Maybe it's because half the dudes behind the counter are just waiting for their band to make it big before they tell the owner, Mr. Kim, to take this job and shove it. Nonetheless, if you're looking for the new pair of Bright Eyes records or to fill in the gaps in your Leonard Cohen collection, you're sure to find it among the huge-yet-selective stock at Kim's. Upstairs, there's a video store that carries everything from the obscure to the less obscure.

### Gimme Gimme Records, 325 E. 5th St.

If you're not looking closely, you'll probably stroll by Gimme Gimme without even realizing it's there. The tiny shop sells only vinyl—mostly punk, jazz and New Wave—and they have huge bargain bins where you can score someone else's throwaway for a buck. The store also has a resident piano teacher, if you want to learn to tickle the ivories. Sadly, Gimme Gimme's hours are prohibitively spare: They're only open on Thurs.-Sun.

### Virgin MegaStore, 1540 Broadway or 52 E. 14th St., www.virginmega.com

Kvetch all you want about how big corporations step on mom-and-pop stores, or how these gigantic record retailers lack old school charm, blah blah blah. There are few better ways to spend an afternoon than browsing the aisles of the vast Virgin MegaStore, sampling oodles of new discs at their listening stations, stocking up on blank CDRs, filling your arms with all three seasons of *Curb Your Enthusiasm* on DVD, or reading Bob Dylan's *Chronicles* in their café without even having to pay for it. Every genre under the sun is represented and you don't have to worry about a hipper-than-thou clerk (or fellow shopper) judging you if you can't resist buying the new Kylie Minogue album. Plus, Virgin goes out of its way to put new releases on sale—often for less than ten bucks—and their "Staff Recommendations" are often much more cutting edge than you'd expect. Which is why Ryan Adams and John Mayer—both NYC residents—can't resist trolling around the Union Square location at every available opportunity. Seriously. I've seen both of them in there more times than I can count.

### Wows!ville, 125 Second Ave.

One thing you can say for Wows!ville is that they do one thing, and do it well: the East Village shop specializes in Sixties psych- and garage-rock, as well as plying the wares of all three decades worth of bands who are stuck in a Sixties garage-rock time warp. If your copy of the *Nuggets* box set has you hankering to expand your collection of platters from the Strawberry Alarm Clock, Them, or the Seeds, make Wows!ville your first stop.

### Breakbeat Science, 181 Orchard

I don't know jack shit about techno music, but I do know that my techno-savvy friends adore Breakbeat Science, the first bona fide drum n' bass specialty shop in North America. Since 1996, Breakbeat Science has peddled tons of the stuff, on CD and vinyl, from the new and hyped to the rare and underrated.

## THE BEST OF THE REST

**For bootlegs:** Bleecker Bob's (118 W. 3rd)

**For punk rock:** Generation Records (210 Thompson St.)

**For house music:** Satellite (324 Bowery)

**For hip-hop:** Fat Beats (406 Ave. of the Americas), or Beat Street in Brooklyn (494 Fulton St.), which carries a seemingly unlimited stock of the latest mix CDs.

**For the Brooklyn-bound indie rocker:** Somethin' Else, owned by Radio 4 bassist Anthony Roman , (294 Fifth Ave., Park Slope), Ear Wax , (218 Bedford Ave., Williamsburg) or Sound Fix (110 Bedford Ave., Williamsburg)

**For selling all the crap you don't want:** Norman's Sound and Vision (67 Cooper Sq.)

## RADIO STATIONS:

**WFMU, 91.1 FM,**
**www.wfmu.org**

A community station in New Jersey whose signal extends into NYC, WFMU is the best kind of freeform operation, one where you never know exactly what you're going to hear, but you have the utmost faith in the DJs to spin an extraordinary mix each and every day. There are no specialty shows, per se, though particular jocks indulge particular preferences. (Dave Spazz spins far-out surf, psych and punk tunes; Noah's Coffee Break for Heroes and Villains focuses on independent and obscure hip-hop tracks.) WFMU has helped define freeform radio ever since legendary DJ Vin Scelsa took over the station in 1968, and it has stuck to its guns ever since. This is radio at its most daring, so if you're looking for easy listening, stick to the homogenous Top 40 stations farther to the right of the dial. Lord knows we've got plenty of those here in New York.

**WNYU, 89.1 FM,**
**www.wnyu.nyu.edu**

The student-operated WNYU is one of the best college stations in the country: Its playlist—though heavy on indie rock—is adventurous; its specialty shows could satisfy virtually any taste imaginable, and it makes educational programming part of its mission. "If you hear it on another station, you probably won't hear it on WNYU," they say. The station also has a reputation for churning out future music industry players, from Atlantic Records vice president of A&R Leigh Lust to punk rock booking agent extraordinaire Andrew Ellis (whose clients include Dashboard Confessional, New Found Glory, Brand New, and a slew of others).

# *MISCELLANEOUS EVENTS:*

**CMJ Music Marathon,**
**www.cmj.com**

Every fall, students representing college radio stations from around the country descend on Manhattan for the CMJ Music Marathon, where hundreds of bands play at dozens of venues during a four-night rock & roll explosion. It's a dizzying affair, and you'll be hard-pressed to see everything you want to see, but the fun is in trying. Bear in mind that you need to have a laminate to get into most of the shows, and that won't come cheap. Which is yet another reason to get a gig at your school's radio station: Free CMJ laminate!

**Siren Fest**

The *Village Voice* has been presenting this one-day festival at Coney Island every summer for the past four years. It's sweaty and overly crowded and you have to haul your ass all the way to Coney Island, but even though I always complain about it, I always go. And how could I not? Siren Fest scores absolutely unbeatable line-ups on its two outdoor stages: previous performers include the Yeah Yeah Yeahs, Modest Mouse, TV On The Radio, the Donnas, the Shins, Sleater-Kinney, and dozens of others. Plus, while you're loitering around Astroland, the amusement park on the Coney boardwalk, you'll have the perfect excuse to indulge in hot dogs and beer before taking a ride on the legendary Cyclone rollercoaster.

## HONORABLE MENTION:

# SUNY PURCHASE
735 Anderson Hill Rd.
Purchase, NY 10577
www.purchase.edu

**S**UNY Purchase College is essentially New York State's answer to the slew of private, super-expensive Eastern art schools in the New York area. That cachet has attracted members of punk and emo bands from the suburbs of Long Island, NY to attend Purchase: Daryll Palumbo, singer for Glassjaw, Brandon Reilly from the Movielife and now Nightmare of You, and Brand New drummer Brian Lane studied at Purchase in the late Nineties. Located a delectable thirty-five minutes outside of New York City, Purchase is home to three main schools of study: visual arts, liberal arts and sciences, and performing arts. The SUNY Purchase Conservatory of Music offers a bachelor of music degree focused on several different areas of study including performance, jazz studies, studio composition, and studio production.

The studio production program is available to undergraduates only, and prides itself on getting students out of lecture halls and into real studios to learn how to man the boards. These students enjoy exposure to musical forms from Mozart to hip-hop and take courses in music theory and musicianship for producers. Graduates of this program must all conceive and produce two original projects, one during their junior year, and another during senior year.

The studio composition program, meanwhile, is one of the first of its kind. The structure of this program is similar to that of the production program—with similar requirements and course work—but with a greater emphasis placed on writing, and the skills that accompany that aspect of the production process. Course offerings encompass film scoring, legal and ethical issues in the music business, record contracts and music publishing, and even a course called Dialogues in which students from varied musical majors enjoy the opportunity to communicate with each other about their studies.

# Oberlin, OH

**Oberlin College** (www.oberlin.edu) has been part of a progressive music scene for generations. Famous concerts have taken place here, such as the Dave Brubeck Jazz at Oberlin show that was recorded in the early Fifties before jazz was widely accepted at colleges. Also, this past year, Bela Fleck and the Flecktones chose Oberlin as the location for the final show before taking an indefinite hiatus from the music circuit. A few recent Obies that have made splashes in the music scene are Liz Phair, the all female hip-hop group Northern State, John McEntire of Tortoise, folk singer Josh Ritter, and Karen O from the Yeah Yeah Yeahs.

Home to, hands-down one of the country's best music conservatories, Oberlin College aims to provide pre-professional training in a variety of music fields to accomplished and dedicated music students. Here students study performance, composition, music education, music technology, music theory, and music history, and as undergraduates, pursue either the bachelor of music degree or the performance diploma. Oberlin students have gone on to illustrious careers in every aspect of the contemporary music world, and those enrolled can be sure that their peers are some of the very best young musicians in the country.

The conservatory boasts an amazing collection of historic instruments including xylophones from West Africa, and classical instruments from China, Turkey, and India. Majors in the conservatory concentrate in performance, music education, composition, music history, technology in music and related arts, and jazz studies. Oberlin also offers an individual major, which allows students to construct their own music-related course of study.

Those interested in music, but not sure they want to pursue a career in performance, or desire exposure to more conventional liberal arts subjects can major in music in the College of Arts and Sciences at Oberlin. These students enjoy the advantage of studying in a program closely associated with one of the preeminent music conservatories in the country, but they also encounter the problems that arise from constantly coming in second to the conservatory's own students. Though most conservatory courses are open to any and all qualified students, enrollment priority is given to conservatory students and in reality, liberal arts students, even if they are music majors, do not gain entrance to most conservatory courses. However, college students do enjoy some music courses specifically designed for them, such as Introduction to Western Art Music and Introduction to Musics of the World, which explores and compares a variety of musical traditions from around the globe.

There are abundant opportunities on campus for rock fans to indulge their interests. For instance, the student concert programming organizations get a healthy budget each year to bring in acts of their choosing. Students get experience booking and hosting bands. Oberlin College's sound department is also almost primarily student run. One supervisor trains students to set up and run professional sound systems as well as how to fix and build certain sound components. After working this job for four years students usually have many of the skills others go to vocational school for, except with a massive amount of field experience, and they got paid for it.

Oberlin's TIMARA department (Technology in Music and Related Arts) is a unique electronic music program hosted by Oberlin's famous Conservatory but open to students in the College of Arts and Sciences as well. Students in this program learn everything from studio recording techniques to making electronic beats. This department produces practical sound editors side by side with atonal electronic composers. The emphasis is placed on developing one's own approach to the field. Creative freedom is dished out by the dump truck full.

**WOBC** 91.5 College and Community Radio, Oberlin's twenty-four-hour, seven-days-a-week freeform radio station has been in action for over fifty years. Since it's freeform, the station's programming includes everything from hip-hop to punk, bluegrass to pop. A number of long-standing community DJs have had shows for years now, but even entering freshmen can nab a show if their playlist is strong enough (although probably in the dead of the night). The station regularly throws parties and sponsors concerts as well. Although there are a lot of unpaid positions for students to hold at the station, such as promotions director or public service announcement director, the four main positions, the station manager, music director, program director and operations manager, are all paid student positions.

And, though Oberlin doesn't have any record stores at the moment, it does have its very own record label! Obedient Pony Records started last year and has devoted its time to putting out an annual compilation featuring local Oberlin bands. They're currently gearing up to start issuing 7-inch records from exciting campus-based groups.

To see bands play, you often don't even have to leave campus: Oberlin's got three main college venues and each has a generous budget for bringing acts. **Finney Chapel** is the largest, and due to its wooden pews and professional-sized stage it is usually reserved for the highbrow acts such as the Cleveland Orchestra. The building is an old church with beautiful stained glass and stone entrances and stunning acoustics. Recent rock performances include Rufus Wainwright, the Indigo Girls, Bela Fleck and the Flecktones.

The 500-capacity **Dionysus Disco**, called the 'Sco for brevity, is smaller and dingier, but books the best indie bands you could hope to see. The school's concert programmers—mostly students with a few full time staff members—have been on a roll when it comes to nabbing up-and-coming acts right before they get way too big to pin down at a small college. Some famous shows include the Magnetic Fields, the White Stripes, Sleater Kinney, Blonde Redhead, At the Drive-In, Apples in Stereo and Mike Watt. Also, the beer here is dirt cheap: every Thursday you can get a cup of Pabst for a quarter. That's cheap. The 'Sco also has a new foosball table, billiard tables, darts, etc. and monthly karaoke nights.

**Cat in the Cream** is a coffee house that sticks primarily to folksy stuff but branches out from that at least once every semester. Students are encouraged to put on their own shows here as often as they can. The only catch is that no show at this venue can have a cover charge. Josh Ritter got his start playing here. Both Bishop Allen and the Moldy Peaches, meanwhile, trashed the stage during recent shows at Cat in the Cream.

## HOUSE PARTY!

Oberlin also has a thriving scene of basement and living room shows. Mindflayer (members of Lightning Bolt), the Fleshies, and the Phantom Limbs are some of the more recognized acts to blow through our parties over the last few years, but countless bands have toured through Oberlin to play for drunken punks and rockers through a gloriously shitty PA. These shows usually cost three bucks or less for the show and you get to drink Pabst from a keg. Since the Oberlin college concert board is run by students but has a sizeable budget, many of the acts touring through actually get paid. There are usually basement shows every other weekend and they tend to be held later in the evening than the ones at traditional venues.

# Olympia, WA

For any students interested in music, **Evergreen State College**'s (www.evergreen.edu) greatest asset is the fact that it's located in Olympia. In part because of the college, Olympia is a haven for artists and musicians and has been home to many of the most influential post-punk and alternative artists of the 1990s. In addition to serving as the place of inception for the riot grrrl scene, over the years everyone from Kurt Cobain to Sleater-Kinney to members of Marcy Playground and the Love Junkies have called Olympia home. The tiny town nestled underneath Mt. Rainier—a giant ice-covered volcano—was also the birthplace of some of the most important indie record labels in the world including Sub Pop (Nirvana, Mudhoney, Soundgarden, the Shins, Hot Hot Heat, Postal Service), Kill Rock Stars (Bikini Kill, Sleater-Kinney, Elliott Smith), and K Records (Chicks on Speed, Kimya Dawson, Modest Mouse).

When Evergreen State College in Olympia, Washington opened its doors in 1971, the then conservative majority of the small town's population was less than thrilled. The school's progressive curriculum centers around team-taught courses dubbed "programs" that combine lecture, laboratory, and fieldwork to create interdisciplinary approaches in less than traditional subjects. Those concerned probably thought that such a school would invite all kinds of crazy thinking liberals into the otherwise quiet, fog-ridden town; it totally did. Everyone from *Simpsons* creator Matt Groening to *Seinfeld*'s Cosmo Kramer (Michael Richards) have attended Evergreen College, not to mention the slew of rock-related icons like all members of Bikini Kill and Sub Pop Records founder Bruce Pavitt, who've also studied here.

The college is publicly funded with an enrollment of approximately 4,400 students and offers several degrees including bachelor of arts in liberal arts and sciences, bachelor of science in liberal arts and sciences, as well as masters degrees in several fields. Students do not receive letter grades, but instead are evaluated by way of written narratives. Public service is integral to Evergreen's educational philosophy and the school has five Public Service Centers focused on everything from labor education to improving the quality of undergraduate education across the nation. Participating in these programs, or others like them (like working the school's own organic farm for example) is a big focus among faculty and students at Evergreen.

Because of the unique courses taught at Evergreen, it's almost impossible to study one and only one subject. For music students this is great because it allows for investigation into not just the history and performance of music but also into the relationship music has on all sort of elements within the culture that creates it. For example, musical students might take Negotiating Cultural Landscapes: Money, Music, Citizens and Stories (in which students look at their culture through their experience as consumers) or Rhythmic Meditations (in which students investigate the relationship between rhythm and creativity).

The main area of interest for rock fans hanging out in Olympia is the 4th Avenue strip. It is, in fact, the only thing in Olympia that qualifies as a "main drag." Many of the city's coolest record stores, clubs, and venues are located here. Both of Olympia's traditional venues, **China Clipper** and **Le Voyeur** (www.levoyeur.netfirms.com), are located on 4th Avenue, as is one of the town's best record stores, **Rec the Place** (www.lastwordbooks.com). (**Rainy Day Records** and **Phantom City**, the town's other noteworthy record stores are not on 4th Ave.). However, most rock shows that happen in Olympia take place at spaces rented by a band or a promoter, and are not arranged by the booking agent at one of the town's two major clubs. The China Clipper and Le Voyeur don't have all ages shows, so for students under twenty-one it's great that many good shows happen independently at spaces like the **Capitol Theater**, **Eagles Hall**, **Art House Designs**, or **Midnight Sun**.

# Omaha, NE

It's common knowledge that Omaha is home to one of the roaring success stories in independent music ... Mannheim Steamroller.

Just kidding, although Chip Davis' cheesy-synth Christmas tunes still convince fans to flock to the local arena for his annual holiday concerts. There's also homegrown alt-reggae band 311, which cut its teeth in Omaha in the late eighties and early nineties before it relocated to California and landed radio and MTV.

But Omaha's true musical identity these days comes courtesy of Saddle Creek Records, which proved to be the little indie label that could—selling hundreds of thousands of units without plugging into the major-label machinery. Conor Oberst of Bright Eyes fame has moved away, but most of the Saddle Creek musicians (in the Faint, the Good Life, Cursive, etc.) remain rooted to their hometown along with the label's business offices.

Such a thriving indie rock underground almost makes up for the fact that this metro of 500,000-plus residents must live in the shadow of the smaller capital city of Lincoln, located thirty minutes southwest on Interstate 80. That flat grid of a city is home to the **University of Nebraska-Lincoln** (www.unl.edu) and its Cornhusker football team—the official religion of Nebraska and much of western Iowa, whose army of believers can be spotted wearing red and white. In spite of its focus on football, UNL offers one of the region's strongest music programs, offering either a bachelor of music or a bachelor of arts in music to qualified applicants. Either program allows students to enroll in classes that study not only classical forms, but also popular, jazz, and rock music. Music majors are also invited to audition for one of UNL's ensembles as well as its renowned Cornhusker Marching Band. This is also where Tommy Lee studied for a semester while filming his reality show *Tommy Lee Goes to College*.

**Creighton University** (www.creighton.edu) in Omaha, meanwhile, enrolls more than 6,000 students and is one of only twenty-eight Jesuit colleges in the nation. Its Department of Fine and Performing Arts offers an undergraduate degree in music that requires forty-three semester hours, or a co-major that entails about half that class load.

And the **University of Nebraska at Omaha** (www.unomaha.edu) includes undergraduate music programs in composition, education, and performance.

Thanks in part to its heritage as a center for stockyards, Omaha still has a reputation as a glorified cow town. But there's more in store for the cultured collegiate than meets the cynical eye. Joslyn Art Museum rewards repeat visits, for instance, and baseball fans can look forward to the College World Series every June. The downtown nightlife district, the cobblestone streets and rehabbed warehouses of the Old Market, rivals similar neighborhoods in Kansas City or Minneapolis-St. Paul, just on a much smaller scale.

The two primary venues for rock shows are the **Sokol Auditorium and Underground** (www.sokolunderground.com) and **The Ranch Bowl** (www.ranchbowl.com). The former—a seventy-five-year-old Czech polka palace and fitness center—has provided the setting for much of this city's Saddle Creek-led indie rock revolution. The larger concerts (1,400 or so fans) take place in the main floor auditorium, where Bright Eyes and the Faint play to capacity on a perennial basis. The nightclub-sized basement (Sokol Underground) plays host to the regular schedule of would-be indie rock superstars. The décor is bare and basic and the lighting is moody, to instill that trademark air of cool detachment in audiences.

A bowling alley and rock club wrapped into one, the Ranch books mostly up-and-coming metal bands, solid blues-rock and the occasional jam band. It's not as if you'll have to dodge gutter balls during concerts—the live music takes place in one of the facility's three indoor bars. There also have been outdoor concerts staged in its sand-volleyball courts, which, as you might guess, are not the best settings for a concert.

As for record shopping, look no further than the Old Market entertainment district, where three superlative stores are all located within a block of each other. **The Antiquarium** is where young Conor Oberst once browsed for vintage vinyl and local CDs in the days when Bright Eyes was a mere twinkle in his weepy eye. The music store, located in the basement, is just one of several reasons to visit. In fact, this place just might be the most satisfying and eclectic music/bookshop in the Midwest. It began life as boxes of books that owner

Tom Rudloff sold out of his own backyard. He moved into his current building in the Old Market district in 1974. Today, its four floors house everything from collectible comics to a regular calendar of homegrown art exhibits—not to mention more than 100,000 used books. Play chess in back, or plop down into one of the worn sofas at the front of the shop, where Rudloff and his friends usually can be found debating philosophy and local politics over coffee and cigarettes. In the mind of any idealistic young college radical worth his/her salt, this is the heart and soul of the Old Market and of Omaha—even if Oberst has long since departed for New York.

**Homer's Music & Gifts** (www.homersmusic.com) is well-stocked with a full range of newly released mainstream CDs. There's a knowledgeable staff, music books and magazines and more trinkets than you'll care to buy. It's one-stop shopping if you're not into vinyl or the more esoteric titles. **Drastic Plastic**, however, oozes pure attitude. It stocks a carefully cultivated collection of indie, punk, and hardcore releases, as well as T-shirts, rare magazines, and posters. The basic black décor of the place will put you in a Goth frame of mind, even in the middle of the day with full sun and balmy temperatures.

*—Kyle Munson*

# Orlando, FL

## FULL SAIL CENTER FOR THE RECORDING ARTS
3000 University Blvd.
Winter Park, FL 32792
www.fullsail.com

An introductory note on Full Sail's website virtually says it all: "You love music, film, video games, design and animation, but do you know how to turn that passion into a fulfilling and productive career in the entertainment media industry?" If you fit the bill, Orlando's Full Sail might be the perfect place for you. The college—which offers associate of science and bachelor of science degrees at an accelerated rate of about a year—gives practical, hands-on training designed to prepare students for life as a producer, engineer, video director, soundtrack coordinator, lighting technician, and even as a roadie. Turns out there's more to that job than schlepping gear and checking microphones. For rock & rollers, the school offers a recording arts program that includes both science and technology components—classes include Audiotronics and Essential Skills for the Audio Industry—as well as courses on Entertainment Business and Law or Music History (which, in its description, references Beck, the Beatles and Stevie Wonder). There's also a degree program called Show Production and Touring, which teaches you to master concert lighting design, rigging and acoustic measurements. Check out Full Sail's website if you're not sure how these classes can be applied in the "real world": for each program, the site features a long list of possible careers, including gigs you probably didn't even know existed.

# STETSON UNIVERSITY
421 N. Woodland Blvd.
DeLand, FL 32723
www.stetson.edu

An hour north of Orlando in DeLand, Florida, Stetson University is a relatively small school—about 2,000 undergrads, and an impressive 11:1 student:faculty ratio—that focuses on doing a few things really well: Its schools of Business Administration and Music are underrecognized gems in the South. In addition to the traditional music curricula, including the bachelor of music in performance, education, theory and composition, and the more broad-based bachelor of arts in music, Stetson offers a digital arts major that lets students interested in using technology to create works of art combine music, sound design, science, literature and fine art. The school—which formerly had a Baptist affiliation—also features a strong church music program, specifically geared toward those who want to study organ. Students within the program get to practice and perform at the Benjamin S. Stetson Memorial Chapel, which houses a rare Beckerath pipe organ that has undergone continual renovation by a team of German experts.

Stetson is unusually supportive of students whose interests don't hew to a particular discipline: honors students in particular are allowed to build their own major by combining various concentrations. Within the School of Music, you can major in theory and composition, voice, guitar, and an assortment of other instruments; but, for the more adventurous, the school includes degree programs that overlap music courses with courses in technology and business. In fact, business students need only complete a fifth year of classes to receive a Masters of Business Administration.

## VENUES:

### House of Blues, 1490 E. Buena Vista Dr., Lake Buena Vista., www.hob.com

It seems appropriate that the beginning of our musical journey around Orlando should center on what put Orlando on the map to begin with. Within the "House of the Mouse" is another house—that in my opinion—gives the locals more pleasure than Splash Mountain. House of Blues, located in Downtown Disney, does the chain thing right. In 2004, *Pollstar* ranked the Orlando venue #3 in the world and #1 in the Southeast in its "World's Top 100 Clubs" list. Night after night, House of Blues brings local and national talent from Pearl Jam to 50 Cent to Dashboard Confessional onto the stage to entertain the mainly local audience. That's right, no tourist shoving—they're too busy on the rides, thank goodness. The music hall, like the others around the country, celebrates blues music and folk art, so that theme is prevalent throughout, especially in the brightly colored artwork that adorns the venue.

### Hard Rock Live, 6050 Universal Blvd., www.hardrock.com

And, in the other corner of the ring, ladies and gentlemen... we have Hard Rock Live. The music venue, located in Universal CityWalk, touts itself as the "Coliseum of Rock," and rock it does. But also rap, spin, and occasionally beat on the bongos for a standing-room crowd of 2,800. Home to the MTV concert specials, Nokia presents Hard Rock

Live, and host to the likes of Elton John, the Pixies, and Nelly, Hard Rock Live is also a very big promoter of the local music scene, having local acts take the stage on a regular basis.

### The Social, 54 N. Orange Ave., www.orlandosocial.com

One of the main venues during the Florida Music Festival, this intimate space that holds 400 at capacity is the source for mainly underground and indie acts about to break. It's that intimate atmosphere that allows the crowd to get up close to acts like Modest Mouse playing back to back sold-out shows. And, if you hadn't heard of the artists before they came to the Social, you'll definitely know about them shortly after they play there. Playing the Social for area musicians is the equivalent to "making it" in the local scene. Because of that reputation, co-owners Michael McRaney and Gerard Mitchell recently started the label Social Recordings, and have already signed local up and comer New Roman Times. But the hipster-cool feel doesn't end with the live shows at the Social: The club is also known for its extensive and yummy martini list.

### Will's Pub, 1850 N. Mills Ave., www.willspub.com

If this town had an equivalent to New York's CBGB—before it became a tourist trap for punk kids—Will's Pub would be it hands down. A home away from home for some, this hole-in-the-wall brings in top local and national blues, punk, alt-country, and rock acts for an audience that sports mohawks, tattoos, and piercings. Most of the music action happens in the back room of the bar where you can see the likes of Lucero and T-Model Ford. Afterward, move the party to the front bar for a game of pool, pinball or darts. But it's not all punk and indie rock; spoken word, poetry, hip-hop and comedy also fill the back room on regular nights throughout the week.

### Copper Rocket Pub, 106 Lake Ave., Maitland, www.copperrocketpub.com

When the downtown crowd is just too much to take, a perfect alternative is Maitland's Copper Rocket Pub, located just ten miles from downtown Orlando. A haven for the rockabilly, bluegrass, and alt-country set, the bar is also known for housing a jukebox that offers up the sounds of David Bowie, Tom Waits, and Elvis Costello. The small space has a capacity of only ninety-nine, but it's just enough room to watch bands such as psychobilly act Th' Legendary Shack*Shakers literally shake their sweat all over the audience circled around the stage. A popular event at the pub is the monthly Bluegrass Bash, which mixes backwoods kitsch with underground cool. Girls in overalls and pigtails jig around the tight quarters with fraternity boys opening their ears to something other than Blink 182.

## RECORD STORES:

### Rock 'N' Roll Heaven, 1814 N. Orange Ave.

Any collector in Orlando knows where to go for vintage vinyl—Rock 'N' Roll Heaven, of course. Nestled in College Park's antique row, Rock 'N' Roll Heaven was bought by the Ehmen brothers, Freddy and Ray, in 1985. The shop's only purpose before the brothers took over was selling out-of-print 45s. Now, vinyl, CDs, Charlie's Angel lunch boxes and Ziggy Stardust posters are just a handful of the items you'll spot in the store. According to Freddy, Michael Jackson and Jello Biafra have shopped there, and when record nut Fred Schneider stops through "The City Beautiful," you'll most likely catch the B-52's vocalist behind the counter helping a customer or ringing up a record at one of his favorite places in Central Florida.

### Park Ave CDs, 2916 Corrine Dr., and UCF Student Union Store, Pegasus Circle Building 52 #102A, www.parkavecds.com

Recently settled in its new location in Orlando, Park Ave CDs has been a fixture in Central Florida for the past twenty years. Its original location was on its namesake Park Avenue in Winter Park, but its popularity surged with the opening of its current spot across from Rollins College and the recent addition of another store on the campus of the University of Central Florida. Yet it was really the music dork knowledge of hard-to-find releases that set this place apart from the rest. Not to mention that Park Avenue single-handedly supports the hell out of local music in this town, selling tickets for many shows at the smaller venues in Orlando and sending out newsletters to loyal customers. Their in-store signings and live performances have brought in Ted Leo, Guided by Voices, and Frank Black among others.

### Retro Records, 59 N. Bumby Ave.

With a section containing close to thirty copies of the Beatles' *White Album*, Retro Records in Orlando lives up to its name, complete with the stereotypical snobs walking the aisles taking notes on new additions to the store. With its dilapidated strip mall location, Retro Records might get by unnoticed initially. Once inside you'll be hard pressed not to return again and again. The usual kitsch memorabilia covers the walls but when it comes to music, the store specializes in vinyl only: If your taste requires that a Britney Spears CD be in your collection, you better head over to Best Buy—enough said.

### Drop Shop, 2422 E. Robinson St., www.dropshop.com

Any DJ around town knows the Drop Shop is the place to go to get the spin on what's new in the scene. House, breaks, trance, and progressive: The store is covered wall to wall in vinyl. Turntables are available throughout the store to test out along with mixers and replacement parts. The Drop Shop also has an in-house DJ booth, and you can schedule an appointment to use the store's soundproof DJ mixing lab to get your demo together.

### Virgin Megastore, Downtown Disney, West Side, 1494 Buena Vista Dr., Lake Buena Vista, www.virginmega.com

Say you're leaving a show at the House of Blues in Downtown Disney and that opening act blew you away. You only need to walk across the courtyard to buy the artists' CD at the Orlando outlet of the Virgin MegaStore. They aren't kidding when they say megastore— with listening rooms dedicated to Latin, jazz, classical, and more, the music behemoth also features more than 300 listening stations and a children's area. The store also teams up with its neighbor House of Blues for autograph sessions in conjunction with concerts taking place and hosts live in-house performances as well.

## RADIO STATIONS:

**WPRK 91.5 FM,**
**www.rollins.edu/wprk**

Touting "the best in basement radio," the Rollins College radio station is also the only game in town. Mainly consisting of volunteer DJs from the school, WPRK plays everything from punk to reggae to local acts.

**WTKS 104.1 FM (Real Radio 104.1),**
**www.wtks.com**

Giving the airwaves to talk radio hosts throughout the week, this station shines during its "Real Music Weekends" where you can hear a variety of alternative and underground artists from 2 P.M. Saturday through the following Sunday.

## MISCELLANEOUS EVENTS:

**Florida Music Festival & Conference**

For four days every May, downtown Orlando becomes a sea of music industry reps, fans, and bands hoping to get signed. *aXis Magazine* produces and programs the festival which began in 2001, in hopes of promoting many of the talented unsigned acts across the nation. But, with more than fifteen live stages set up around town and five electronic venues, it's not all business.

*—Kelly Fitzpatrick*

# Philadelphia, PA

## DREXEL UNIVERSITY
3141 Chestnut St.
Philadelphia, PA 19104
www.drexel.edu

**D**rexel University in Philadelphia is home to one of the most inventive music industry programs around. Drexel's College of Media Arts and Design offers a variety of programs for the artistically inclined student in disciplines ranging from film and video to graphic design, dramatic writing to photography. Meshed in with all those creative disciplines is the music industry program, which requires its students to take courses in both the business and the technology side of the industry. Music industry students declare a specialization in either music business and law, or music technology and production. But even non-music industry students are able to dabble in the courses offered by this institution, which cover topics of wide interest like rock music and popular culture. Examples of the courses offered by the music industry program include Sound Reinforcement and Enhancement, Modern Arranging Techniques, Songwriting, American Popular Music, The Recording Industry, and The Publishing Industry among others. Drexel is also home to MAD Dragon Records (www.maddragonrecords.com) one of the only student-run record labels in the country.

## UNIVERSITY OF THE ARTS
320 South Broad St.
Philadelphia, PA 19102
www.uarts.edu

**T**he University of the Arts is known for bringing explicitly creative people together under one roof. The university prides itself on integrating the artistic interests of dancers, designers, screenwriter, and musicians and encouraging its students to influence each other's work. The music program at the University of the Arts focuses on the skills needed to pursue a hands-on musical career in fields such as composing, arranging, music education, and performance. Students may choose from one of three official majors: instrumental performance, vocal performance, and composition, and all of these majors emphasize jazz and contemporary music as the focus of study. Interesting courses available at the University of the Arts music program include Business of Music, Careers in Music, Vocal Styles and Diction, all of which are supplemented by courses like Introduction to Modernism, and First-Year Writing.

Music education students can combine their performance or composition major program with their music education studies, which allows students to graduate with a music education minor. Those students who are certain they want to teach music in K-12 schools pursue the minor while simultaneously enrolling for an additional year beyond completion of the requirements for the bachelor of arts degree, and graduate with a master of arts in teaching with an emphasis on music.

# THE CURTIS INSTITUTE OF MUSIC
1726 Locust St.
Philadelphia, PA 19103
www.curtis.edu

The Curtis Institute of Music is emblematic of Philadelphia's old-world style. Founded in 1924 with the intention of providing young gifted classical musicians with the chance to train for performance careers on the highest level, the Curtis Institute—legendary conductor Leonard Bernstein's alma mater—has been serving this mission for the last eighty-plus years. Having firmly established its position as one of the most prestigious conservatories in the world, the school now focuses on keeping its reputation intact by limiting enrollment to a mere 180 students, and by maintaining one-on-one study between Curtis students and today's leading musicians (many of whom are principle players in the world-renowned Philadelphia Orchestra.) And get this, all Curtis students, once accepted, receive full-tuition, merit-based scholarships; a fact which in part explains why Curtis students travel from nineteen different countries to study here.

Undergraduate Curtis Institute students pursue a diploma or a bachelor of music degree, and vocal students have the additional option of seeking a master of music degree or professional studies certificate. The Curtis Institute curriculum centers on loads and loads of performance time. In addition to private instruction, students participate in coursework including diction coaching for singers, or chamber music sessions for instrumentalists, plus master classes that are frequently taught by distinguished visiting artists. Curtis Institute students are also expected to take required liberal arts courses to ensure that their education is well rounded, and those who have completed their liberal arts requirements may enroll (at no extra cost) at the University of Pennsylvania for any additional liberal arts related courses not offered at the institute.

# UNIVERSITY OF PENNSYLVANIA
201 South 34th St.
Philadelphia, PA 19104
www.upenn.edu

The University of Pennsylvania has the reputation of being the least self-conscious of all Ivy League schools. Penn's music program, while not one of its strongest departments (try English, history, anthropology, and business) is very much in keeping with the university's overall adherence to practicality. Students who major in music can declare as late as the spring of their junior year—technically the program can be completed in two rigorous years. However, to work at a more moderate pace, students should get started during their freshman or sophomore years.

Required courses include Introduction to Western Music, Introduction to the Musical Life of America, and Introduction to Global Music, among others. Compelling electives range from Psychology of Music, Studies in African American Music, Music Cultures in Southeast Asia, Listening to Literature, Pop Music in Theory and Practice, to Anthropology of Music, among others. All majors are required to complete at least four semesters as participants in one of Penn's performing groups, which include Ancient Voices, Madrigal Singers, and the University Orchestra. All Penn students, regardless of major are invited to audition for these groups.

# TEMPLE UNIVERSITY
Esther Boyer College of Music and Dance
Philadelphia, PA 19122
www.temple.edu

The Boyer College music program at Temple University aims to offer sophisticated professional training within the "context of a modern research university." Boyer College does not ignore the potential music interests of non-music majors; in fact, the school considers itself duty-bound not only to train adept performers, but also to promote a culture of good listenership by getting general university students to study music as well. The Boyer College Music Program is broken down into several different areas of emphasis, which include but are not limited to classical guitar performance, music technology, composition, and music history, music education, and music therapy. As a classical guitar student, you might take anything from choral ensemble, to intellectual heritage. A music history major would enroll in Music in History or Basic Conducting. The school also offers a bachelor of science degree in music, which is designed to prepare students for developing aspects of the music industry such as publishing, communications, and computer software.

## *VENUES:*

### The Khyber Pass, 56 South Second St.,
### www.thekhyber.com

This magnificent hole-in-the-wall is famous for catching soon-to-be huge bands just before they've started attracting celebrity fans and cultivating drug habits. The club, which has excellent sound for such a diminutive room, features a chintzy dinette set on the makeshift stage during the day. When the bands show up for load-in, the table and chairs are moved, the French doors that double as the club's back wall are opened, and the band literally hoists their gear in from the street to the stage. So, if you want to catch today's version of the Strokes or Black Rebel Motorcycle Club struggling with their drum kit on the street, or you want to buy them a beer after the show, the Khyber is the place to do it.

### The Trocadero, 1003 Arch St., 21,
### www.thetroc.com

"The Troc," as the kids call it, is the most Philadelphian of all Philly's venues because it's a gloriously decrepit kooky spot that also happens to be listed in the National Register of Historic Places. The building became the Trocadero Theater in the early part of the twentieth century, and enjoyed lives as a movie house, a nightclub, and a burlesque club before being restored in the late Seventies and embracing its current incarnation as a music venue. The theater hosts the same kinds of acts as its similarly-sized (1,200 person capacity) but slightly more corporate cousin the TLA, but Troc shows tend to be a little less organized, the bouncers a little scrawnier, the drinks a little stiffer and a little cheaper. The bands that play here run the gamut of goth, indie, punk, and rock acts, and have included the Doves, Stephen Malkmus and the Jicks, the White Stripes, and Motorhead. Another great feature of the Troc is "Movie Mondays," where the three-dollar cost of admission gets you into the balcony section and goes toward the price of your first cocktail or snack. Play pool in the back, then claim a space on the red-carpeted floor of the balcony and watch movies like *Say Anything*, *A Clockwork Orange*, and the *Creature from the Black Lagoon* on the Troc's giant projector screen.

### The Theater of the Living Arts, 334 South St.,
### www.theateroflivingarts.net

The Theater of the Living Arts started out in the early Sixties as the primary performance space for an experimental theater group that included Danny DeVito, Judd Hirsch, and Sally Kirkland among others. South Street in Philadelphia was then a hotbed of countercultural creativity, but eventually the performers moved on, and the theater was converted into a repertory art movie house. TLA enterprises grew (they now operate several artsy video stores in Philly and New York, plus a film distribution company and an online store) and in the theater began its life as one of the premier places to see bands in Philadelphia. This mid-sized venue still holds true to its liberal roots by hosting alternative rock, indie, punk and emo bands such as Dashboard Confessional, the Strokes, From Autumn to Ashes and the Arcade Fire.

### First Unitarian Church, 2125 Chestnut St., www.R5productions.com

Punk bands in a church basement? No, seriously. The Unitarians are an open-minded lot, so there's no need to repent after seeing a sinfully sweaty rock show downstairs from this house of worship. Unlikely a spot as it is, the First Unitarian Church often has the best shows that roll through Philly, and for relatively cheap. In the past few years, Bright Eyes, Cursive, and the Yeah Yeah Yeahs have all taken the stage in the spacious wood-paneled rec room. The space is actually rented by R5 Productions, a production company run by Philadelphia-based entrepreneur Sean Agnew. R5 is responsible for many DIY shows in the Philadelphia area, which take place in essentially any space available—from warehouses and clubs, to universities and, well, churches. Door prices are kept low and many of the annoyances of corporate shows, like expensive bottled water and surly bouncers, are absent. R5 (along with Philly's kingpin of cool, DJ/promoter Dave Pianka) is also behind Philly's number one hipster drink-, dance- and make-out fest, known as **Making Time**, which happens every so often (read: roughly monthly) when a really great, impossibly cool band (read: Franz Ferdinand or the Rapture) comes through town.

### North Star Bar, 2639 Poplar St., www.northstarbar.com

This smallish laidback spot in leafy North Philadelphia near Fairmount Park is a great spot to see lower-tier indie rock bands such as Clinic, the Stills and Spoon. The best North Star Bar night involves getting to the show on the early side and snagging a spot at the cozy upstairs balcony where you can see every move the band makes without being jostled in the front row.

### The Electric Factory, 421 North 7th St., www.electricfactory.com

With its freestanding brick walls, and frosted, multi-paned windows, the Electric Factory resembles a prison and, sadly, it doesn't get much better inside. The Electric Factory, and Electric Factory Concerts represent the Clear Channel venues in Philly. Even the beloved TLA is a part of this group! (A complete list of Electric Factory Concerts' venues, including the Liacouras Center at Temple

University and some rock-friendly venues in Atlantic City, is available on the Electric Factory website.) Once a band is into its second album (Interpol) or has a huge radio hit (Scissor Sisters) they start playing this 3,000 capacity spot in Philly's Northern Liberties neighborhood. The sound at the Electric Factory is passable, but compared to the baroque feel of many Philadelphia venues, the Factory seems stiff and corporate. But if you like rock & roll and live in Philadelphia, now and again you are going to find yourself here.

### The Tower Theater, S 69th St & Ludlow St., Upper Darby

The coolest venue in Philly is so far away from downtown that it's hard to believe you're still in Philly. This seventy-plus-year-old club is located waaaaay into West Philly on the 69th Street strip that, in its heyday, was the center of the city's swinging vaudeville, blues, and jazz scenes. This decadent venue, with its red velvet seats and marble staircases, still makes you feel like you're seeing Billie Holiday instead of Ashlee Simpson. David Bowie famously played four nights at the Tower on his Ziggy Stardust World Tour in 1973, and the list of stars drawn to this spot since is staggering: Jill Scott, the Strokes, Ryan Adams, Bob Dylan, Sigur Ros, Morrissey, Mötley Crü, and Elvis Costello, among many others, have performed here. The Tower also hosts non-musical guest such as comedians Margaret Cho, Ellen Degeneres, and Dave Chappelle. The best thing about the Tower, other than its rich history and killer performers, is the fact that the best way to get there from downtown Philly is on the mostly elevated Market-Frankford Line subway train, which lets you enjoy the scenic view of Philly's skyline.

### Tweeter Center, 1 Harbor Blvd, Camden, NJ
### www.tweetercenter.com/philadelphia

The Tweeter Center is technically in New Jersey, on the east side of the Delaware River, clearly visible from Philly's Old City neighborhood. The venue includes a huge amphitheater, put to use primarily during the sticky summer months, and features a great sound system for an outdoor spot, a huge, well-groomed lawn, and several giant video screens. Let's not kid ourselves: It's a run-of-the-mill corporate amphitheater. But this is where artists cooler than that description implies—John Mayer, the Pixies, Santana—take the stage to play for audiences of up to 25,000. During the fall and winter, the Tweeter Center converts to an enclosed, climate-controlled venue with a smaller, 1,600-person capacity.

## RECORD STORES:

### Spaceboy Music, 409 South St.

This tiny record store on Philly's South Street has new CDs on its ground floor and an impressive selection of vinyl and used CDs upstairs. The shop specializes in indie rock, dance music, and anything imported, rare, officially unreleased, or otherwise unavailable. Another great feature is the 99-cent bin, in which you can always find something you forgot existed but suddenly must have. Spaceboy is in with the Philadelphia rock & roll scenesters and as evidence of this, fans can come here to buy tickets to shows put on by R5 Productions.

### AKA Music, 7 North Second St.

AKA has the most expansive collection of any independent record store in Philadelphia, plus cheaper prices than the corporate monoliths. Located in the swanky Old City neighborhood, the store is sleek, its selection highly browsable, and its stock comprehensive enough to include Boards of Canada, James Brown, Run DMC and David Bowie. Listening stations in the back always feature interesting releases from a variety of genres, and up front, placed temptingly close to the register, is a selection of the staff's best new releases picks.

### Tower Records, Avenue of the Arts, 100 S Broad St, www.towerrecords.com

If you are feeling nostalgic for your suburban roots, Tower Records is the best place to indulge that sensation. Racks and racks of well-organized CDs plus the requisite vinyl and singles sections characterize the basic organization at both of Philly's Tower outlets. The best part about Tower Records is its extensive listening stations: If you're not sure you want to buy the whole album by some band whose single you like, Tower is bound to have it set up for you to fully check out. The Tower on South Street is something of a landmark and has been known to host artist signings, and stay open late the night before a major release, allowing fans to line up and buy their eagerly anticipated record the absolute minute it comes out.

**Spruce Street Records & Tapes, 4044 Spruce St.**

This is the one independent music source available on campus for Penn's students. The owner is usually around, and is very knowledgeable and eager to chat you up about whatever music you're into. If you want to order something weird, this is a good place to go. Also, the used collection here is so big it almost eclipses the new stuff. So if you have a bunch of old CDs to unload and you want to get something in return, this is the spot for you.

**Penn Bookstore, 3601 Walnut St./ Barnes and Noble Booksellers, 1805 Walnut St.,**
**www.barnesandnoble.com**

The Penn Bookstore is Barnes and Noble disguised as a college bookstore, and as such it's got the extensive offerings and prices you'd expect from a corporate outlet. Still, the Penn Bookstore and the Rittenhouse Square Barnes and Noble are two of the only places in town where you can get your hands on British music magazines like *Uncut* and *Mojo*, plus the music store upstairs will order anything you want. (You can also find rare and imported magazines of all sorts down the block from the Penn Bookstore at the European newsstand Avril 50, 3406 Sansom Street.) If you are a Penn student you'll learn all about the virtues of the Penn Card, which allows you to charge whatever you want from the bookstore to you school account. Be careful, students have had to take out extra loans to pay for all the CDs they ordered here.

**Repo Records, 538 South St.,**
**www.reporecords.com**

Another of the South Street record store elite, Repo Records specializes in punk and indie rock rarities and b-sides. Find the *No Thanks* punk rock box set, early Hives singles on Swedish label Burning Heart, and spend hours blissfully perusing the used vinyl and CDs. A big plus at Repo is that the staff is usually knowledgeable but not snotty, making the shopping experience a non-ego-crushing affair.

*—Elizabeth Goodman*

# Portland, OR

## LEWIS AND CLARK UNIVERSITY
0615 SW Palatine Hill Rd.
Portland, Oregon 97219
www.lclark.edu

L ewis and Clark's Department of Music prides itself on supporting a curriculum that caters both to serious music students and those looking to have fun with an interesting class or two. Music majors at Lewis and Clark study musicianship, literature, and theory, and coursework is supplemented by weekly lessons in the student's particular performance area. Majors are, of course, invited to specialize in the usual band or orchestral instrument but Lewis and Clark also offers lessons in the harpsichord, organ, and instruments from India, Japan, and Java. In keeping with this world-music oriented theme the college owns one of the only Javanese gamelans available in the entire United States.

Lower-level music courses such as Sound and Sense: Understanding Music, and Music Fundamentals focus on topics that might be interesting to anyone from a child prodigy violinist, to the hardcore Marilyn Manson fan who failed band in elementary school. The school also offers training in arts management, allowing music majors who wish to get into the recording industry to take business courses and pursue internships at labels, management companies and the like.

Music majors are also required to study conducting, instrumentation, and world music and work closely with a faculty advisor on a senior project of their own design during their final year. The very well equipped Evans Music Center houses most of the practice rooms, faculty offices, studios, and classrooms for the department. Included in the building's facilities is an electronic music studio that allows students to record whatever sonic experiments they undertake.

Lewis and Clark music majors have gone onto to such distinguished positions as violinist in the Oregon Symphony, arranger and composer for television and motion pictures, and president of Polygram Classics and Jazz. Recent guest artists at the school include sitarist Ravi

Shankar and jazz guitarist John Scofield, among other distinguished performers.

## REED COLLEGE
3203 Southeast Woodstock Blvd.
Portland, OR 97202-8199
web.reed.edu

**R**eed College is one of the most serious and intellectually ambitious colleges in the country. The campus is situated right outside of Portland on a hundred-acre spread complete with rolling hills, salmon-filled creeks, and 125 different species of trees. Students come to school here because they want to embrace the work ethic found at Ivy League paragons like Harvard or Yale, but seek a less traditional context in which to do so. All students, after declaring a major, must pass a qualifying exam administered by the major department at the end of the junior year. After passing this exam, students are able to move on to their senior thesis—a year-long investigation into a topic intimately related to the student's major.

The good news for prospective students a little overwhelmed by Reed's oh-so-serious curriculum is that students do not receive grades unless they request them. Professors submit conventional grades to the school's registrar, but as long as the student's performance is considered to be above C level they receive only written evaluations, though their performance is reviewed six times a year, rather than the conventional two times a year.

Music is not one of Reed's strongest programs (those would be biology, chemistry, psychology, and English, to name a few) but the department is respectable, and considering the school's proximity to Portland (five miles from the center of the city) plus its creative and eclectic student body, you're guaranteed at least a few fellow music geeks as classmates. Musically inclined Reed students will find many resources waiting for them, including a well-equipped media center that functions as a music listening room and houses a collection of audio recordings, music scores, and video tapes, plus individual student listening and viewing stations.

# VENUES:

### Ash Street, 225 SW Ash St.,
### www.ashstreetsaloon.com

Portland's Old Town neighborhood, a seedy collection of nineteenth-century buildings just north of downtown, has long been the epicenter of the city's rock scene. That's changing, as tube-top-dominated meat markets take over Old Town and the rock action moves closer to the hip 'hoods east of the Willamette River. (Portland's east side/west side divide is way too petty to get into here—you'll catch on.) But a couple of places are keeping it real in the city's oldest district. Ash Street, a cozy bar with an unpretentious hard-rocker vibe, shares a hopping block with Berbati's Pan and the infamous Voodoo Donuts (open pretty much around the clock for all your fried dough and quirky-scene needs). Loud, metal-tinged local acts dominate, but the club makes frequent forays into underground hip-hop.

### Berbati's Pan, 231 SW Ankeny St.,
### www.berbatis.com

Berbati's Pan is a 500-capacity stronghold in an ancient brick building, roughly horseshoe-shaped and Siamese twin to a Greek restaurant of the same name. The club juggles a diverse array of local, regional and touring talent, moving from the ultra-grimy punk-gothic-blues of Federation X one night to the real-live blues of Bo Diddley the next. For up-and-coming national and international acts, this is often the last stop before graduating to truly big venues; Berbati's gave Portlanders their last intimate looks at the White Stripes, Rufus Wainwright, and Franz Ferdinand. Conversely, this is where local bands often have their first flirtation with real rock glory. The atmosphere is fittingly dark and (for casual Portland, anyway), glamour-tinged—the imposing carved mahogany bar fits well with Old Town's decayed Victorian feel, while the ever-present conversational buzz sometimes overwhelms anything remotely shoegazey on stage. If somehow this fails to satisfy your social itch, check out the atmospheric underground bar at Shanghai Tunnel just down Ankeny Street's narrow alleyway.

### Bossanova, 722 E Burnside,
### www.bossanovapdx.com

This classic refurbished 1920s ballroom is part of an emerging nexus of cool on a once-desolate stretch of Burnside, Portland's main east-west drag. With its upstairs lounge pool hall overlooking a cavernous stage and dance floor, the bossa nova drips speakeasy-esque elegance, yet still manages to throw all-ages shows in a state bedeviled by uptight liquor regulators. Booking is an extremely mixed bag—Gogol Bordello and Kottonmouth Kings both played here in the space of a couple months, and tango and salsa classes take over a couple of nights a week.

### Crystal Ballroom, 1332 W Burnside, www.danceonair.com

Love them or hate them (local opinion is mixed), it's virtually impossible to live in Portland without spending time in the domain of the McMenamin Brothers. These craft-brewing hippies-gone-capitalist have made a cottage industry of taking over distressed old buildings and retrofitting them into taverns, theaters, and venues in a signature style that mixes classic Americana with a dippy Grateful Dead aesthetic. The Crystal Ballroom is the music flagship of the McM's vast chain, and though Portland showgoers live to complain about its echoey sound, it's become an essential part of the scene. With a capacity of about 1,500 and four bars, this century-old wedding cake of a building snags most touring talent. Northwest faves like Modest Mouse and Built to Spill have taken to selling out four or five consecutive nights at the Crystal, but it's hardly indie-exclusive: Hip-hop, nu-metal, big-time punk bands, alt-country—hell, maybe even Merle Haggard—are all pretty much guaranteed to grace the Crystal's stage in a given year.

### Dante's, 1 SW 3rd Ave., www.danteslive.com

This is the place your mother warned you about—or, at least, it wants you to think so. The décor keynotes here are midnight black and hellfire red; an always-burning gas fireplace bolted to a table near the door gives the place the same lighting scheme as the average Neolithic cave. The bar itself glows neon red. There's velvet-a-plenty, a "lingerie modeling" joint upstairs, and dancers from the Portland-based alt. softcore site SuicideGirls.com put on a "sinful circus of debauchery" every Sunday night. Aside from all the nocturnal lustiness, Dante's books a pretty straightforward mix of local rock acts and smaller touring bands.

### Douglas Fir Lounge, 830 E Burnside

Opened in the fall of 2004, this place just a few blocks east of the Bossanova Ballroom threatens to raise the stakes in Portland's nightlife arms race in a big way. Upstairs, a smashing high-design bar and restaurant transfuses Fifties modernism into a woody lumberjack's lounge—and draws one of Portland's most mixed crowds of scenesters, slumming suburbanites and people who dress like (and may actually be) LA refugees. Downstairs, a converted parking garage hosts blue-chippers like the French Kicks, the reunited Helmet, and Royal Trux, as well as local big guns like the Thermals and Decemberists.

### Holocene, 1001 SE Morrison St.

This ultra-cool, spare warehouse space is cut from a slightly different cloth than Portland's rough-'round-the-edges rock venues, and plays to slightly swanker party impulses. The food is great, the cocktails are top shelf, the crowd is pretty, the music leans heavily to the electronic and experimental—Bollywood beats, avant jazz, and deep house, among many other flavors, grace the wide-roaming sonic menu. Renowned for its chilled-out Sunday brunch and a luxe lesbian club night called Tart, Holocene could be the sleekest club in town.

### Loveland, 320 SE 2nd Ave.,
### www.themeowmeow.com

It would take a bastard with a heart of flint not to love Meow Meow, a club that's defied the short lifespan that afflicts the species. After five years and one change of location, the ex-warehouse in a mostly ungentrified industrial district just east of the river recently expanded, adding a restaurant and an intimate mini-stage called Loveland. Higher profile bands like the Explosion and Hot Hot Heat lace a line-up heavily weighted with local high school hopefuls and the collegiate indie-poppers Portland grows in droves.

### Nocturnal, 1800 E Burnside,
### www.nocturnalpdx.com

All-ages upstairs, full-service bar downstairs—what's not to love? Nocturnal's spic'n'span wood dancefloor is always polished to a high gloss; its basement lounge is as cozy as a suburban den. All this combines with the earnest cheeriness of everyone who works here and decidedly twee leanings (yoga class? Knitting night?) to create the sense that rock & roll is good clean fun. With its art shows, community events, classes and, oh yeah, A-grade rock (the K Records crowd from nearby Olympia considers this a virtual home away from home), Nocturnal takes its mission as an all-purpose Portland gathering place seriously.

### Sabala's at Mount Tabor, 4811 SE Hawthorne Blvd., www.sabalasmttabor.com

This converted movie palace at the base of Mount Tabor, a pint-sized extinct volcano in the middle of the east side, was a hippie haven for years. That changed last year, when a former booking agent for Austin's legendary club Emo's took the place over. Now it's the adopted home of Portland's balls-out, tattoo-heavy hard rock and punk scene. The occasional weirdo variety act—an over-the-top pro wrestling parody, a live talk show conducted by a masked freak—mixes up the sonic mayhem. This place is in the middle of a little cluster of bars known affectionately as the Stumbling Zone.

## RECORD STORES:

### Everyday Music, 1931 NE Sandy Blvd. and 1313 W Burnside

This mini-chain's no-frills CD emporia are nothing special—just fluorescent lights, semi-surly employees and scads of music, new and used. But they buy just about everything (should those student loans run dry) and they're open, like they say, every day.

### Jackpot! Records, 203 SW 9th Ave. and 3736 SE Hawthorne Blvd. www.jackpotrecords.com

This record store is so nice, they opened it twice. Jackpot!, a luscious smorgasbord of new and vintage vinyl, CDs, DVDs, and magazines catering to every genre under God's blue sky, boasts two killer locations. Downtown, it shares a block with indie-culture staples Reading Frenzy and CounterMedia; meanwhile, the original Jackpot! stakes its claim in the east side's bustling Hawthorne District. A deep, nondenominational love for music powers everything Jackpot! does—

its employees can steer you toward unknown avant-Sixties-jazz-psych-funk as easily as they can fill you in on the new Bright Eyes release.

**Mississippi Records and Repair, 4007 N Mississippi Ave.**

Vinyl junkie, welcome to heaven. This tiny, well-run shop on one of north Portland's coolest streets is a vision out of those *High Fidelity* dudes' fever dreams. Rock, punk, jazz, blues, classical, folk, country… everything up to and including Balkan Gypsy balladry finds its way into Mississippi's neatly organized stacks. You'll find the stray, wallet-cleansing collector's item, but most slabs are priced well within reach of, say, you. Bonus round: the bulletin board is a good place to find out about under-publicized shows at houses and small clubs; the always-hopping Fresh Pot coffee shop next door slings some of the finest java in a coffee-obsessed city.

**Music Millennium, 801 NW 23rd Ave., 3158 E Burnside, www.musicmillenium.com**

The granddaddy of Portland record stores (it claims to be the oldest operating record store in the Northwest), Music Mill's pair of locations offer just about everything in their deep CD racks. The kind of place where you can score a Christmas present for your mom, plus one for yourself, and not feel guilty about funneling money into a big-box monstrosity.

**Powell's City of Books, 1005 W Burnside, www.powells.com**

No inventory of Portland's charms would be complete without a mention of Powell's—the city's cultural Ark, perhaps the largest bookstore in the world. Smack in the middle of downtown, this titanic three-story, nine-room maze contains a literally incomprehensible trove of books. Its sections on music, the entertainment industry, and pop culture are, like just about everything else, large and lovingly tended.

## RADIO STATIONS:

One drawback to not having a major university: Portland radio sucks. The two true bright spots in the wasteland are **KBOO** (90.7 FM), a venerable collective-run station steeped politics, and **KPSU** (1450 AM), Portland State's excellent student-run station. Both are hyper-eclectic, veering from ethnic hours (KBOO broadcasts in Italian, Persian, and Yiddish on the weekends) to bristling punk to reggae and ska to meandering freeform.

—*Zach Dundas*

# Providence, RI

## BROWN UNIVERSITY
1 Young Orchard Ave.
Box 1924
Providence, RI 02912
www.brown.edu

**B**rown University is known for being the artsy ivy—filled with crunchy smart people obsessed with political correctness and recycling. This perspective on Brown, while very limited, is neither entirely false nor as negative as you might think, and the Department of Music perfectly showcases why. The Brown University Department of Music offers its students a general music degree with supplemental concentrations available in theory and composition, history, ethnomusicology, and computer music and multimedia. The study of ethnomusicology is one of this program's most interesting offerings. Students examine the role music plays in the identity of different cultures by studying basics like theory and the history of Western music, plus courses in seemingly unrelated fields like cultural anthropology. The computer music and multimedia concentration focuses on "the technical, aesthetic, and cultural issues surrounding music made by electronic means" which means students take courses in everything from music composition and computer programming to sound synthesis and cultural studies. Students seeking a traditional approach to the study of music can concentrate in music theory and composition at Brown, but with courses like Ghanaian Drumming, Orientalism and Primitivism in Western Music, and Music and Modern Life available, the program is really designed for those interested in a serious, truly interdisciplinary approach to studying music.

# RHODE ISLAND SCHOOL OF DESIGN

Two College St.
Providence, RI 02903
www.risd.edu

**L**et's be clear about this: RISD does not have a music department but it still totally belongs in this book. Here's why: This quirky Providence fine arts school has a reputation as a safe haven for the truly serious burgeoning artist, and as such, draws some of the most creative students in the country to its campus. RISD kids study everything from glass blowing to jewelry design and metalsmithing, and though there is no academic music program at RISD, history shows this hasn't been much of an impediment for bands like Les Savy Fav, the Black Dice, and the Talking Heads, all of which formed during their time at RISD. In addition to this impressive list of rock-related alumni, RISD can also claim fashion designer Nicole Miller and film director Gus Van Sant as alumni, further presenting the college as the kind of place cool people just flock too, regardless of discipline.

## *VENUES:*

### Safari Lounge, 103 Eddy St.

Dirty, tiny, and draped with all sorts of cheetah tapestries, the Safari is a long-standing, downtown club that is hanging onto economic solvency by the skin of its teeth. Hopefully it will keep its doors open and continue to bring live shows by Providence heroes like Lightning Bolt, Arab on Radar and the Chinese Stars. There's a bar with cheap pitchers, the requisite pool table and a jukebox—even though the venue's hardly big enough for the stage or the loud sounds emanating from it.

### The Call/The Century Lounge, 15 Elbow St.,
### www.thecallnightclub.com

Promoter Rich Lupo, owner of the now defunct club Lupo's Heartbreak Hotel, books smaller artists like the Stills, Saul Williams, and Ratatat at the Call for an 18+ crowd of indie kids. The bar wraps around the entire room and the stage is set in a sort of pit so that everybody in the venue can see artists perform without having to crowd up front. The floor is a lovely blond wood a la the middle school gym, and the windows have grates that break the light from outside into awesome geometric shadows. Probably one of the chillest venues in Providence, with the most appeal for Brown and RISD kids.

### The Living Room, Rathbone St.

When it opened, the Living Room had plush couches and chairs lining the walls and looked more like the place you'd come home to after hitting the bars. But the most recent incarnation of this Providence mainstay is as no-frills as a live music venue gets. With an alleged capacity of about 1,000, you'll get mighty sweaty at a show here, but you won't be sweating the four-dollar cover charge.

### AS220, Empire St.,
### www.as220.org

An art space, gallery, café, non-profit and music venue, AS220 showcases local electro-sleaze favorites Mahi Mahi and experimental electronic pioneers such as the Lucky Dragons. Some nights at AS220, a Sun Ra Arkestra concert will screen before Brown professors get on stage to play experimental jazz. Other events at the space include openings in the various galleries complete with box wine and finger food. The space looks as multi-use as it acts. There are semi-permanent walls, chairs and tables near the bar (which serves beer and coffee) as well as outside.

### Club Hell, 73 Richmond St.

Primarily a goth club, Hell attracts the most diverse crowds imaginable. Goth nights bring in a punky twentysomething crowd while typical club nights on the weekend attract the Johnson & Wales set, which tends to be decked in halters and Abercrombie and listens to chart hip-hop and R&B. On Tuesdays, hipsters from RISD and Brown show up along with a bunch of wild high school kids with fake I.D.s looking to party to Eighties New Wave classics from artists such as Human League, Gary Numan, the Smiths, and Echo and the Bunnymen. Though all but an underground spot, Hell is a great party most nights with gothic gargoyles, blood red velvet and torches set near the dangerously raised dance floor. When you get tired, hit one of the two bars or just sack out on a velvet armchair in the chill-out area, and when you get hungry pop outside to grab a real Rhode Island weiner or cheese fries from Spike's Hot Dogs.

### Diesel, 79 Washington St.

One of the largest clubs in Providence, Diesel—formerly The Strand—is housed in an old theater complete with a gorgeous balcony and enormous chandelier. On show nights, bands are booked by Rich Lupo, and include national artists as diverse as Erykah Badu, Ani Difranco, the Slip and the Faint. There is gay night and a beach-themed night, but most are typical club nights featuring R&B, trance and hip-hop deejays. Rock shows on the weekends end early to make way for the dancing. Death Cab for Cutie singer Ben Gibbard lamented the fact that the crowd for his band's show was drunk at 7:00 P.M., but having an early show means more weekend bang for one's buck.

### Art Bar 171, Chestnut St.

Art Bar is a trendy nightclub tucked away in the jewelry district. They have a strict dress code (black everything) and pride themselves on their serious demeanor. The crowd is a late-twenties professional set. The coolest thing about Art Bar is the indoor skate park upstairs, but that's hardly part of the club atmosphere.

### The Green Room at Snookers, 145 Clifford St.

The Green Room is a small bar inside a fabulous pool hall renowned for its reggae- and dancehall-themed parties on Wednesdays, as well as for showcasing up-and-coming artists like the Unicorns and Chromeo. Green drapes and pulpy, vintage posters on the walls lend an air of mobster depravity to the Green Room, which has a large lounge area as well as a bumping dance floor. The Thursday night indie party is a blast (you're as likely to hear vintage Blur as Khia's "My Neck My Back"), making this club one of the best 18+ hosts in Providence.

## RECORD STORES:

### Newbury Comics in the Providence Place Mall, 74 Providence Pl., www.newburycomics.com

Newbury is the best chain music store in Providence. It carries inexpensive new releases, a wide variety of imports, tons of DVDs, merch from Emily the Strange, Paul Frank, and Ben Sherman and other novelty wares ("Seed of Chucky" action figures anybody?) Housed on the third floor of New England's largest mall, buy your movie tickets at Providence Place Cinema, then shop while you wait for the show.

### Cathartic Records, 5 Steeple St., www.cathartic.anewlanguage.org/store

On the sprawling, railroad-style, third floor of an impossibly old building off the eastern skirt of downtown Providence, this record shop services a ton of vinyl to those interested in punk, hardcore, metal and emo. And since this is Providence we are talking about, there's the requiste stash of noise records by artists on Load and Corleone.

### Armageddon Record Shop, 436 Broadway, www.armageddonshop.com

An outlet for the best local music, 'zines, and screen-prints coming out of the Providence underground. They also have used discs and a selection of new vinyl supplementing a fully stocked hardcore section. Local and unsigned bands frequently sell their demos or screen prints from the front counter, and Armageddon is the hangout-of-choice for Providence's townie scenesters.

### Tom's Tracks, 281 Thayer St.

Tom's has a great selection of old bootleg recordings from Bob Dylan and The Traveling Wilburys that they will lend you for a price, but it also sells concert tickets for shows downtown and carries a large stock of new and used indie music. It's the only remaining record store on Thayer Street, but still competes heartily with the Brown Bookstore, which sells new mainstream releases.

## RADIO STATIONS:

### WBRU 95.5, www.wbru.com

WBRU is a major-league alt-rock radio station run by Brown students. It has a corporate board of directors with student representation, but all of the programming, promotion, and staffing is done by Brunoians. The WBRU news department is a breeding ground for future radio journalists and the rock department exposes even the most inexperienced jocks to the highest radio listenership in southern New England. Their promo department also puts on shows for cheap by artists like Muse, MC Lars, Doves, Ok Go, Lit and the Presidents of the United States of America. A great place to start your radio career, the station also boasts an alumni network plugged into the industry. Jazz and roots shows at night are stellar because they are freeform, and the 360 Black Experience, which airs on Sundays, is the highest-rated program in the region.

**WBSR 88.1,**
**www.brown.edu/Students/WBSR**

The oldest student-run radio station in the country uses The Wheeler School's frequency at night, which means that the Warwick-based signal they share is hard to pick up on or off campus. However, the station's website lets you stream its signal live in Real Player from anywhere on the planet, so you can hear all the local slices (including transistor-radio bike tours), alt-country, and underground hip-hop whenever you damn well please. The best place to hear local music, as well as great creative journalism by Brown students.

## MISCELLANEOUS EVENTS:

### Spring Weekend

Every April you can look forward to Brown's Spring Weekend, which is widely acknowledged as the Ivy League's best party. Past performers during Spring Weekend concerts have included artists on the edge of the mainstream such as Luna, the Donnas, Blackalicious, and Ozomatli, as well as marquee acts from Bob Dylan to Jurassic 5 and the Roots. After the shows, wind down with a drunken performance by the Jabberwocks, Brown's oldest a cappella group, singing their greatest hits, in drag!

### Brown Concert Agency

BCA gets a large chunk of change each year from the university to bring live music to campus and plan major music events such as Spring Weekend. Depending on who's holding the purse strings at any particular time, extra money not spent on the festivities aforementioned goes to shows by artists as diverse as the Virginia Coalition, the Indigo Girls, Dabrye (of Ghostly International), and Black Dice.

### Cobab, or the Coalition of Bands at Brown

Organizes and provides practice space and instruments for musicians in bands at Brown for a small monthly fee

### The Underground

The on-campus bar in the basement of Brown's center for student life, Faunce House, is where many bands at Brown play during the weekends. Held together by green and black two-by-fours, the Underground offers a dart board, cheap beer on tap and a place other than the frat houses to hang out on campus.

—*Micah Salkind*

# St. Louis, MO

## ST. LOUIS UNIVERSITY
221 N. Grand Blvd.
St. Louis, MO 63103
www.slu.edu

**M**usic majors at St. Louis University—a Jesuit school that enrolls approximately 11,000 students at a time—are required to perform an entrance audition for the music faculty before being accepted into the department. But, if you pass the audition, you are not only admitted into the program, but also qualified to receive a one-year scholarship from the Father Guentner Fund, which covers the expenses for private lessons on the instrument of your choice. Once you're in, you can either work towards a bachelor of arts in music with a performance emphasis or with a musical studies emphasis.

Music courses run the gamut, from foundation-level topics such as Approaching the Arts—an introductory, and required music class that seems general in scope but creates a framework for the program—to advanced courses such as Music of Women Composers and Music Literature Seminar, the latter of which teaches formal analysis and criticism. Non-majors, or music majors seeking music-related pop-culture-influenced classes outside the music department, check out the course listings in the Communications Department. There you'll find a class called Analysis of Pop Culture, plus all types of journalism and feature writing classes. For aspiring critics, think about double majoring, or focusing on journalism, especially criticism and opinion-writing courses, in addition to the music curriculum.

# WASHINGTON UNIVERSITY
One Brookings Dr.
St. Louis, MO 63130
www.wustl.edu

**W**ashington University is located just minutes from the Loop, St. Louis' hip commercial district, which is studded with boutiques, vintage shops, arty movie theaters and concert venues. And the school's music program isn't too shabby either: Music majors at Wash U have the benefit of a school that believes in teaching music "as a liberal and fine art, one of humanity's central creative and communicative activities, rather than as an isolated, separate subject." That means musicians-and non-majors interested in dabbling in music history, theory and performance—study in a program ensconced in the university's esteemed liberal arts program. Music majors can pursue either a bachelor of arts in music degree, which focuses on music curriculum, but leaves room for a second major (for those considering a career in the music industry, think about a double major in business, especially since Wash U's business school is considered to be among the best in the country), or a bachelor of music. The bachelor of music is perfect if you imagine your future as a member of an orchestra, music professor, music historian, or music writer.

The school's philosophy stresses a critical approach to the basics of music education. But that doesn't mean stilted coursework. Study composers Philip Glass and John Cage (largely seen as an influence for many rock musicians) in a class called Music From Cage to Glass and Beyond.

Outside of the music department, there are more areas to concentrate on popular culture and pop music's social impact. The interdisciplinary American Cultural Studies program is divinely suited for those who dig all types of media—film, music, literature—and wish to apply it in an academic way. Popular Music in American Culture, for instance, may be your only chance to listen to heavy metal in a college classroom. And Black Power and Black Arts provides a critical look at black culture, including music, and protest in the Sixties and Seventies.

## VENUES:

### Blueberry Hill, 6504 Delmar Blvd., www.blueberryhill.com

Blueberry Hill alternates between being the best bar in St. Louis on weeknights and being the most frightening and Molotov cocktailable tourist trap on weekends. The joint consumes an entire block of the thriving boho heart of St. Louis, the University City Loop, and contains not only a huge booze main floor, but two venues at either corner of the basement: the Elvis Room, where hilarious karaoke action occurs four nights a week, and the Duck Room, an intimate, comfortable space with a capacity of 250 and a pristine sound system that supports both loud rock and gentle, lovin' and/or touchin' music. On this stage, Iron and Wine brought the ladies (and at least one man) to tears. Cat Power electrified this room, the Flaming Lips freaked fellow Midwesterners out with a pre-*Zareeka* boombox experiment, and even Lenny Kravitz once snuck down here for an impromptu gig. Every Friday the Duck Room hosts a party called the Science, where area DJs, breakers and freestylers throw down the best in indie and classic gems. Everyone dances, and the whole shebang is broadcast live on community station KDHX. Nota bene: The club refuses to bend its 21-and-over admission policy and the doorguy is pretty savvy about fake IDs, so don't say we didn't warn you.

### Cicero's, 6691 Delmar Blvd., www.ciceros-stl.com

Cicero's has a storied past. It was here that Uncle Tupelo and the Bottle Rockets helped birth the alt-country movement, and where history recorded the first-ever Wilco performance. Well, not here. That was down the street, before Cicero's was forcibly relocated (Blueberry Hill needed, ahem, more space), and before the club moved from booking Beck, Luna, and Yo La Tengo to bringing all things jam-band-y. At Cicero's the guitar solos sometimes last for days, and the facial grimaces are legendary. The room itself is small, and has a rec-room feel to it. It's just a windowless rectangle, nothing more, with a stage that sits only slightly above the dance floor, a bar on one side and John-John the soundman in back. But although the space itself is bland, the room is acoustically perfect; nothing bounces, nothing clangs, and bongos sound sweet in here.

### The Creepy Crawl, 412 North Tucker Blvd., www.creepycrawl.com

All ages all the time, with a punk 'tude, a knack for wanton rebellion and a concrete floor ripe for head-kickin' and drunken wrasslin', the Creepy Crawl is an aptly named downtown hole-in-the-wall. Over the course of its decade-long life, the club has been punk-proofed: All breakables have already been broken and a chain-link fence separates the youngsters from the drinkers. Slamming is *de rigueur*, of course, as is a little blood; and like most punk clubs, they tend to book about ten bands per night. The Creepy caters to the fast and the furious. Fans of the labels Hopeless, Lookout!, Fueled by Ramen and Asian Man will find their every wish fulfilled. The Fall tried to play here last year, but Mark E. Smith got bored a few songs in, muttered something about his crutches and hobbled away. Add to that a dose of prescience—the White Stripes gigged here mere months before they exploded with *White Blood Cells* and !!! set the room on fire—and you've got an essential St. Louis club.

### Frederick's Music Lounge, 4454 Chippewa St., www.fredericksmusiclounge.com

You'll get a good sense of Frederick's Music Lounge by simply ordering their specialty drink, called Cock Soup: whiskey and chicken broth served in a Campbell's Soup can and garnished with a chicken bone that owner Fred Friction nibbles clean himself. Consider that an honor, because Mr. Friction is a singular St. Louis presence—part Tom Waits, part Mickey Rourke, all Casanova—who inherited this bar from his father, ditched the bumper-pool table and proceeded to transform a corner bar for career alcoholics into a tiny live music venue for budding (21-and-over) drunks. Located in South City, the club occupies a former split-level ranch house; drinking and rocking on the left side, Friction's sleeping quarters on the right. When he took over from his father in the late-90s, Friction still used an intercom/buzzer system just for the hell of it; patrons walked to the front door, rang the bell, he queried you through the speaker ("Yeah, what do you want?" "Uh, umm, could I come in?" "I guess ..."). But the club soon took off, hired a doorman and started booking the twang. Frederick's is the place to go for *No Depression*-style alt-country. At one time or another the entire Bloodshot Records roster has played here. Calexico crammed seven people on this tiny stage, and the Handsome Family crammed two. On Thursdays, they open the mic to ragtimers early in the evening, and to singer-songwriters later. In all, Frederick's is one of the best, most authentically St. Louis, clubs in town.

### Lemp Neighborhood Arts Center, 3301 Lemp Ave., www.lemp-arts.org

The rebels run the Lemp Neighborhood Arts Center, located in the heart of the city's leftist/activist south city neighborhood. It's across the street from the old Lemp Brewery complex, home to the city's late-Nineties tunnel raves, in a semi-struggling but architecturally gorgeous north Cherokee neighborhood. The Arts Center occupies a simple storefront that's been converted into an art and performance space. It holds a hundred lithe indie rockers, and the low budget vibe draws a great mix of musicians and artists. Because of its proximity to homes, the evenings begin early, at 8 P.M., and end at 11 P.M. (midnight on weekends). Although their national booking is sporadic, they tend to strike gold when they mine for it. Among others, Wolf Eyes, the Animal Collective, Black Dice, and the Flying Lutenbachers have graced the stage; local acts reflect this adventuresome, free-floating aesthetic.

### The Pageant, 6161 Delmar Blvd., www.thepageant.com

Owned by Joe Edwards, the same fellow who founded Blueberry Hill, the Pageant is the best concert venue in town—if not the entire Midwest. The vast 1,500-seat club was built from the ground up by a true music geek who decided that what St. Louis needed was a nice room to see Bob Dylan and all those performers who so often passed by St. Louis on their way to Chicago—Elvis Costello, the Magnetic Fields, the Scissor Sisters, Sonic Youth, Dashboard Confessional, Outkast,

Dave Chappelle. Sure enough, he built it, and they came. It's big, it's got a balcony, it serves good beer semi-cheaply, the bouncers are friendly and the atmosphere is transcendent. What's best, there's not a bad seat in the house; even at sold-out shows, the Pageant seems intimate.

**The Way Out Club, 2525 South Jefferson Ave.,**
**www.wayoutclub-stl.com**

The Way Out Club has a great stage, a boss room, kick-ass owners (Bob and Sherri) and a stubbornly rigid rule about booking local bands as opposed to touring ones. But in a room this great, it'd be nice to be able to enjoy the Arcade Fires and Yeah Yeah Yeahs of the world. Occasionally they'll break their own rule and book, say, Le Tigre or Hasil Adkins, but not often. Anyone into rock and/or punk, however, should make a beeline for the Way Out Club—but only if you're twenty-one or over, alas—because you'll find a mass of kindred spirits on any given night.

## RECORD STORES:

**Vintage Vinyl, 6610 Delmar Blvd.,**
**www.vintagevinyl.com**

Located in the former movie theater where a teenaged Michael Stipe used to dress up as Frank N. Furter to act along with Rocky Horror, Vintage Vinyl is the premier music store in St. Louis. (Full disclosure: I worked there for seven years.) The name is a misnomer; although the store still buys and sells vinyl, and stocks a vast quantity of collectible fare, it's mainly a CD store. That said, New Yorkers looking to make a quick buck during their semester break from Washington University would be advised to scour the LP racks before departure; I've seen fifty-dollar disco plates marked at three dollars, and their ninety-nine-cent bin is a joy. But it's their CD selection that draws the masses, mainly because Vintage Vinyl employs the obsessive geeks who can tell you which early Bright Eyes CD to buy, which other Saddle Creek release is just as good, and which Cursive offshoot you simply must own. Got a question about the best Keith Richards tracks on Rolling Stones records? They'll rank them one by one. Ditto Kool Keith. Keith Hudson? Owner Papa Ray is one of the nation's foremost authorities on all things Jamaican. Jazz, blues, great. Techno and house—excellent. Hip-hop? It's the only St. Louis shop still trading in 12-inch vinyl.

**The Record Exchange, 5230 Hampton Ave., 2831 Cherokee St.**

The Record Exchange's two locations are for the diggers, for the bored, desperate, and/or obsessed junkie looking for surprise at the risk of disappointment. For years the two stores, the better being located in a big former library, have paid pennies for every DJ's crate o' crap 12-inch collection, and the proof lies within the vast walls and shelves. Scour for an hour and nothing but subpar Bobby Brown wannabes and a million Benzino and Obie Trice 12-inches. But then, suddenly, heaven in a white cardboard jacket: someone's discarded early Miami bass collection. Yowza. Honestly, nine times out of ten you're going to leave the store empty handed or with something that'll only plug the longing for an hour, but that's part of the fun, isn't it?

**Euclid Records, 601 East Lockwood,**
**www.euclidrecords.com**

Euclid Records is in the inner-ring suburb of Webster Groves, home to excellent liberal arts college Webster University. The shop is almost as good as Vintage Vinyl—especially when it comes to used LPs and CDs. It's a big store whose strength is in jazz and blues, with a respectable folk section (Webster Groves is kinda sorta the "folk" part of town), a strong rock section but little hip-hop and funk. Generally, Euclid pays a bit more for used CDs than Vintage Vinyl, but they're a bit more selective. What's best, though, is that because they're a bit more out-of-the-way, their used CD bins are less picked-over than their competition, so you can usually walk out with something you never thought you'd find cheap.

## RADIO STATIONS:

**KDHX 88.1 FM,**
**www.kdhx.org**

Listener-funded KDHX is one of the jewels of the city, where very good-looking DJs (like myself) and obsessive freaks (ditto) run wild through their collections and broadcast the results to the area's 2.3 million residents. The station, located in the Tower Grove neighborhood of South St. Louis, resides in a converted Victorian two-family. Ethics prohibit me from slobbering too much—I've had a show (um, Sovereign Glory ... um ... Wednesdays, 10 P.M. to midnight) for over a decade. But the proof is in the playlists. "Bob's Scratchy Records" moves from the Buzzcocks to Buck Owens to the 5,6,7,8's seamlessly; "Suffragette City" offers Serge Gainsbourg, Beck, Rufus Wainwright, and the Kinks; "All Soul, No Borders" brings fringe jazz and new improvised music to the forefront; and "Radio Rio," features all Brazilian music.

### KWUR 90.3 FM,
### www.kwur.wustl.edu.

Proudly, ironically, boasting its 10,000 milliwatt signal (a mere ten watts), KWUR is the Washington University student-run station. Unfortunately, unless you've got a good antenna or live within a mile of the Wash. U. campus, you'll only get it while driving around University City and the Central West End. KWUR's no different than any student-run college station: they dole three-hour blocks to students, who do bong-hits, then waltz in and play their favorite records to a few hundred college buddies. The result, of course, is amateur and defiantly unprofessional, but who cares? The station rocks, a place where RJD2 sits comfortably next to AC Newman, who shares bandwidth with Boom Bip, Clouddead and Pinback.

### The Beat, 100.3 FM,
### www.100.3thebeat.com

Evenings at hip-hop station the Beat are pretty great thanks to J-Nicks, "The Young One In Charge," who hosts a prime time mix show. St. Louis is a rap town, after all, and The Beat has led the charge; for better or worse, it broke Nelly, Chingy, J-Kwon and Murphy Lee. Of course, like all rap stations, they grind songs into the ground with repetition; if you missed the new Snoop at 2 o'clock, stick around and you'll hear it at 2:30.

## MISCELLANEOUS EVENTS:

### Twangfest
### www.twangfest.com

It stands to reason that Twangfest, the country's foremost alt. country festival (excluding South-by-Southwest), would be held in St. Louis. Now in its ninth year, the festival, held over the course of four early-summer nights at Blueberry Hill's Duck Room, has drawn the nation's most defiantly Southern-drawled acts, an annual snapshot of a movement that has collected both the torchbearers and the renegades of twang-infused rock, country and western music. Although the festival at this point could pack each night with five luminaries, the Twangfest organizers book both the "big" names and the up-and-comers. Past acts have included Bobby Bare, Jr., the Waco Brothers, the Handsome Family, Tift Merritt, Marah, Kelly Hogan, and the Ass Ponies.

—*Randall Roberts*

# St. Peter/Mankato, MN

**Gustavus Adolphus College** (www.gac.edu), a small Lutheran college situated an hour south of the Twin Cities is dedicated to providing students a broad, liberal arts foundation while also hewing to spiritual values. Apart from a nationally touring choir and orchestra, the college encourages music majors and members of ensembles to participate in community-based activities. For their bachelor of arts in music, students can complete a music theory, history or pedagogy program, a major in performance, or a major in music education. Courses such as Church Music, Liturgies and Hymnology reflect the college's religious affiliations and History of Western Music focuses on all eras, with a concentration in modern music; composers from the twentieth century will be studied and music will be considered in its cultural, social, and historical perspectives.

**St. Olaf College** (www.stolaf.edu) in Northfield, MN, may not have the kind of music program geared at serious rockers, but the school does lay claim to a world-renowned choir, the St. Olaf Choir. If singing hymns is your bag, you could do much worse than to audition for this prestigious group, which travels extensively for performances both in the States and abroad.

St. Peter itself is not a frequent tour stop for national acts, but there are opportunities for even non-music majors to indulge their fandom on campus, around St. Peter and in neighboring Mankato. In the spring, Gustavus Adolphus' **Earth Jam** festival offers a full day concert outdoors. In addition to the student bands that perform during the day, Earth Jam's nighttime headliners have included Jack Johnson and Pete Yorn. And Gustavus Adolphus' Campus Activities Board organizes one big concert every other year or so. The board has a knack for booking artists before they become too huge to play this kind of gig: Jason Mraz played for a few dozen students before his song "The Remedy" broke at radio, and Ryan Adams, Something Corporate, Five for Fighting and Semisonic have also given shows for Gustavus students. Throughout the year, C.A.B. puts on a series of intimate performances at the campus' **Courtyard Café**. These gigs, held amid twinkling candles and latte-sipping hipsters, tend to feature Twin Cities-based acoustic musicians of the lo-fi variety. Off campus, Saint Peter hosts the annual Rock Bend Folk Festival during early September. For the past fifteen years, Rock Bend has treated Saint Peterites to a full-weekend of music, food, and dancing. In spite of its name, the fest brings in an array of genres including folk, jazz, rock, bluegrass, blues, and swing.

Mankato, the nearest town with amenities like Starbucks and Target, is only a short drive from Gustavus Adolphus. Home to one branch of **Minnesota State University** (www.msnu.edu), Mankato offers at least a couple of options for fans of live music—including the **Midwest Wireless Civic Center** (www.midwestwirelessciviccent er.com), an arena that draws the biggest of the big, from Tom Petty to Guster. With a student body of nearly 10,000 students, MSU has enough money to bring in acts such as the Black Eyed Peas and MTV's Campus Invasion Tour. Shows are held at the campus' field house or at the Midwest Wireless Civic Center, and both Gustavus and MSU students are offered tickets at discounted prices.

As for smaller venues, the **What's Up Lounge** (www. whatsuplounge.com) has established itself as the only opportunity in southwest Minnesota to hear indie acts. Though What's Up used to host local metal bands on most nights, they have recently been bringing in more diverse acts and a large number of jam bands. This shift is due in large part to the locally based Two Fish Recording Studios, who now does the booking for What's Up. Boutique café the **Coffee Hag** puts on a handful of acoustic shows each month, usually by local singer-songwriters. Then there's the **Venus Lounge**, an upscale martini bar that traditionally caters to an older crowd because of its reputation for bringing in jazz and lounge acts, such as Martin Zeller. Fun fact: The Venus Lounge has a baby grand available for open mic nights and when Poison was in town a few years ago, Brett Michaels decided to stop in prior to the show. Due his unkempt appearance, most patrons believed that he was just a very talented homeless man.

You'll have to do most of your record shopping online, at the mall, or during treks to Minneapolis, but Mankato's **Tune Town** offers a large selection of new and used CDs and vinyl. The store is planning to add an indie movie rental section, and they also sell music memorabilia, movies, posters, and even homemade handbags featuring classic *Rolling Stone* covers.

# San Diego, CA

## UNIVERSITY OF CALIFORNIA, SAN DIEGO
9500 Gilman Dr.
Department 0021-A
La Jolla, CA 92093-0021
www.ucsd.edu

**T**his beachside university offers B.A.s in music, music humanities, and an unusual program called Interdisciplinary Computing and the Arts. The latter combines studies in computer science, art and cultural theory and teaches students how to use computers in the creation of both visual arts and music. Straight music majors can shape their course load to focus on composition, performance, literature, technology or jazz and the music of the African Diaspora. UCSD's performing groups include choral, orchestral, wind, and jazz ensembles.

Though selections vary from semester to semester, UCSD's music department has plenty of classes that cater to students interested in contemporary and popular music, including courses on electronic music, jazz and the blues. Popular Music: Reggae, Bob Marley and Globalization looks into the roots of Jamaican pop music and examines its influence throughout the world. Another class, Popular Music: 10 Great Rock Albums can be taken twice, as the albums taught vary from semester to semester. Hip-Hop: The Politics of Culture explores everything from rap music and lyrics to dance moves, graffiti, advertising and music videos.

For both ICAM students and general music majors, UCSD's Computer Music series offers instruction on modern recording techniques such as waveshaping, sampling and MIDI control. Classes on audio production, mixing and editing encompass a wide variety of topics from semester to semester.

## VENUES:

### The Casbah , 2501 Kettner Blvd.,
### www.casbahmusic.com

The Casbah calls itself the "only cool place in San Diego." Thank God that's not true, but it is by far the best venue in town. Located right near the airport, this is where legendary nineties punk bands—and SD locals—Rocket From the Crypt and Drive Like Jehu got their start. Local musicians like Mitch from No Knife, Pall from Black Heart Procession, Rafter Roberts and Adam Gimbel of Rookie Card all hang out at the Casbah, and any band worth seeing has played or will play here. It's got a meager capacity of 200 and you have to be twenty-one to get in. But it's a good hang even on nights when there's not a band you want to see: The back room has pool tables, pinball, and a classic Galaga game.

### Soma , 3350 Sports Arena Blvd. Ste. I,
### www.somasd.com

An all-ages venue in Point Loma near San Diego's sports arena, Soma puts on the biggest and best indie and punk shows in town. This converted movie theater holds just shy of 1,000 people and has played host to bands including Interpol, the Ataris, and PJ Harvey. They still use the old movie theater curtains, but the concession stand has been converted into a merch booth where the bands sell their wares.

### Mira Mesa Epicentre, 8450 Mira Mesa Blvd., www.epicentre.org

If you can get over the fact that this youth recreation center lacks much rock & roll ambiance, you're likely to see some damn fine shows at Mira Mesa Epicentre. It's a short drive up the 15 to get there, but they sell slushies inside to make up for the lack of alcohol and the abundance of teens. Snow Patrol, Starsailor, and Rilo Kiley have all played here recently, and the ticket prices are always on the cheap side.

### Cane's, 3105 Ocean Front Walk, www.canesbarandgrill.com

Aesthetically, this Mission Beach club is a mess, but it's hard to fault their lineup of heavily buzzed indie rock acts such as the Shins, Badly Drawn Boy, and Blonde Redhead. The venue switches back and forth from all-ages to 21+, so give a call before heading over. Cane's boasts four bars, yet the dance floor is tiny and the crowd often gets squeezed onto the stairs or balconies. Try to ignore the remnants of the outmoded tropical motif and the autographed photo of Stuttering John, and you'll be fine.

### Che Café, on UCSD campus

Che Café is actually a small house located on the UCSD campus that functions as a music venue, vegan café, and punk rock commune. Bands are booked into the Che a few nights a week, and they're usually fairly obscure: Recent shows came care of lesbian punk folkie Mirah and post-rock outfit Xiu Xiu. The place is really small, so get there early or you'll end up hanging out in the courtyard, smoking cloves with all the other hipsters. The café doesn't serve beer, but you're probably too young to drink anyway.

### 4th and B , 345 B St., www.4thandb.com

San Diego's biggest small venue, 4th & B is where bigger acts play when they roll through town. Wilco, Ryan Adams, Guided by Voices, Nas, Gov't Mule and Ronnie James Dio have all graced the stage at 4th & B. Between the floor seating and mezzanine, the place holds about 1500 people, and though tickets and drinks are pricier than at the small clubs, locals say the sound is pretty good and rate it as a decent concert experience overall.

### Kensington Club, 4079 Adams Ave.

The Ken Club is a small but charming dive bar that occasionally hosts live shows. Local bands play here from time to time, as well as touring acts like Drag the River and John Cougar Concentration Camp. Shows and drinks are cheap, so it's a great neighborhood haunt for those nearby.

### Scolari's Office, 3936 30th St. (North Park)

Says one UCSD student: "You don't go to shows in San Diego if half of them aren't at Scolari's." We don't know where he got his fake ID, and we're not asking. The bar is 21+, but there's never a cover charge. Small touring bands and pretty much every local band plays at this dingy sports bar, where you can pass the time playing pool, darts, or a golf arcade game and try not to think about how the ceiling looks like it might collapse at any moment.

## RECORD STORES:

### M-Theory, 3004 Juniper St.,
### www.mtheorymusic.com

Cattycorner from the Whistle Stop, the hippest bar in town, M-Theory specializes in indie rock, stocking inventory from labels such as Matador, Touch and Go and Barsuk. The shop, located in South Park, has frequent in-store performances by the kinds of bands whose albums they sell: the Delgados, The Stills, and Interpol. M-Theory is also the only record store in town to do midnight sales on Mondays for new releases. It's a small store, but it's well organized and—in spite of the hipness of its stock—the staff is friendly and approachable.

### Off The Record, 3849 5th Ave.

For new vinyl enthusiasts, Off the Record is a great place to blow your paycheck. The walls are covered with new albums and singles, and they have loads of bins full of used vinyl—some of which is rare or collectible. The CD selection is separated into subcategories for "mod/garage," "hardcore," "goth," and "dub." Local bands occasionally pop by for in-store performances, but you only have to look at the Polaroids near the cash registers to see that national acts including Sunny Day Real Estate, Blur, and Nirvana have all played in Off the Record.

Once you're a regular, you'll notice that members of SD bands Kill Me Tomorrow and Plot to Blow Up the Eiffel Tower work there when they're not on tour.

### Record City, 3757 6th Ave.

Record City can be found a few blocks from Off the Record in Hillcrest, a predominantly gay neighborhood in SD. Though OTR is best for new vinyl, Record City is tops when it comes to the used stuff. While the clerks blast vintage punk on the stereo, you can thumb through the store's vast assortment of jazz, rock, blues and r&b platters. Everything is in pristine condition, and most of it is modestly priced.

### Lou's, 434 N. Highway 101, Encinitas, www.lousrecords.com

Don't mind the half-hour drive to the beach town of Encinitas: Lou's is worth the trip. From CDs to vinyl, there's nothing you can't find at this San Diego county staple. Lou's is split in two stores—one for new, one for used. The used store is overflowing with vinyl, cassettes, and CDs, and they have a turntable in the front so you can sample an LP before you buy it. The new store is even more expansive, with highly specialized sections like the one for only new British albums. All the CDs are placed in vertical shelves stretching across the length of the store and in between, which is quite a sight to see—if a little overwhelming. Says one local: "It's a great place to go after surfing and having some tacos a few doors down."

## RADIO STATIONS:

### 91X 91.1, www.91x.com

The longest-running modern rock station in the county has been broadcasting from Tijuana for more than twenty years. It's your basic run of the mill station, playing the usual suspects, but Tim Pyles hosts a local show called "Loudspeaker" that's worth hearing for its showcase of great local bands.

### FM 94.9, www.fm949sandiego.com

A competitor to 91x, with a somewhat better selection of music.

They do play decent music, especially considering the more loosely formatted shows like "Big Sonic Chill" and "FTP," which avoid the big hits. They veer slightly more toward indie rock than 91x, but still could branch out a bit further. Just because Blink 182 are from San Diego doesn't mean they really need to be played as often as they are.

### KCR (Cox Digital Cable 956, Time Warner Digital Cable 957)

San Diego State University's campus radio station is all student-run, with a few community DJs. They have lots of specialized shows, where playlists should appeal to fans of emo, punk, goth, indie rock, and underground hip-hop.

## *MISCELLANEOUS EVENTS:*

### Street Scene

R.E.M., X, James Brown, Love, and Wilco are among the acts who have performed at Street Scene, an outdoor music event held downtown at the end of summer. It's a big, crowded mess, but there are usually several bands worth seeing.

# San Francisco, CA

## SAN FRANCISCO CONSERVATORY OF MUSIC
1201 Ortega St.
San Francisco, CA 94122-4498
www.sfcm.edu

The San Francisco Conservatory of Music is one of only a few major conservatories on the West Coast. Enrollment is deliberately limited to just over 300, to ensure that faculty can lavish enough personal attention on each student. The conservatory offers a bachelor of music degree and a music diploma in composition, guitar, keyboard instruments, orchestral instruments, and voice. Bachelor of music students at SFCM study performance, as well as traditional liberal arts subjects like history, literature, and philosophy. Music diploma students, who have fewer total requirements, are exposed to exactly the same core courses as the bachelor of music students, but without the general liberal arts requirements. Essentially, any undergraduate at SFCM is going to get a stellar musical education, filled with core requirements such as Keyboard Skills, Practical Aspects of a Career in Music (a pretty comical and wise inclusion) and private instruction courses.

The conservatory offers two compelling specialized areas of study: baroque performance studies and new music studies. Students who want to learn how to play period instruments like the harpsichord, organ, or baroque flute can do so here, supplemented by courses that look at the musical, stylistic, and technical aspects of literature from the corresponding historical periods. Students interested in new music can take courses in twentieth-century composition, trends in twentieth and twenty-first century composition and performance techniques. They are also welcome to play around in the Wiegand Electronic Composition Studio, which is stocked with equipment for student use.

## SAN FRANCISCO STATE UNIVERSITY
1600 Holloway Ave.
San Francisco, CA 94132
www.sfsu.edu

Though not known primarily for its music program, SFSU allows students to pursue undergraduate professional degrees in classical and jazz performance, composition, music education, and music history, plus liberal arts programs in world music and jazz, electronic music, music history, and classical music. In a given year, the school is officially involved with nearly 200 performances of professional, semi-professional, and student groups that range in focus from big band to string quartets to world music ensembles.

Anyone interested in popular music should check out San Francisco State's concentration in music history and literature. In addition to being exposed to courses in music history and ethnomusicology, students can select classes focused on Latin American or Middle Eastern music, and the school offers a number of pop-culture friendly classes such as Minimalism, American Iconoclasts, The Roots of Rock, Rock Since 1965, and The Beatles.

## VENUES:

### Bottom of the Hill, 1233 17th St.,
### www.bottomofthehill.com

This small club is lodged at the bottom of Potrero Hill, but it's tops with eclectically minded indie rock fans. Apparently inspired by PeeWee's Playhouse, with its crooked windows and faux architectural touches, the quirky space has played host to artists on the verge of breaking out such as Arcade Fire, Interpol, and Andrew W.K., as well as big names returning to their roots such as the Beastie Boys, Elliott Smith, and Billy Joe Shaver. Otherwise, the venue is crammed almost every night of the week with local and touring mall-punkers, psych-rockers, screamo trios, forest folkies, dream poppers, electronic experimentalists, shoegazer hillbillies, noise mavens, art rockers, no wavers, singer-songwriters, and representatives from just about every rock microgenre you can imagine.

### Slim's, 333 11th St.,
### www.slims-sf.com

Co-owned by 1970s hitmaker Boz Scaggs and boasting some of the best sound in the city (so good that Built to Spill allegedly will play nowhere else), the 550-capacity venue offers two or three bands almost five nights a week. Indie rock, punk, singer-songwriters, and experimental units all find spots on the bills here. The bookers also have an uncanny knack of attracting breaking overseas media darlings like Franz Ferdinand, the Hives, and Darkness on their first spin through town. Otherwise, take in acts such as the Distillers, Chingy, Scissor Sisters, Iron and Wine, and the Locust. One caveat: Sold-out shows can get humid, and the pillars scattered throughout the venue block some views.

### Great American Music Hall, 859 O'Farrell St.,
### www.musichallsf.com

Once a bordello and later owned by fan dancer Sally Rand (who is rumored to haunt its gracious spaces), the Great American Music Hall continues to seduce all comers with its ceiling murals, gold leaf trim, marble touches, rococo woodwork, balconies, and grand mirrors. Recently purchased by the owners of Slim's, it now showcases local and international players such as Neurosis, I Am Spoonbender, the Rapture, Low, Jane Birkin, Black Heart Procession, Hot Hot Heat, Paul Westerberg, Ted Leo and the Pharmacists, Pedro the Lion, and the Fall.

### Cafe Du Nord, 2170 Market St., www.cafedunord.com

Descend the stairs of this former Prohibition-era speakeasy and you'll find one of the cozier and more charming venues in all of SF. This almost-100-year-old subterranean space sports red velvet walls and a mahogany bar in the main room, a pool table, and Victorian couches perfect for canoodling. Deeper into the club, in a second room, everything from jazz, spoken word, folk, rock, and punk can found, including recent residencies by no-wavers Erase Errata and boomer folkie Donovan. Upstairs, above the club, owner Guy Carson showcases quieter music, sans a bar, in the quaintly austere Swedish American Hall; performers have included Rilo Kiley and M. Ward.

### Hemlock Tavern, 1131 Polk St., www.hemlocktavern.com.

Anthony Bedard—local drummer, art-making instigator, and Hemlock booker—makes Hemlock Tavern, located below the Grammy-nominated remix studio Moulton in the space once occupied by historic gay bar the Giraffe, the spot to catch edgy, smart, and experimental music. Well-soundproofed and partially designed by co-owner, sound engineer, and Fuck guitarist Kyle Statham, the tiny, intimate live room is cordoned off from the rest of the bar by heavy curtains and moving panels—at a capacity of 100, it fills up quickly when cool, on-the-rise artists like Comets on Fire, Deerhoof, Wolf Eyes, and Six Organs of Admittance are in the house. Expect the surprise appearances by major performers such as PJ Harvey, Cat Power, and Smog, playing the occasional down-low show. Outside, the rest of the bar is usually teeming with art-school hipsters, random trendoids, creative professionals, and weekend warriors who vie for attention around the central bar and huddle in the open-air smoking room.

### The Independent, 628 Divisadero St.,
### www.theindependentsf.com

This beloved big black box has been serving up the live goods for more than thirty years under various monikers: the Half Note, the VIS Club, the Kennel Club, and the Justice League. Mazzy Star, Urge Overkill, and the Boredoms caroused there in the late Eighties and early Nineties, while DJ Spooky, De La Soul, and Money Mark kept the space hopping through the '00s. The new owners have given this joint the makeover it deserves, installing a state-of-the-art sound and light system and pushing the once-central bar back against the wall. The seats are still few and far between, lining the two walls beside the stage, but the music now sounds fantastic, from wherever you're sitting or standing. In honor of the many genres in the club's past, the calendar is filled with a blend of national and local indie rock, pop, jazz, Americana, and generally unclassifiable offerings including the Soundtrack of Our Lives, Jesse Malin, the reformed MC5, DJ ?uestlove, and Soul Coughing's Mike Doughty.

### 12 Galaxies, 2565 Mission St.,
### www.12galaxies.com

Nearly all the sightlines are stellar at this relatively new and thoughtfully appointed Mission District venue, nestled among the fruit stands, taquerias, and discount stores of the working-class yet increasingly gentrified area. Take in the stage from the shining art deco-style bar, tuck yourself into a dark cranny, or gaze down from the second-floor mezzanine. Upstairs, there's a pool table and a conversation nook around a small fireplace. The owners are still tweaking the mixture of acts at this space: these days, the lineup tends to be heavy on local acts.

### Thee Parkside, 1600 17th St.,
### www.theeparkside.com

San Francisco's rock & roll roadhouse began life as a lunch spot for dot-commies and a showcase for country acts. Then the pink slips started flying, and that business plan went the way of free workplace breakfasts and massages. Never fear—Thee Parkside has found a second life as a raucous spot that specializes in garage rock and occasionally roots and country. In the tiki-decorated patio out back, hard rockers and Pabst drinkers can indulge in bouts of ping-pong. Don't be surprised if you run into artists like Ryan Adams, the Donnas, the Hives, the Dirtbombs, and the Jon Spencer Blues Explosion, soaking up the atmosphere before they play at bigger joints in other parts of the city.

### Milk, 1840 Haight St., www.milksf.com

Don't believe those jaded club kids—there *is* such thing as a second chance in nightlife. Consider the Milk, which replaced the lackluster lousy-band showcase Galaxy, which took the place of the only slightly better Boomerang. With the passing of those two previous clubs, live rock & roll has been all but banished from the once-groovy Haight, the historic bastion of the San Francisco sound. To make up for it, Milk is providing something that's a rarity in so many other parts of the Bay these days: a legit, cozy crib for turntablists and underground DJs. The club is appointed with a streamlined, modern décor; a lively roster of club nights (among them Fresco and Hella Tight); and a dance floor with enough room to stylishly grind up against a loved one—rather than a half dozen strangers. World-class jocks such as DJ Shadow and well-regarded rappers such as Dudley Perkins have dropped in for a last-minute set or two, and ambitious hip-hop collectives such as Future Primitive Sound have set up shop with MCs from local groups.

### Fillmore Auditorium, 1805 Geary Blvd., www.thefillmore.com.

Initially slated as a dance hall when it opened its doors in 1912 and later cultivated as a black music showcase by promoter Charles Sullivan, the Fillmore began its storied life as a rock ballroom when the late producer Bill Graham took over in 1966. It became the site of many an important Sixties-era Bay Area rock artist's debut (Grace Slick performed there with Jefferson Airplane for the first time) and a favored locale for live recordings including Cream's *Wheels of Fire*. Still appointed with a tub of red apples at the entrance, the Fillmore remains a beloved space for renowned players and their fans, admired for its fairly intimate feel—in spite of its 1,200 capacity—and the fact that it's become a shrine to S.F. musical history: check the concert photos and artist portraits in the lobby and the zany array of vintage and recent show posters lining the walls of the upstairs lounge and hall.

**Warfield Theater, 982 Market St.,**
**www.thefillmore.com/warfield.asp.**

The 1922 theater was renovated in the late Seventies and soon after provided the stage for a series of controversial gospel concerts by Bob Dylan, produced by Bill Graham. Broadway road shows, the Grateful Dead (who recorded a live album there), and a weekend warriors' disco found their way to the venue until Bill Graham Productions set up shop for good, presenting major national and international acts such as Elvis Costello, Neil Young, Prince, PJ Harvey, Guns 'N Roses, Nick Cave and the Bad Seeds, Sonic Youth, and Kraftwerk.

**Bill Graham Civic Auditorium, 99 Grove St.,**
**www.billgrahamcivic.com.**

Renamed for the concert promoter after his death in 1992, the former San Francisco Civic Auditorium doesn't come with a fabulous reputation as a concert venue—the 5,000-seat venue is a sprawling box with poor acoustics, suitable for only a few arena-sized big names. Still, it does have a pedigree: a youthful Franklin D. Roosevelt was nominated for Vice President in the hall when the Democratic National Convention was held at the hall in 1920. The San Francisco Opera was born there in September 1923, and the NBA's San Francisco Warriors found a home in the space in the 1960s. Now it's the urban point to play for performers like the Beastie Boys, Radiohead, the Strokes, Maxwell, and Beck.

# RECORD STORES:

**Amoeba Music, 1855 Haight,**
**www.amoebamusic.com.**

The biggest independent music store in San Francisco happens to be the best in terms of its selection of new and used CDs, prices, and the general savvy and sophistication of its music-fan staff. The rest of the nation is catching on: when the owners opened a mammoth branch in Hollywood, the news broke out—brick-and-mortar music emporiums aren't dead after all! San Francisco's mammoth store fills the onetime Rock 'N' Bowl alley at the end of Haight Street, on the edge of Golden Gate Park, and its music stock, ranging from Kraut rock to hip-hop to J-pop, is unbeatable. Vinyl, music posters, DVDs, and videos are plentiful, as are in-store performances by acts such as Sonic Youth, Black Keys, Brother Ali, Moving Units, Handsome Boy Modeling School and Ted Leo and the Pharmacists. The store has also put out compilations of its favorite local music and highlighted Bay Area bands under its Homegrown banner.

### Aquarius Records, 1055 Valencia St., www.aquariusrecords.org.

Trimmed with ivory curtains and armed with a homespun DIY aesthetic, the oldest independent music shop in the city is also the hippest—to the point that they've been accused of being far too cool for school. The staff's alleged music-snob elitism is legendary in underground circles. Still, it's hard to deny the well-edited music in the bins and on the new releases board, as well as the passion of the Aquarius employees, who have counted among their number members of I Am Spoonbender and the Husbands.

### Grooves, 1797 Market St.

A veteran light show maestro during the Summer of Love daze, Ray Andersen now shines a light on vinyl of all varieties in a store jam-packed with bins, boxes, and lots and lots of records. Overlooking a major freeway artery from a white storefront decorated with many-colored discs, Grooves is known for its well-priced collection of rock, jazz, and classical rarities as well as a notable array of world music. Chalk it up to Anderson's never-ending collecting bug—the ace storyteller regularly drops choice items from his personal record stash into Grooves' inventory—and if you stick around and ask questions, he'll also drop gossipy tidbits about the colorful characters he's encountered in his travels.

### Virgin MegaStore, 2 Stockton St., www.virginmega.com

It's hard for any store in SF, no matter how "mega" to compete with Amoeba, but Virgin can't be faulted for that. This three-story outlet offers a jaw-droppingly vast selection of new releases, as well as DVDs, videogames, books, magazines, and apparel. Listening stations allow you to sample most anything before you buy it. And, hell, it's not a bad way to kill a couple of hours between classes.

# RADIO STATIONS:

### KUSF 90.3 FM,
### www.kusf.org

San Francisco State University's radio station is home to both student and community DJ's and is that much richer for it, considering the provocative tastes of the raging music fiends behind the board. Local indie and underground artists including Deerhoof, Devendra Banhart, the Gris Gris, Tussle, Soft Pink Truth, N. Lannon, and Tarentel get plenty of airplay here, along with collegiate favorites such as Wilco. Specialty shows delve into Hawaiian sounds, hip-hop, oldies, electronic music, and more.

### KITS 105.3 FM,
### www.live105.com

Modern rock is the game for this Infinity Broadcasting station—and they do it well, with plenty of sassy 'tude and specialty shows that focus on up-and-coming local artists and electronic sounds. The Shins, the Killers, and Interpol have made it onto playlists with emerging major label prospects the Bravery, Louis XIV, and Kaiser Chiefs hot on their heels. The station also hosts summer and winter arena concerts of hot modern rock performers every year: their recent Not So Silent Night show at Bill Graham Civic Auditorium featured headliners Modest Mouse as well as Franz Ferdinand.

# MISCELLANEOUS EVENTS:

### Noise Pop Festival

Indie rock artists rule this longtime music festival, though the organizers also like to showcase at least one "event" reunion by an indie precursor group like Big Star, Television, or Camper Van Beethoven. The multi-venue, three-night event includes panels and film screenings, but otherwise count on the programming to emphasize the buzz artists of the moment. Those have included Death Cab for Cutie, Bright Eyes, Cat Power, Blonde Redhead, Spoon, Magnetic Fields, Superchunk, the Faint, Beulah, and Beachwood Sparks.

**Mission Creek Music Festival**

Named after the buried trickle of a creek that courses beneath the cracked pavement of the hipster-heavy Mission District, this upstart fest wants to eat Noise Pop's lunch, showcasing mostly local artists while the other event has looked beyond city borders. Led by ex-Zrmzlina honcho Jeff Ray, MCMF reflects the idiosyncratic tastes and whims of its volunteer producers. Last year saw players re-creating the life of bedroom rockers, performing on stage in pajamas on a mattress.

—*Kimberly Chun*

# Seattle, WA

## UNIVERSITY OF WASHINGTON,
Box 353450
Seattle, WA 98195-3450
www.washington.edu

The University of Washington School of Music is a nationally recognized center for the study of both the academic and the performance aspects of classical music. The faculty is distinguished and accomplished as musicians or scholars in their own right, and the students who come here are working towards similar levels of achievement in their fields. The School offers three undergraduate degrees: bachelor of arts, bachelor of music, and the concurrent bachelor of arts/bachelor of music degree.

The school boasts an array of unusual ensemble groups like the Collegium Musicum, a group committed to the study of early tonal music, or the Contemporary Group, which explores the "notation and performance problems in contemporary music" in addition to a baroque chamber ensemble, among many others. The school also offers several student music associations such as the ethnomusicology Student Association and the American Musicological Association.

Students enrolled at the University of Washington School of Music should come prepared to work very hard in one of many relatively traditional areas. Though non-majors are welcome to participate in most ensembles and can take instrument and voice lessons at the school, this is not the place for kids looking to dabble in the occasional music history course.

## CORNISH COLLEGE OF THE ARTS
710 East Roy St.
Seattle, WA 98102
www.cornish.edu

**C**ornish College of the Arts offers all the attributes of your typical art school—a creative faculty and student body, eclectic course selections, and innovative curriculum. Graduates include John Cage and Lou Harrison, and recently the college has featured guest performers such as Philip Glass and Laurie Anderson. Music department students pursue a bachelor of music degree, with a focus in composition, instrumental performance, or vocal performance, and with further concentrations in jazz or classical music performance, opera-musical theater, performance-composition, electro-acoustic music, and world music. The program really does concentrate on individualized instruction—students work on their particular musical craft with a primary instructor, and then supplement their performance practice with academic music courses as well as classes in the humanities and sciences.

## SEATTLE PACIFIC UNIVERSITY
3307 Third Ave. West
Seattle, WA 98119-1997
www.spu.edu

**F**or students looking to merge their Christian faith with their interest in music, Seattle Pacific is a great choice. The school's curriculum includes a prominent group of required classes, which are taken throughout the student's time at SPU and which are designed to bring a sense of the Christian perspective to each students experience here. Music majors are required to participate in ensembles, as well as to pursue a particular instrument. Performance work is supplemented with core courses like musicianship and survey of music, plus additional classes in everything from theory and literature to music technology. Any SPU student who wants to be a part of the campus music scene is welcome to seek out the same ensemble and studio instruction resources available to majors.

## VENUES:

### The Crocodile Café, 2200 2nd Ave., www.thecrocodile.com

As the dust covering its decorative papier mâché swamp creatures proves, the Crocodile is no newcomer to the club scene. Owned by the wife of R.E.M. guitarist Peter Buck, the Belltown destination has become a cornerstone of the Northwest music scene. Its popularity stems from a mix of indie-friendly booking (everything from garage rockers the Dirtbombs and the Mooney Suzuki to the cult favorites the Wrens, shoegazers Ambulance Ltd., and post-punkers Futureheads packed in crowds here) and its relative proximity to popular dive bars dotting 2nd Ave. One of the best things about this club, though, is the layout. A separate bar and "dining area" leave plenty of room to socialize between (or during) acts.

### The Showbox, 1426 1st Ave., www.showboxonline.com

The Showbox is one of the larger mid-sized venues in town. With a sweeping red and black interior, gargantuan chandeliers, and three bars for the properly ID'd, it's also one of the nicer places to see live music. Audiences can sport heels and vintage fur or denim and cocked baseball caps and both count as appropriate attire here—a treat in a city where the grunge days' club aesthetic has held on tight. Acts that grace the large Showbox stage span from blues giant Bo Diddley to large-scale cover bands such as Super Diamond to reggae heroes Spearhead and indie siren PJ Harvey. Drinkers can escape the showroom for cocktails and finger food in the Green Room, a smaller bar inside the club that often hosts shows of its own; mostly local acts and singer/songwriter types.

### Neumo's Crystal Ball Reading Room, 925 E. Pike St., www.neumos.com

A bi-level club with a bar on each floor, Neumo's brings in a lineup that is fairly eclectic and incredibly popular—leaning towards the tastes of the young and music savvy—with shows from Iron and Wine and Saul Williams bookending performances by the Locust, the Melvins, and Ted Leo. Neumo's booker favors touring acts just as they're about to blow—bands such as the Scissor Sisters and Arcade Fire can later say they played here back in the old days—but also mixes in standbys ranging from Guided by Voices (who played a farewell show here) to budding local bands. Neumo's also hosts one of Seattle's regular hip-hop events, Yo, Son!, which turns the space into a dance club on Saturday nights. One word of warning: Neumo's tends to pack crowds like sardines for the more popular acts, so arrive early for sold-out shows.

### The Vera Project, 1916 4th Ave., www.theveraproject.org

If you're under twenty-one in Seattle, you'll quickly become familiar with the Vera Project. Located in Belltown, the black-walled club may not be much to look at, but its members put a lot of energy into bolstering the underage world and the indie music community at large. This non-smoking, alcohol-free space hosts shows by local and touring bands (everything from power pop to punk to arty noise bands, and hard rock shows) geared towards musicians on smaller labels. Vera also hosts art shows and workshops on nearly every angle of the music industry. This is the spot where you can find free to low-cost classes in punk rock yoga, and instrument instruction as well as opportunities to get your foot in the door of the local club community by working as a volunteer for this popular non-profit.

### Chop Suey, 1325 E. Madison St., www.chopsuey.com

Chop Suey's red and black/Asian-themed décor may not break ground in modern club design, but it does add a bit of class to Seattle's live music scene. The club offers a slightly smaller space than venues such as the Crocodile but still attracts plenty of quality acts, from radical hip-hop crew the Coup to Carlos D. from Interpol and dance punks Death from Above 1979. Chop Suey also helps balance out Seattle's indie rock-heavy market: its calendar boasts big and buzz-worthy names in hip-hop and electronica, and it hosts two popular club nights—the monthly Comeback, a gay event with four regular DJs, and Juicy, a weekly Sunday night hip-hop party.

### Comet Tavern, 922 E. Pike St.

For fans of sweat-soaked punk and garage rock, the Comet is an infrequent but important host in this city. The Pine St. beer-only bar gained unfortunate notoriety as the last place where Mia Zapata, frontwoman for Nineties punk band the Gits, was seen alive before her brutal 1993 murder. It remains a popular spot for the punk- and rock-friendly types. Although Comet shows are far from regular, hit this bar if you're a fan of record labels like In the Red and Sympathy for the Record Industry and crave wildly spastic performances (where more often than not the band and crowd share floor space).

### The Fun House, 206 5th Ave. N.

Located across from the Seattle Center, the Fun House is an unpretentious dive where the quality of the shows depends on who's booking them. If KEXP DJ Brian Foss is leading the charge, expect an exciting, eclectic mix of punk, garage, electro-trash, and synth experimentation. The bar is small enough that becoming a regular is all too easy and their concrete outdoor courtyard is perfect in the summertime.

### Gorge Amphitheater, 754 Silica Rd. N.W., www.hob.com/venues/concerts/gorge/

Few venues can compete with the scope or scenery of the Gorge Amphitheater. Located along Washington's Columbia River Gorge, 150 miles southeast of Seattle, the shed's majestic views more than make up for the traffic you'll hit on the way there. Due to its size and location, the Gorge hosts only the biggest of summer tours—shows by the Who, Britney Spears, Lollapalooza, Metallica, and the annual Sasquatch! festival have all taken place here. It's a good idea to camp or stay nearby if you do hit a performance here, as it's a long drive back. Nearby Soap Lake is a quirky, creepy town to explore before or after a show.

**El Corazon, 109 Eastlake Ave. E.,**
**www.gracelandseattle.com**

Generally considered one of the grimier venues in Seattle, Graceland is a hive of activity when it comes to national and local new metal, pop-punk, hardcore, and all the crusty centers in between. Occasionally an indie rock band will slip into their calendar, but for the most part this place is run, operated, and frequented by the black hoodie and tattooed sleeve types. Graceland is a comfortable, smoky spot located in enough of a no-man's land that appropriately high decibel levels won't disturb the neighbors.

**The Paramount, 911 Pine St.,**
**www.theparamount.com;**
**The Moore Theater, 1932 2nd Ave.,**
**www.themoore.com**

When Ashlee Simpson, Air, Al Green, or Interpol tour Seattle, they usually hit one of these two opulent venues. Both are vintage performance halls, home to musical theater, comedy, and big-ticket performances. Under the umbrella of the Seattle Theater Group, these roomy theaters offer balcony, general admission, and/or floor seating, depending on the show.

**The Paradox, 1401 NW Leary Way,**
**www.theparadox.org,**

Along with the Vera Project, the Paradox is a standby for those too young to hit bar shows. This volunteer-run Ballard venue is a little more out of the way than Vera, but it's accessible from a number of bus lines. The Leary Way space is the Paradox's newest home, but the organization has had an impressive history in Seattle, hosting shows by such bands as Death Cab for Cutie, Hot Hot Heat, Converge, Cursive, Low, Rilo Kiley, and others since opening in 1999.

**Re-Bar, 1114 Howell St.,**
**www.rebarseattle.com**

Although Re-Bar isn't technically a gay bar, this hole in the wall hosts plenty of queer-friendly mischief. From lowbrow theater to drag shows and house music nights, Re-Bar has long been a destination in Seattle for both the out-of-the-closet and the open-minded. Its pitch black, no frills interior, friendly bar staff, and quirky art openings only add to the bar's homey vibe. Live shows usually focus on local bands, but expect everything from annual Seattle productions of *Hedwig* to new wave glamazon queens to grace the stage.

### Tractor Tavern, 5213 Ballard Ave. NW, www.tractortavern.com

Ballard is Seattle's *de facto* twangtown, where members of the local alt-country scene (such as Jesse Sykes & the Sweet Hereafter) congregate at bars like Hattie's Hat through the wee hours of last call. A couple of doors down, the Tractor hosts most of this city's roots and Americana music, be it rockabilly, blues, honkeytonk, folk, cosmic country, or acts that mix all of the above. Bobby Bare, Jr., Tift Merritt, and Deke Dickerson have all hit this venue on their swings through town.

### Sunset Tavern, 5433 Ballard Ave NW, www.sunsettavern.com

Whether it's the Ballard location, the chatty bar staff, or the strong cocktails they serve at the nearby dive bars, the Sunset Tavern—which books mainly garage, punk and alt-country bands—has always maintained more of a basement-party vibe than that of a strictly regulated music venue. As an added bonus, the Sunset screens music-related movies for free most Monday nights.

### The Triple Door, 216 Union St., www.thetripledoor.net

Aside from occasional indie acts such as the Concretes and Joanna Newsom—or mass appeal artists like Nancy Sinatra—the Triple Door keeps its roster stacked with music that appeals more to the well heeled and well on in years. The non-smoking dinner club has intimate booth seating and a crystal-clear sound system, but as the offer of "private suites" (which go for a couple hundred bucks a pop) make clear, this is more of a place to take the parents (if the folks appreciate jazz) than a hotspot for college kids.

## NOT A VENUE, BUT STILL ROCKIN':

Few bars in town have the hipster pull of the Cha Cha Lounge (506 East Pine St). Populated by well-loved local musicians and a destination watering hole for touring bands, the Cha Cha is a dimly-lit haven for musician and groupie activity. Adjacent burrito joint Bimbos also employs—and feeds—much of the local guitar-wielding population.

## RECORD STORES:

### Bop Street Records, 5219 Ballard Ave. NW

With half a million records in stock (and over 100,000 7-inches), Bop Street offers hours of collector-style escapism in nearly every genre. Though the store also carries CDs, cassettes, and 8-tracks, this place is all about the vinyl. Expect to find everything from roots to ragtime, new wave to blues and psychedelic to punk here, and they offer trade if you're worried about breaking the bank.

### Sonic Boom Records 2209 NW Market St.; 514 15th Ave. E; 3414 Fremont Ave. N., www.sonicboomrecords.com

Sonic Boom may be a chain, but they're local and only three links long. Their knowledgeable employees—many of whom play in local bands—and music selection come highly recommended. With frequent in-stores and entertaining reviews on their website, there are plenty of good reasons why this is one of Seattle's most popular music geek haunts.

### Singles Going Steady 2219 2nd Ave., Ste C., www.singlesgoingsteady.com

Seattle is generally very supportive of independent businesses, and the music scene is especially keen to the DIY attitude. Singles Going Steady is one of the best local resources for indie musicians in the punk, hardcore, ska, and garage genres—and all the places in between—specializing in singles, as the name implies. The store's employees know a lot about the music they sell (you can read their recommendations at www.singlesgoingsteady.com) as well, turning this Belltown store into a welcome community hub.

### Easy Street Records, 20 W. Mercer St.; 4559 California Ave. SW, www.buymusichere.net/stores/easystreet/

With a wide selection of CDs and vinyl, and plenty of big-name in-stores, Easy Street is paradise for both the big music collector and the casual fan. The store stocks a solid variety of music magazines and music-related merchandise as well, and its West Seattle location also houses a small café that's a popular weekend destination.

### Everyday Music, 112 Broadway Ave. E.

The Seattle wing of this Portland chain offers new and used CDs, a local music section, and a small collection of used vinyl. Not only is it a good place to shop, but since Everyday Music buys all kinds of used CDs and DVDs, it doubles as the place to unload those bands you rarely listen to.

### Tower Records, 4518 University Way NE; 701 5th Ave N., www.towerrecords.com

With so many well-stocked, independently owned record stores in town, the only reason to hit a place like Tower Records is its location. With two stores in Seattle (one in the University District and one near the Seattle Central) both locales are accessible to the college student and visiting tourist alike. The U-District space carries new and used vinyl.

### Jive Time, 411 East Pine St.; 3506 Fremont Ave. N.

Jive Time is a vinyl hunter's wet dream, specializing in used records across the ages and the genres—specializing in hard to find Sixties and Seventies rock and soul. Out-of-town bands often make special trips to collect rare finds here—as do Japanese collectors, who fly in especially to pick up bagfuls of vinyl.

## SPECIALTY RECORD STORES:

One of a handful of specialty stores in Capitol Hill, **Respect Records** (www.respectrecords.net) focuses on vinyl of the jazz, in funk, and soul varieties, both new and used. Further down the street, **Wall of Sound** (www.anomalousrecords.com/wos) shares space with indie comic/zine store **Confounded Books**. It's the place to hit for world- and adventurous music—noise, IDM, sound recordings, dub, and more. And then there are the DJ specialty stores. **Platinum Records** (www.platinum-records.com) peddles mainstream rap, drum 'n' bass, techno, and house, along with technical DJ supplies; **Zion's Gate** (www.zionsgate.com) features a wealth of reggae, dub, and death metal.

## RADIO STATIONS:

**KEXP 90.3 FM, 91.7 FM in Olympia/Tacoma,**
**www.kexp.org**

Hands down, this is the best radio station Seattle—and really the whole Northwest—has to offer. The web-savvy, listener-supported, commercial-free station broadcasts terrestrially and through their website, offering a broad mix of genres to the public. Specialty programs include shows focused on reggae, African music, world pop, roots music, hip-hop, punk, and avant jazz, while their regular programming leans heavily on indie rock buzz bands. The station is very Seattle-focused as well, supporting and breaking local artists as much as it boosts national acts.

**The End 107.7 FM,**
**www.1077theend.com**

The End has vastly improved its playlists since 2004. The station now broadcasts music by bands like Interpol, the Yeah Yeah Yeahs, and Death Cab for Cutie along with the "classic alternative" fare. It also sponsors and throws a number of concerts in the Northwest, including the summer's Endfest and the holiday Deck the Hall Ball, both of which have offered impressive lineups in past years.

## MISCELLANEOUS EVENTS:

**Bumbershoot,**
**www.bumbershoot.org**

For very reasonable ticket prices, Bumbershoot offers four days of access to a dozen different indoor and outdoor stages showcasing everything from local up-and-comers, honky-tonk and Top 40 artists. (Past years have included appearances by Nickelback, the Pixies, Public Enemy, Nas, Modest Mouse, Mötörhead, the Killers, the Walkmen, and the Shins, among others.) Plus there are stages/spaces for comedy, breakdancing, emcee battles, visual art shows, author readings, and more.

### Capitol Hill Block Party,
### www.capitolhillblockparty.com

Hands down, this is one of the best local music events Seattle has to offer. The Capitol Hill Block Party occurs every summer on the corner of 11th and Pike St., hosting a wide range of Northwest talent on multiple outdoor stages as well as beer gardens, local food and clothing vendors, and other surprises. Past performers include Mudhoney, the Melvins, Pretty Girls Make Graves, El Vez, the Blood Brothers, and more.

### Hempfest,
### www.seattlehempfest.com

Bands are rarely the reason people hit Hempfest, but most stoners appreciate some sort of music. If you plan on mingling with the hippies, burnouts, and marijuana motivators, Hempfest usually offers a variety of world music, rock, and reggae.

### Pho Bang

If you consider yourself open minded to both truly alternative music (art punk, seedy garage rock, avant metal) and to wacky divas who play in new wave bands, Pho Bang is one of the best things going in Seattle. Hosted by crass queens Jackie Hell and Ursula Android, and usually featuring one or two bands, this popular club night shifts venues but retains its notoriety in this town—even the White Stripes played a Pho Bang back in the day. Pho Bang's schedule has grown a little irregular recently, but it's worth the trip out when you see one listed.

### Sasquatch! Music Festival

This is the weekend Northwest indie rockers die and go to heaven—or at least hit the road for the Gorge Amphitheater. Past artists who've performed here include Coldplay, Modest Mouse, the Shins, Flaming Lips, the Roots, Jurassic 5, and Sleater-Kinney, and there's usually a smattering of smaller Seattle acts on the bill as well.

### The Experience Music Project and Science Fiction Hall of Fame,
### www.emplive.com

Microsoft co-founder Paul Allen's passion for music—and spending his millions on it—is undeniable in Seattle. The Experience

Music Project (recently renovated both in name and in scope for some reason to also include the Science Fiction Hall of Fame) is his baby, designed by Frank Gehry and housing memorabilia from artists spanning rock, country, blues, punk, folk, and disco. Reactions to the space are mixed, as it comes off alternately as an overpriced Hard Rock Café or an impressive interactive learning venue, depending on your appreciation for, say, seeing the boots of Paul Stanley under glass. (The permanent Northwest music section is worth checking out when touring the museum). Although it houses a large live music venue, EMP hosts fewer shows as the years progress, but it does have a number of music-related workshops, the annual Elvis Impersonator Invitationals, as well as changing exhibitions that in the past included the Beatles and Bob Dylan.

— *Jennifer Maerz*

# State College, PA

Hitting the books in a Pennsylvania cowtown celebrated for its football, ice cream, and surplus of popped collars seems like a questionable option for any sane rock aficionado. But that jibe about State College's anemic music scene just doesn't hold true. If you know where to look, State College—home to nearly 40,000 Penn State students—offers some hipper-than-thou auditory alternatives that might make your undergrad years here bearable (however many there may be).

The music department at **Pennsylvania State University** (www. psu.edu) offers a gaggle of degrees for your learning pleasure: There's the bachelor of music in both performance and composition for those invested in a particular field, the bachelor of science in music education for those so scholastically inclined, the bachelor of arts for anyone who digs a broad-based, liberal arts approach and the bachelor of musical arts for the interdisciplinary kid looking to attain some outside skills. There's also a music minor for those audiophiles hankering after a major that's a bit more wallet-friendly and parent-approved.

Off campus, State College has its fair share of visit-worthy concert venues. Problem is, the best of them are bars, so unless you're twenty-one, you're caught between rock and a hard place. For the underclassman crowd, you're sure shot is the **Crowbar** (www.crowbarlivemusic.com), which stages a slew of out-of-town acts—these days, of the emo, metal, or punk persuasion. The multi-level venue has hosted some recognizable artists before they broke big, in addition to some still-indie acts. Past performances include GWAR, Saves the Day, Broken Social Scene, the Drive-By Truckers, Ol' Dirty Bastard, Kittie, and, um, Vanilla Ice.

A (colossal) step up from the Crowbar is the **Bryce Jordan Center** (www.bjc.psu.edu), which comfortably seats more than 5,000 screaming fans of stadium rock. The concrete arena with questionable acoustics sees shows by massive acts like Prince, Weezer, Ludacris, Pearl Jam, Kenny Chesney, and the Dave Matthews Band, a sure fave in this Abercrombie town.

Step outside the Crowbar and Jordan Center routine, though, to experience the thriving underbelly of State College rock. This scene's heart can be found at none other than the **Darkhorse Tavern** (www.darkhorsetavern.com), home to the weekly, sometimes twice-weekly, indie rock showcase that goes by the rollicking name of **Roustabout!** (www.roustabout.net). The dim, smoky basement bar hosts a never-ending slew of local, regional and ever-increasingly national acts, including Yo La Tengo, Matt Pond PA, the Washington Social Club, Bishop Allen, and the Spinto Band. Also, Roustabout!'s where you'll catch the best local artists, including early-R.E.M. Brit-poppy quartet the Bullet Parade.

Roustabout! aside, **Zeno's** is a swell site to catch a stray show. A couple times a semester, the basement bar (yes, another basement) with a monstrous selection of on-tap beers hosts acts that'll remind you why you love rock & roll as much as that Joan Jett minx. In distant past, there's been Marah, Rogue Wave, Two Gallants, and American Minor, but there's also that fabled Ryan Adams performance of yesteryear.

Then, the highlight of any self-righteous, rock-lovin' Penn Stater's year might be **Movin' On** (www.movinon.org), a free music fest that invades the student union lawn every spring. Sonic Youth, Jimmy Eat World, Ben Folds Five, Sarah Harmer, Guided by Voices and Wilco have played the event in the past. But so have a lot of crappy bands not worth mentioning. No matter. It's free, so deal.

If you haven't frittered away all your cash on concerts, squander the rest at **City Lights Records**. It, too, is located in a basement storeroom—directly under the town's biggest sorostitute clothing retailer, so you can't miss it. City Lights is small, but teems with the organized chaos of drool-inducing albums you'd be hard hit to find at a Best Buy. The twenty-year-old shop, owned and operated by quite possibly the coolest oldish dude in town, might not sell every album in the world, but it sells every album worth listening to.

The other music shop in town is **Arboria Records**, which has a fine selection of new and older releases plus a decent collection of used albums at reasonable prices. Arboria certainly lacks as many smirk-worthy indie gems as City Lights, but it's the kind of store where you can buy an Ashlee Simpson disc and maintain your sense of dignity. This may or may not have something to do with the fact that Arboria is not located in a basement, but in a storefront across the street from the community library and an old folks' apartment complex.

So when you've had enough of those frat-tastic cover bands that dominate the above-ground town, dive into State College's indie rock scene, where "underground" takes on a quite literal meaning indeed… Catch ya in the basements.

*—Caralyn Green*

# Syracuse, NY

## SYRACUSE UNIVERSITY
201 Tolley Administration Bldg.
Syracuse, NY 13244
www.syr.edu

In 2004, Syracuse University made headlines when the school began offering a class analyzing the lyrics of raunchy rapper Lil' Kim. Taught by professor Greg Thomas, the English department class, Hip-Hip Eshu: Queen B@#$H 101, may sound like pop culture puffery, but—in keeping with everything about this esteemed university—the course is as academically ambitious as it is unique, inviting students to "study Queen B in the context of a culture that goes beyond any music genre or generation; beyond the colonial confines of Plantation America; and beyond erotic conventions of Western heterosexual patriarchy. In place of bourgeois literature, and even more bourgeois criticism, there will be rap audio and lyrics, oral history, ethnomusicology, folklore or spoken word, magazine articles, interviews, film and video." It isn't the only unconventionally contemporary class among Syracuse's offerings both in and outside the school's music department. Another English course—a two-part series, actually—Reading Popular Culture involves analyzing film, music, TV, video games, advertising and even theme parks. How many schools let you watch *8 Mile* and *Queer Eye for the Straight Guy* in the classroom? Not many.

As such, the Setnor School of Music tends to get eclipsed by Syracuse University's more famous communications programs and its highly distinguished S.I. Newhouse journalism school. Nonetheless, SU offers a lot for musicians looking for something a little broader than a conservatory experience. Undergraduate courses aim to instill a picture of things beyond just clefs and meters, covering music's psychological aspects and contributions by women and minority composers. But proficiency is a big part of the well-rounded Setnor experience, too. Majors take up both a primary and secondary performance area, which can help out later in the unpredictable world of professional playing. Weekly lessons are balanced out with courses in music theory, dictation, history and writing, and whatever else a student's particular major requires.

The university also allows students to focus on the record business by achieving a bachelor of music in Music Industry—a degree that requires classes in sociology, live sound and economics. Students can also shoot for their B.M. in composition, performance or music Education, or the more general bachelor of arts in music. Music industry majors can benefit from working with Syracuse University Recordings, a fully operable record label with its own 24-track recording studio. Setnor prides itself on its high job placement rate; graduates have gone on to such noted careers as booking agent for Artists Group International and publicist at Blue Note Records, and include two star singers of the opera world, Julie Newell and Phyllis Bryn-Julson. The well-qualified faculty includes members of the Syracuse Symphony Orchestra and teaches most band and orchestral instruments including the organ, with which SU has a distinguished history—Setnor Auditorium even houses a 3,283-pipe colossus built by master organ-smith Walter Holtkamp in the Fifties.

For most of its programs Setnor also offers a master's degree option, and adds Conducting to the list. But those headed for higher learning might also find SU's Goldring Arts Journalism program appealing. The brand-new venture trains future music, film, architecture and theater critics through the S.I. Newhouse School of Public Communications. The inaugural class of 2005-06 will be up for the first-ever M.A. in Arts Journalism from an accredited journalism school. Enrollment is just ten students per year, but will almost definitely expand as the early crops of tastemakers sally forth into the market.

## VENUES:

### Club Tundra, 5863 Thompson Rd., www.tundratavern.com

Club Tundra is a remnant of what was once a teeming live music scene along Erie Boulevard, Syracuse's main east-west strip. The venue was previously known as the Lost Horizon, an endearingly filthy dive that managed to host almost every touring band of note in the punk and metal scenes in the Eighties (Black Flag! Slayer!). Since changing names and owners a couple times, the bar has cleaned up substantially and nixed its flagrantly rude bouncers, but preserves what was always good about the Lost: its devotion to balls-out rock & roll. Frequent Budweiser-sponsored showcases tap local assets such as Brand New Sin, while city floor is sure to lure more national acts along the lines of recent bookings Mastodon, Authority Zero and the *Girls Gone Wild* road show.

### Awful Al's Smoke and Whiskey Bar, 321 S Clinton St.

Awful Al's is the best spot for weeknight music in fashionable Armory Square, the former warehouse district-turned hipster entertainment enclave just west of Downtown. Jazz-oriented live music, ranging from local Afro-Cuban fusion to downstate instrumental soul and funk, unfolds in Playboy mansion-meets-hunting lodge ambiance, with plush carpeting, nature paintings and a liquor array so big it requires a sliding library ladder. Al's is one of the last places it's legal to smoke indoors in smoke-free New York, which means you'll probably leave smelling like Dutch Masters, but high ceilings and good ventilation keep your lungs relatively happy.

**Bull and Bear Pub, 125 Water St.**
**www.bullandbearpub.com**

Open since 2002, the Bull & Bear has raised the musical stakes in Hanover Square, the most historic of Downtown's business districts, culling a seemingly endless supply of groove-friendly acts from Massachusetts hip-hop to local zydeco legends Los Blancos. There's no stage, just a corner where the bands practically belly up to the crowd in quarters so close your buddy can fill up the guitarist's beer glass without leaving his seat. Friday and Saturday nights, it's a beautifully hectic madhouse of frat types playing pool, people who look like extras from a trucker documentary keeping bar seats warm and couples cutting the rug up front. To top off the venue's amazing energy, a beautiful staff serves up affordable brew and the best sweet-potato fries you've ever tasted.

**Coffee Pavilion, 133 Water St.,**
**www.coffeepavilion.com**

A docket of mostly acoustic local folkies and singer/songwriters reel in crowds on weekends, but the venue's calling card is its Friday night jazz jams, where a house trio of aspiring high school musicians invites guests on a sign-up basis to swap chops. By all accounts they're the real deal, with some of the city's most revered jazz cats sitting in now and then. Late hours accommodate partiers from the next-door Bull & Bear looking to sober up with some java.

**Dinose, 246 W. Willow St.,**
**www.dinosaurbarbque.com**

Blues is Syracuse's specialty, maybe because the city is one of the rainiest spots in the Northeast. But the Dinose's fanatical devotion to the genre might have something to do with it, too. Local and touring national blues acts take the stage six nights a week in front of a mostly potbellied crowd, with a big biker constituency reflecting the roots of this den of blues bacchanalia. (As the story goes, three wanderlust pork enthusiasts perfected their sauce recipes at fairs and festivals across the East Coast using a halved fifty-five-gallon drum and a lot of love, before swapping nomadic life for stability in Syracuse.) The food is as famously heaping as the live music roster, slathered in the Dinosaur's five specialty sauces, which are now bottled and marketed nationwide.

### Half Penny Pub. 321 W. Fayette St.

In its past life the Half Penny Pub was known as the Stag Hotel, the black sheep of Armory Square venues with a sleazy staff and an aversion to any live music remotely marketable. The former nineteenth-century hotel seemed bound for conformity when it was bought by the owners of a local dance hovel for urban twenty-somethings, but miraculously, the subversive vibe survived a renovation and a name change, and Syracuse's outré punk/art-rock scene has once again adopted it as its stomping grounds. There's nothing special about the mostly domestic brew selection, the bare-bones décor or the tinny in-house sound, but it's a refuge for the uncompromising Thunderosas and Undergangs of this town, who've lovingly nicknamed it "Stag Penny."

### Mezzanotte Café & Lounge, 658 N. Salina St., www.mezzanottelounge.com

Mezzanotte was part of the beautiful new streetscapes that emerged when Little Italy became the center of North Side gentrification not long ago. The lounge/bar's ever-growing live roster is the result of its reputation for open bookings and for actually paying bands at the end of the night, while students and in-the-know locals come to partake of the comfortable, laid-back vibe. Java and drinks ranging from Riesling to blue moons are fairly priced. Mezzanotte ("midnight" in Italian) has picked up much of the slack left by the closing of the SU-area institution Planet 505, with long-running Wednesday open mics that are secret hipster oases.

### The Stoop, 309 W. Fayette St.

No venue makes you feel like you're unwinding on the fire escape of a Brooklyn tenement more than The Stoop, and that's a good thing. Painted window scenes grace the brick-walled stairway entrance of this postage stamp-size margarita den, with a displaced doorway framing the stage like a set from *West Side Story*. Bookings tend toward innocuous acoustic rock, which reflects the slightly upscale clientele, but you can usually count on a choice Violent Femmes or Clash cover—not to mention a renewed love for triple sec and starry nights.

## RECORD STORES:

### The Sound Garden, 124 Walton St.

The Sound Garden's staff members are invariably in local bands or hang out with them, which gives the store the feeling of a scenester pow-wow den. Extensive and lovingly tended racks of LPs and new and used CDs run the gamut from vintage black metal to Top 40 artists, and if somehow you still can't find what you're looking for, a near-miraculous catalog of titles can be special ordered. Upstairs, a carefully screened assortment of new and used DVDs ranges from typical Hollywood stuff up to and including exotic midget porn. In-store performances have recently featured Hot Hot Heat and a showcase for local station WWDG (105.1 FM).

## RECORDS ALONE WILL NOT SUSTAIN YOU...

### Books and Memories, 2600 James St.

High-piled tomes loom like the Red Sea around Moses in this treasure trove of used wares—two stories, ten rooms and literally Biblical proportions of books, LPs, magazines, and games. Regular new arrivals reward vigilance, but if that Sun Ra biography doesn't surface, the congenial staff can usually point you toward a great Salman Rushdie or Saul Bellow read instead.

## RADIO STATIONS:

Like most radio markets, Syracuse is pretty well staked out by Clear Channel, but two bastions of noncommercial programming live healthily on the SU hill. **WAER** (88.3 FM) flows between popular jazz and National Public Radio programming, while the student-run **WERW** (1570 AM) veers intrepidly from indie rock to improv comedy and almost everything in between, including sports commentary that's a big hit in this Orange-centric town.

—*Nathan Turk*

# Tampa, FL

## UNIVERSITY OF SOUTH FLORIDA
4202 E. Fowler Ave., FAH 110
Tampa, FL 33620
www.usf.edu

The University of South Florida is a thriving research institution with campuses around west central Florida, with the primary campus in north Tampa. USF's School of Music, a distinguished program within the College of Visual and Performing Arts, is well regarded for its jazz studies program and the opportunities for private study with professionals—namely members (even some principals) of the Florida Orchestra, who serve as faculty. Music majors can pursue degrees in performance, music education, jazz studies, composition and piano pedagogy. Regardless of the concentration, students are expected to complete a balance of performance-based classes, music theory, and music history. Students in the music education program, will master theory and performance, but also concentrate on research and skills that will prepare them for teaching.

USF's department also offers classes such as Music in Your Life, a class open to non-majors curious about how, with limited theoretical knowledge, they can approach, understand, appreciate and talk about music. Music in the United States promises a dynamic approach to the historical subject by using recordings, videos and texts to study music from colonial times to the present. And another one of USF's perks is SYCOM, its own electronic music studio. Students interested in electronic music, as well as techno-fans, might enjoy a course called Electronic Music—Digital Synth. This composing class promises to let you tackle ambient and possibly new wave arrangements a la Philip Glass or even Depeche Mode.

Speaking of electronic and experimental music, the Tampa Bay area hosts the BONK experimental music festival each March where composers from around the world present their work (imagine: symphonies for city buses, performers wearing shower curtains and performing oboe compositions with electronic enhancement). USF plays an integral role, with university ensembles often hosting an evening and/or performing; and USF faculty also compose for the thriving festival which is a highlight for the local arts scene.

In terms of pop music, USF brings in bands for students to its Special Events Center. The intimate theater space has hosted acts such as Marilyn Manson, Garbage, and even Beck. These concerts are either exclusively for students, or really cheap.

## VENUES:

### Orpheum, 1902 E. Eighth Ave., Ybor City

Every city needs a sweaty, hole-in-the-wall nightclub. The Orpheum is the spot in Tampa to catch getting-bigger-by-the-minute indie rock acts such as Rilo Kiley and Modest Mouse. Located in Ybor City, Tampa's primary nightlife district, the Orpheum packs 'em in and, in the spring and summer especially, can be pretty sweltering. But at least the shows are cheap and intimate. The room is tiny and the acoustics are good. A caution for shorter concertgoers, though: the room is not tiered, and with a sold-out crowd, sightlines can be kind of shitty. Still, the Orpheum is practically living room-sized, so it's not tough to inch toward the stage. Saturday nights feature an all-you-can-drink special with DJs playing rock and dance hits from the likes of the Faint, the Streets, and Franz Ferdinand, among others.

### Jannus Landing Courtyard, 200 First Ave N, St Petersburg, www.jannuslanding.net

The Tampa Bay area offers several smaller outdoor venues. In St. Petersburg (only a twenty-minute drive from downtown Tampa) this New Orleans-style courtyard is a local treasure. The venue hosts bands such as Bad Religion and Taking Back Sunday, legends such as Blondie and Iggy Pop, and contemporary, critical favorites such as Cake and Lucinda Williams. Since the Florida weather is typically charming, this venue operates nearly year-round.

### Skippers Smokehouse, 910 Skipper Rd.

A wacky seafood restaurant, Skippers is a favorite among blues and folk lovers, though it gets occasional pop and rock acts, including Calexico and Tegan and Sara. The stage is outdoors, the vibe is low-key (picnic tables sit under a thatched, palm frond-studded roof and sandpit) and the beer is cheap. Plus, the parking lot—more like a narrow ravine adjacent to the restaurant—makes leaving a crowded show sometimes feel like a game of bumper cars.

### Tampa Theater, 711 Franklin St., www.tampatheater.org

Want to catch a concert under the stars but not deal with the Florida heat? The 1,300-seat Tampa Theater, with its bright blue ceiling and twinkling stars was built to resemble an outdoor villa, complete with an exposed sky and ornamented balconies. Built in the 1920s and restored with a pristine sound system, Tampa Theater is primarily a movie house that screens art and indie flicks. But concerts occasionally pass through. The theater has hosted folkies Natalie Merchant, Steve Earle, and Ani DiFranco, and alternative acts such as Bright Eyes and Wilco.

### Masquerade, 1503 W. Seventh Ave., Ybor City

The Masquerade, also in Ybor City, is Tampa's most eclectic concert venue in terms of the bands it books. The club has hosted everybody from David Benoit to Slayer to Melissa Etheridge to the Killers. Despite its diverse lineup, the Masquerade is not big on décor. Think skate park: there's concrete, concrete and more concrete. But with five bars, it shouldn't matter. The main room is spacious and can reasonably handle large crowds and its tiered floor creates ample sightlines; the other rooms are primarily used as poolroom bars with house/hip-hop/techno DJs or karaoke.

### USF Sun Dome, 4202 East Fowler Ave., www.sundome.org

Located on the campus of the University of South Florida, the Sun Dome does a swell job netting the acts college students want to see, including the White Stripes, Britney Spears (admit it: you love "Toxic"), and the Pixies. As with all stadium venues, most of the pricing, from the beer to the T-shirt, is relatively expensive; plus, this isn't a "student-only" venue. The stadium seats about 8,000, so it's not as large as other arenas, and you don't have to be on the floor to feel like you're part of the concert.

# RECORD STORES:

### Vinyl Fever, 4110 Henderson Blvd,
### www.vinylfever.com/tampa

Vinyl Fever has been a vital part of Tampa's music scene since it opened in 1981. Unlike the bland chain stores all over Tampa, this independent business is passionate about good music. If a band does an in-store concert and signing, it's going to be at Vinyl Fever. The store features a wide range of new, underground music as well as mainstream stuff. The shop also maintains a respectable stock of used CDs, DVDs, and, of course, a decent selection of new and used vinyl. Plus, scavenge the bargain bin (with used CDs ranging from one to six dollars) and you're certain to find records you didn't know you needed but can't resist buying anyway.

### The Sound Exchange, 14610 Livingston Ave,
### www.soundexchangemusic.com

The Sound Exchange is a reliable poor man's version of Vinyl Fever. If you've just got to have that new and obscure release, your chances are better at Vinyl Fever, but this store features plenty of quality products at a cheaper cost.

# RADIO STATIONS

### WSUN 97.1 FM,
### www.97xonline.com

Fans of alternative music love 97X for its dedication to contemporary music as well as its yearly concert called "Next Big Thing," an outdoor festival that boasts a lineup with bands inches away from big time success.

### WMNF 88.5 FM,
### www.wmnf.org

This community radio station might be a little more granola than, say, California's famous KCRW (which prides itself on finding new pop/rock acts), but in between the blues, folk and talk shows, this station is your best chance to hear indie rock and pop that mainstream radio stations don't play. Plus, the DJs are responsive, so call in and request whatever you want to hear. Each May, the station sponsors

Tropical Heatwave, a night-long, party-cum-concert in Ybor City where, for a small fee, you can catch sets from the station's favorite artists.

*—Brian Orloff*

# Tempe/Phoenix, AZ

## ARIZONA STATE UNIVERSITY
PO Box 870112
Tempe, AZ 85287
www.asu.edu

With three campuses all located in and around the Phoenix metropolitan area, Arizona State University is a large, thriving public university with a focus on research and creative, liberal arts studies. The main campus, located in the college town of Tempe, hosts the majority of students and activity, though there are satellite campuses in Phoenix and Mesa. At the Tempe campus, music students can enroll in the Herberger College of Fine Arts. Advanced students will find ample opportunities to collaborate with faculty on research and aid in writing journal articles, study ethnomusicology and engage in composition projects.

Students may earn a bachelor of music, which focuses on theory and skill development, a degree perfect for teaching, composing, performing, arranging, or, later, graduate study. This degree has various, specific concentrations, including music education, jazz performance, music therapy, musical theater, performance, piano accompaniment, and theory and composition. Unique facets of the program include the music therapy concentration, which, in addition to the history, theory and performance courses other concentrations take, also gives equal weight to psychology and sociology programs. The Jazz concentration requires courses such as Recording Studio Techniques, Jazz Ear-Training and Music and Culture.

Non-classical courses include a History of Jazz class and a History of Popular Music class that, according to the School of Music's website, cannot be counted toward the music degree but may be taken as an elective. For non-music majors, ASU offers courses related to rock music, including a communications class called Communication Approaches to Popular Culture that incorporates an interdisciplinary approach to the subject; music related elements include studying MTV and pop music in general.

## VENUES:

**Rhythm Room, 1019 E. Indian School Rd., Phoenix, www.rhythmroom.com**

This small and laidback club is a must visit for any blues fan. Adorned outside with a canopy and some tables where you can snack on BBQ from the Rack Shack Blues BBQ next door (it's open till 2 A.M. and serves a shitload of food, cheap), the venue itself it so tiny that you'll never be more than fifty feet from the stage. The stage is even itty-bittier, but they somehow manage to pack as many as eight musicians up there during sweaty blues jams. The audience has no reservations about dancing—and, often, badly—while artists such as R.L. Burnside, Kim Wilson, Henry Gray, Mojo Buford, and Sonny Rhodes heat things up onstage.

**Celebrity Theater, 440 N. 32nd St., Phoenix, www.celebritytheater.com**

Rock & roll in the round! At the Celebrity Theater, artists such as Ani DiFranco, Social Distortion and Violent Femmes perform on a circular stage that slowly rotates to give everyone in the two tiers of seats a front-and-center view. For smaller shows, the stage doesn't spin, but there's still not a bad seat in the house. Speaking of seats, another perk: Your chair comes with a cup-holder—movie theater style—so you don't have to balance your drink on your lap.

**Marquee Theater, 730 N. Mill Ave., Tempe, www.luckymanproductions.net**

Within walking distance of Arizona State University's Tempe campus, the Marquee is where most buzzworthy national acts stop when they come through town. Artists including the Darkness, Le Tigre, Ben Kweller, and even Eminem have graced the stage at the Marquee, which used to be a legit playhouse. The theater seats that used to be anchored to the sloping floor were removed when the venue converted to a rock club, so the sightlines are great even in the back. And when it gets too hot inside (as it did one summer during a Strokes show that had concertgoers complaining of "crotch-heat") you can always head to the outdoor patio for some fresh air or a smoke.

### Modified, 407 E. Roosevelt, Phoenix, www.modified.org

For teetotalers and those with an avant-garde sensibility, Modified is hard to beat —a multi-purpose art gallery and rock club with stark white walls and not a drop of liquor to be found. Their adventurous tastes bring in cutting-edge touring bands such as Death From Above 1979, Xiu Xiu, and the Arcade Fire. The space is tiny (holding fewer than 200) but that's just fine: This is the kind of place where the truly in-the-know go to see tomorrow's "next big thing" before anyone else catches on.

### Old Brickhouse Grill, 1 E. Jackson St., Phoenix

This aptly named brick-walled venue is one of the few in Phoenix that has a section for those who choose to drink alcohol and a section for those who can't or don't. Of course, most people hang in the boozy section, providing an unexpected perk: Go to the dry side for an easier view of the stage. The club's bookings are spotty—lots of local and regional acts—but it occasionally brings in a cool national artist like Ambulance LTD or Fantomas.

### Dodge Theater, 400 W. Washington St., Phoenix, www.dodgetheater.com

The Dodge benefits from the deep pockets of its corporate owner. This recently constructed venue, built explicitly as an arts center, has impeccable acoustics and lights and everything in it is new, shiny and state-of-the-art. Depending on the event, the Dodge seats between 1,900 and 5,000. It may be lacking in old-world ambiance, but when David Bowie or Alicia Keys take the stage, you'll likely be too caught up in the sonic majesty to give a damn.

### The Clubhouse, 1320 E. Broadway Rd., Tempe

This place used to be Tempe's grungy stomping grounds for metal and rock bands. But a change in management brought the Clubhouse a feminine touch, and it's been spiffed up with the addition of candles on the tables and a fancier vibe, overall. Their bills are divided between rock and country acts—mostly local or regional artists—but if you're bored with whoever's on the stage there are TVs, videogames and cheap snacks to distract you.

## RECORD STORES:

### Eastside Records, 217 W University Dr., Tempe

Drop by Eastside and you'll feel like you just walked into the wood-paneled, orange-carpeted basement rec room of a friend with an amazing record collection. And like many cluttered basements, the store can be difficult to navigate. The long aisles full of albums go only one way, so when you get to the end, you've gotta turn around and head back out again. As a result, Eastside tends to feel congested even when there are only a few people browsing. But Eastside rewards the patient: Their selection of vinyl is huge, encompassing rock, jazz, country, hip-hop, and reggae, as well as oddball soundtracks and other miscellany. Once you stock up, you can pick up an old board game or record player on your way out.

### In the Groove Music, 2700 W Baseline Rd. # 103, Tempe

One local says that In the Groove reminds him of a tiny record store that was uprooted from New York City and plopped in a plaza next to a dry cleaner and hot wings restaurant. More importantly, In the Groove has a strong assortment of R&B, soul and hip-hop albums for sale. Prices are negotiable, and the store regularly has in-store autograph sessions with acts such as Dilated Peoples and Slum Village. And here's something unusual: In the back of the store there's a barbershop where you can get your hair dyed. Beat that!

### Stinkweeds, 1250 E Apache Blvd # 112, Tempe, www.stinkweeds.com

One of the best independent record stores in the Southwest, Stinkweeds boasts an extensive local music section, t-shirts for sale,

CD listening stations, a DVD viewing station and an almost infallible selection of indie and alternative rock. It's a little farther from campus than some other shops, but well worth the trip.

**Zia Record Exchange, 105 W University Dr., Tempe,**
**www.ziarecords.com**

The Tempe outlet of this five-store chain packs every inch of its small space with new and used CDs, vinyl, and DVDs. Though it can get cramped and cluttered, the stock tends to be easily navigable. New and used discs are mixed in together, so you can flip through until you find either a shrink-wrapped new copy or a cheaper used one. Zia also recently installed a "Touch Stand" that lets shoppers preview discs, search for songs in its database or watch snippets of DVDs. Plus, Zia puts out its own free 'zine, which includes CD reviews and interviews with local bands.

**Hoodlums New & Used Music, ASU Campus, Memorial**
**University Building,**
**www.hoodlumsmusic.com**

Hard to beat when it comes to convenience, Hoodlums is actually on the ASU campus, in the basement of the Memorial Union and across from the food court. Similar in layout and aesthetic to Zia, Hoodlums carries a wide array of new and used rock records, as well as a sizable DVD section and listening stations where you can sample up-and-coming local acts. Best of all, the store offers coupons on its website and rewards frequent buyers with discounts and free t-shirts.

# Washington, DC

## HOWARD UNIVERSITY
2455 6th St., NW
Washington, DC 20059
www.howard.edu

If it was good enough for Sean "P. Diddy" Combs, soul legend Donnie Hathaway, and "Killing Me Softly" diva Roberta Flack—not to mention a slew of noteworthy musicians, celebrities and scholars—are you going to tell me Howard University isn't good enough for you? This distinguished 138-year-old black college is dedicated to providing students with research and academic opportunities at a reasonable cost. Students studying music have the benefit of a program that became the first in Washington, DC to gain membership to the National Association of Schools of Music. Apart from the research and performance-based aspects, the school also promises to "preserve, publicize and disseminate music of people of African ancestry." Facility-wise, the school boasts a Keyboard Laboratory with nine electric pianos, a music education/therapy laboratory and a Jazz Studies Digital Music Laboratory that allows students to record and playback performances. Howard offers the usual variety of music majors—in performance, theory and education—but also allows students to specialize by taking elective studies in business.

## GEORGE WASHINGTON UNIVERSITY
Department of Music
Phillips Hall, Rm B-144
801 22nd St. NW
Washington, DC 20052
www.gwu.edu

George Washington University—located in Foggy Bottom, and only a few minutes from DC's fancy-schmancy Georgetown commercial district—is a large, private research institution that offers students ample opportunities to study and perform music. The school stresses individuality, allowing students to work closely with mentors and professors to achieve goals at unique paces. Students working toward a bachelor of arts in music must also take courses from a core curriculum and, apart from the typical requirements such as music theory, composition, music history, and performance, majors must, as seniors, participate in a capstone project which becomes an opportunity for individualized research. Students can also minor in music, or jazz studies, but even non-major can get in on the act: Classes open to the entire student population focus on a variety of composers, American music, and even the history of music in the District. The department also offers courses on electronic and computer music and allows students to use technology labs in conjunction with their composing.

# AMERICAN UNIVERSITY
Department of Performing Arts
4400 Massachusetts Ave. NW
Washington, DC 20016
www.american.edu

Despite its name, Washington D.C.'s American University is actually quite international in focus. The small school—with only 5,000 undergraduates—regularly hosts world leaders and enrolls students from over 150 countries. Musicians should turn to the Department of Performing Arts for a music program that can be tailored to suit each student's needs. The school's philosophy: push music outside the classroom, rehearsal room, and concert hall. Students are encouraged to pursue research, internships and jobs at cultural institutions within the city as part of their education. And the school offers an arts management degree, demonstrating the weight it places on mastering the business of music. Another unusual distinction: students can put together their own individual music concentration. Can you design a pop culture-oriented music major? Submit a proposal, the school says.

## VENUES:

### 9:30, 815 V St. NW,
### www.930.com

When this club opened on F St. in 1980, it was a tiny room propped up by a pole that partially blocked the view of future legends like Minor Threat, the Replacements and Smashing Pumpkins. And locals still talk about the time Einsturzende Neubauten set the stage on fire. So there was some relief when the club moved to grander digs (1,200 capacity) on V St. that allow unobstructed views from three levels, a vast beer selection and pristine sound. Visitors such as Wilco often play two cozy nights rather than one in a theater or arena. The club also welcomes locals such as Chuck Brown, godfather of the indigenous DC sound called go-go—a mixture of funk, soul and hip-hop over a signature huckabuck beat.

### Black Cat, 1811 14th St. NW,
### www.blackcatdc.com

Black Cat is the younger cousin to the 9:30 Club. It's run by former Grey Matter drummer Dante Ferrando with backing from area native Dave Grohl, who not only started his career in DC legends Scream, but also played in a couple little bands you might have heard of called Nirvana and the Foo Fighters. Despite its smokey, divey vibe, the kitchen offers delicious vegetarian and vegan dishes by Dante's dad. This is the place to catch local and touring buzz bands in the smaller downstairs room, or monsters of indie rock such as the Hives or Yeah Yeah Yeahs upstairs. The Red Room bar sports a great jukebox, its own brand of ale, and no cover.

### DC9, 1940 9th St. NW,
### www.dcnine.com

The new kid amongst the town's rock clubs, DC9 offers a welcome alternative to the sometimes scenester-heavy rooms down the street. If you just sat in the long downstairs bar you might not notice the stairs hidden behind a curtain. They lead up to a performance space that comfortably fits a couple hundred. Upcoming local acts often find their foothold here before moving up to bigger rooms, which means those who pay attention can claim early bragging rights.

### Velvet Lounge, 915 U St. NW, www.velvetloungedc.com

If you like heavy riffs, the Velvet will quickly become an extension of your living room. It's got a bare bones bar downstairs with a narrow room upstairs that hosts the legions of stoner rock, wayward songwriters, and those who don't dig the clubbiness of the local punk scene.

### Galaxy Hut, 2711 Wilson Blvd., Arlington, www.galaxyhut.com

Sometimes you wanna go where everybody knows your order before you sit down. The tiny Galaxy Hut has bighearted bartenders, hip regulars, and approximately a bazillion beers. And there's never a cover even when some indie band is stuffed in the corner.

### Iota Club and Cafe, 2832 Wilson Blvd., Arlington, www.iotaclubandcafe.com

If you like Americana, roots rock, alt-country or whatever you call under-recognized songcraft from around the block, this is your joint. Alejandro Escovedo, Tift Merritt, and Jay Farrar are practically fixtures. Excellent wines and modern cuisine grace the restaurant side, from which you can hear (though not see) music from the club side through the shared bar.

### Birchmere, 3701 Mt. Vernon Ave., Alexandria, www.birchmere.com

The Birchmere is an institution as much as a venue. In its nearly forty-year history it has helped launch the likes of roots rock and country artists including Lyle Lovett, Emmylou Harris, Shawn Colvin, and Mary Chapin Carpenter. Of course, it has diversified over the years, with recent offerings spanning from soul legend Solomon Burke to ex-Husker Dü mastermind Bob Mould. Audiences skew older than many DC clubs, but it's no home for nostalgia acts. It's a lab for living, breathing artists in all their career phases.

### Eighteenth Street Lounge, 1212 18th St. NW, www.eslmusic.com/lounge/lounge.html

As electronica stars, label honchos, and local restaurateurs, Eric Hilton and Rob Garza—aka Thievery Corporation - have built an empire of modernist chic under the ESL moniker. The tiny plaque on their flagship bar's otherwise unmarked door suggests in-the-know snobbery. Yet the space is disarmingly lived-in and friendly, with couches, a fireplace, and retro record covers on the wall. It's not the expected sterile, space age martini bar (that's across the street at Firefly, another venue in the ESL conglomerate). The music includes downtempo deejay selections or excellent live Afro-Cuban and Latino music.

### Dream, 1350 Okie St. NE,
### www.welcometodream.com

Much has been made of Dream's multi-million dollar interior and sound system. No doubt it's swank, and its themed rooms, impeccable accoutrements, and a dress code attract an upscale set. But that set throws down to the likes of Nas, Bell Biv Devoe, and Beyonce without reserve. It's set well off the Metro line in a dodgy neighborhood, which requires a car or a cab—and a watchful eye. But that's part of the adventure.

### Madam's Organ, 2461 18th St. NW,
### www.madamsorgan.com

Their motto is "Where the beautiful people go to get ugly," which pretty much says it all. It's trashy, fun, soused, with loads of blues, bluegrass, and Americana. And it's centrally located in the Adams Morgan strip, which becomes an alcohol theme park on weekends.

### Warehouse Next Door, 1017 7th St. NW,
### www.warehousenextdoor.com

The Warehouse is equal opportunity: theater, art, edgy music and uncategorizable happenings can be found in this compound of three adjacent buildings. The Next Door space typically receives local and touring bands, poetry slams, and whatever else requires a barebones space with a bar. The new convention center across the street has taken some edge off the grungy neighborhood, but this place has earned its right to be called "an avant-garde Kennedy Center."

### Nation, 1015 Half St. SE,
### www.primacycompanies.com/nation/index.cfm

Located in a sketchy waterfront neighborhood, Nation is basically a big empty box with the capacity to host raves with top international DJs or live acts such as Outkast and Limp Bizkit. In warm weather, turntablists transform the outside deck into an excellent, chill space to have a drink.

## RECORD STORES:

### Smash Records, 3285 1/2 M St. NW, www.smashrecords.com

Your one-stop punk outlet, ironically located in frou-frou Georgetown where the rich and beautiful browse designer boutiques. You can get a Ramones mousepad, hair dye, new Doc Martens, and just about any album (vinyl or digital) that exudes bad attitude. Somehow the fancy neighborhood is the perfect foil for this palace of snarl.

### Orpheus Records, 3173 Wilson Blvd., Arlington, www.orpheusrecords.com

A veritable institution, for twenty years Orpheus has sold collectible vinyl to dudes even dorkier and more obsessed than Jack Black in *High Fidelity*. It's a thing of beauty, really. That said, you pay for quality. Owner Rick Carlisle has a global clientele and a photographic memory for back issues of *Goldmine*. Happily for the rest of us, Carlisle also butters his bread with sales of current CDs.

### Capital City Records, 1020 U St. NW, www.capitalcityrecords.com

This is a great place to drop the needle on all those obscure electronica sides you've read about but can never find. Just to enter the room is an education in beats, bloops and blips from around the world. Vinyl is the mainstay, but prices are competitive.

### Crooked Beat Records, 2318 18th St. NW, www.crookedbeat.com

A clean, well-lit space that appeals to both the collector and the fan, Crooked Beat is all killer, no filler: Every item inspires covetousness. Their specialty is underground sounds and major label records that never cracked the mainstream. The operation relocated from Raleigh, NC and landed in the building where Bad Brains, Minor Threat, and other legends played their first shows. Naturally.

**Revolution Records, 4215 Connecticut Ave. NW,
www.revolutionrecords.net**

Picking up the baton from the late, lamented Now! Music and
Fashion, Revolution's hallmark is its in-store gigs. And though indie
rock is the staple here, performances range from soul to jazz and singer-
songwriters. Its second-floor location works out better than might be
expected, thanks to the store's modern living room vibe. Revolution
is the kind of place where you want to sink into the stuffed chairs and
hang out. Super-extra bonus points for their delivery service to work
or home—a godsend on those days that you simply must hear the new
Meal of Poodles album during your lunch hour.

—*Bob Massey*

# Top Ten Lists

For those with a short attention span, a quick guide to
the best of everything, and some noteworthy runners-up

## *TOP TEN MUSIC SCENES*
### *(IN ALPHABETICAL ORDER):*

1. Athens, GA
2. Austin, TX
3. Boston, MA
4. Chapel Hill, NC
5. Chicago, IL
6. Los Angeles, CA
7. New York, NY
8. Portland, OR
9. San Francisco, CA
10. Seattle, WA

## *TOP TEN RADIO STATIONS*

1. WNYU (New York, NY)
2. Indie 103 (Los Angeles, CA)
3. WRAS (Atlanta, GA)
4. WXYC (Chapel Hill, NC)
5. WLUW (Chicago, IL)
6. KCRW (Santa Monica, CA)
7. WBRU (Providence, RI)
8. WYBC (New Haven, CT)
9. KEXP (Seattle, WA)
10. KDHX (St. Louis, MO)

## TOP TEN VENUES

1. Bowery Ballroom (New York, NY)
2. Slim's (San Francisco, CA)
3. Emo's (Austin, TX)
4. Troubador (Los Angeles, CA)
5. Black Cat (Washington, DC)
6. 40 Watt Club (Athens, GA)
7. The Metro (Chicago, IL)
8. Magic Stick (Detroit, MI)
9. The Crocodile Café (Seattle, WA)
10. Berbati's Pan (Portland, OR)

## TOP TEN RECORD STORES

1. Amoeba (Berkeley, CA)
2. Vintage Vinyl (East Brunswick, NJ)
3. Waterloo (Austin, TX)
4. Schoolkids (Chapel Hill)
5. Newbury Comics (Boston, MA)
6. Other Music (New York, NY)
7. Dusty Groove (Chicago, IL)
8. Sonic Boom (Seattle, WA)
9. Vintage Vinyl (St. Louis, MO)
10. Grimey's Record Shop (Nashville, TN)

## MUSIC DEPARTMENT: GOOD. SCENE? NOT SO MUCH.

1. **Stanford University** (Stanford, CA)—If you like to tinker with your iTunes and you think Grand Theft Auto and the Velvet Underground are equally compelling, Stanford—just a thirty-five mile drive south of San Francisco—might be the place for you. In addition to traditional concentrations in theory and performance, among others, music majors can students can also pursue the MST or Music, Science, and Technology specialization, which is designed for those interested in computer music technology, digital audio, signal processing, and the acoustic foundations of music. As a student in this area of Stanford's music program, you will gain exposure to the work being done at another of the coolest and geekiest music institutions in operation today—Stanford's CCRMA, or the Stanford University Center for Computer Research in Music and Acoustics. Basically, this place is like Mecca for techie musicians and composers who are dying to merge the art of making music with advances in technology. Areas of interest at the Center include some heavy-sounding subjects like synthesis techniques and algorithms, signal processing, and psychoacoustics and musical acoustics.

2. **University of Dayton** (Dayton, OH)—Composition, education, performance, and therapy are the main tiers of the University of Dayton's Music Program but the music therapy division is most noteworthy. Study everything from conducting to music literature, then graduate to a job with one hundreds of community programs that employ music therapists to work with children and serve those with disabilities.

3. **SUNY Geneseo** (Geneseo, NY)—The School of Performing Arts at SUNY Geneseo offers a bachelor of arts in music, a bachelor of arts in musical theater and a liberal arts degree with corresponding concentration in music.

Students in these programs enjoy original courses like Folk Music in New York State and Studies in Keyboard, Vocal, or Instrumental Literature. Another highlight is Geneseo's Special Talent Admissions, which admits students who are highly gifted but my have slightly lower grades than the average student accepted to the school.

4.  **SUNY Potsdam** (Potsdam, NY)—Even though it's basically in the middle of nowhere, SUNY Potsdam's Crane School of Music houses some of the most well respected programs in the country. In 1886, the Crane Institute of Music became the first school in the U.S. to implement a music education curriculum designed to prepare music teachers for public schools, and it has since continued to lead as an innovator within the field.

5.  **Smith College** (Northampton, MA)—The music department at Smith, the country's oldest liberal arts school for women, specializes in renaissance and baroque studies, gender theory and feminist studies. Check out Music and Gender in a Cross-Cultural Perspective, a class that explores the ways music reflects social constructions of gender or Metal and Punk: Rock History Out Loud, which looks at the connections between the two genres.

6.  **Hampshire College** (Amherst, MA)—This small, non-traditional school—where the late, great singer-songwriter Elliott Smith studied in the late Eighties is designed for self-motivated students. There are no grades here: Instead, faculty members offer personalized written assessments. The music program is equally unconventional: Past courses have included Music Now, Rhythm Meets Blues: A Social History of Rock 'n' Roll and Sonic Networks: Discourses and Practices in Music Today.

7.  **University of North Carolina, Greensboro** (Greensboro, NC)—Apart from featuring a yearly school-sponsored New Music Festival, UNC also was the first school in the south to offer a degree in music education, a fact that

predates the school's current housing of the prestigious North Carolina Music Educators Association on campus. The school also offers an accelerated masters program, combining a bachelor of arts with masters in business administration, which prepares students for music business and performance careers.

8. **University of Rochester, Eastman School of Music** (Rochester, NY)—Eastman stresses a community atmosphere, combining scholarly pursuits with performance opportunities for students, including the chance to study abroad in a unique conservatory-exchange program with schools in France, Scotland, Sweden, Austria, England, and Germany. The 3+2 program also allows students who wish to be certified in music education to receive both a bachelor's degree and a master's degree in only five years.

9. **Rice University** (Houston, TX)—Rice University's Shepherd School of Music is a nationally recognized music program with an international student population and the tony Alice Pratt Brown Hall, which houses both concert venues and recording studios. Students will earn a bachelor of music in performance, music theory, music history or composition.

10. **Carnegie Mellon** (Pittsburgh, PA)—Carnegie Mellon's School of Music prides itself innovative teaching styles: Students learn improvisation and participate in the creation of new music, and are taught by professors who are themselves professional composers. Within a student's concentration, he or she can further specialize in the following eclectic areas: Dalcroze Eurhythmics, piano pedagogy, accompanying, conducting, jazz performance, music education, or music technology. And Pittsburgh's rock scene is nothing to sneeze at: Most touring bands, big and small, hit one of the city's venues on their way through the Northeast.

# TOP MUSIC BUSINESS DEPARTMENTS

1. **New York University** (New York, NY)

2. **Belmont University** (Nashville, TN)

3. **Full Sail Center for the Recording Arts** (Orlando, FL)

4. **Drake University** (Des Moines, IA)

5. **Drexel University** (Philadelphia, PA)

6. **Columbia College** (Chicago, IL)

7. **Pomona University** (Claremont, CA)

8. **University of Texas, Arlington** (Arlington, TX)—The University of Texas at Arlington's Business of Music degree interrelates course work from UTA's Department of Music, the School of Business, and the Department of Communication.

9. **University of Evansville** (Evansville, IN)—Evansville's music department merges fundamentals of music with fundamentals of business. In addition to basic courses you'll get to take stuff like Techniques of Music Merchandising, Legal Environment of Business, and The Creative Dimension.

10. **University of Miami** (Miami, FL)—The University of Miami offers a music business and entertainment program that provides a minor in marketing. The school also touts programs including music engineering technology, music education and a major called Studio Music and Jazz.

# SCHOOLS THAT OFFER FREE NAPSTER ACCESS

1. **Eastern Michigan University** (Ypsilanti, MI)

2. **University of North Carolina** (Chapel Hill, NC)

3. **University of Tennessee, Knoxville** (Knoxville, TN)

4. **Penn State University** (State College, PA)

5. **Cornell University** (Ithaca, NY)

6. **George Washington University** (Washington, DC)

7. **Middlebury College** (Middlebury, VT)

8. **University of Miami** (Miami, FL)

9. **University of Rochester** (Rochester, NY)

10. **University of Southern California** (Los Angeles, CA)

11. **Vanderbilt University** (Nashville, TN)

12. **Wright State University** (Dayton, OH)

# Contributors

**Steve Appleford** was born in Los Angeles and is now the editor of *Los Angeles CityBeat*. His work has also appeared in *Rolling Stone*, the *Los Angeles Times* and *GQ*.

When **Ricardo Baca** isn't rocking the mic via his day job as the lead music critic at the *Denver Post*, he's freelancing for other national magazines. Haters beware: Ricardo jigs better than Ashlee Simpson and MCs hotter than Talib Kweli.

**Kimberly Chun** is a senior arts and entertainment editor and music columnist at the *San Francisco Bay Guardian*. She has also written for the *San Francisco Chronicle, East Bay Express, AsianWeek, Magnet* and *Devil in the Woods*, among others. Chun has played badly in Hawaii's first all-female punk band and recently go-go-danced in a chubby panda costume onstage at the Fillmore alongside XBXRX as they opened for Sonic Youth and Wolf Eyes.

**Eric R. Danton** lives in Hartford, Connecticut, where he has been the rock critic for the *Hartford Courant* since 2002. His work has also appeared in *No Depression*.

**Dominic J. DeVito** has called the central part of Virginia his home for his entire life. He writes reviews for *9x Magazine* online and spends most of his waking hours hanging out at a record store.

**Zach Dundas** is a staff reporter (and used to be the music editor) for *Willamette Week*, Portland's weekly paper. He covers city hall, the nightlife industry and people who wish they were hobbits. Really.

**Jenny Eliscu** is a New York native and graduate of Queens College, CUNY, and she sincerely believes that her town has the best rock & roll scene on Earth. She is a contributing editor at *Rolling Stone*, where she has worked since 1999. Her work has also appeared in *Elle Girl, Time Out New York, CosmoGirl!* and Britain's *NME*, among others. She lives in Brooklyn, where she spends most of her time petting her cat, Lena, and watching *Law & Order* episodes.

**Kelly Fitzpatrick** is on a personal mission to prove there is more to Orlando, Florida, than theme parks and boy bands. Having lived in the city for ten years, she is the music editor for *OrlandoCityBeat*.com and the bars & clubs columnist for the *Orlando Sentinel*. She has also contributed to *Florida Magazine* and the Travel Channel.

**Steve Forstneger** has been the associate editor at the "Illinois Entertainer" in Chicago for three years, and lived in the area for all 24 years prior to that. While also contributing to London's *SoundGenerator*. com, *Randee Magazine* and the *Village Voice*, his ears belong to the rigamarole and scuttlebuttin' of the Second City.

**Pete Gershon** edits and publishes *Signal to Noise*: the journal of improvised & experimental music. He lives in Winooski, Vermont and Houston, Texas.

**Richard Gintowt** is an entertainment writer for *Lawrence*.com. In his six years in Lawrence, he has been music director for KJHK college radio, a booking agent for the Bottleneck and a fixture on the Mass. St. circuit with his band OK Jones. He looks forward to moving to Austin someday and realizing that Lawrence was actually a whole lot cooler.

**Elizabeth Goodman** is a freelance writer based in New York. She writes a weekly column for the *New Musical Express*, and is a frequent contributor at *Spin* magazine. Her work has also appeared in the *New York Post*.

**Caralyn Green**, who hails from the lovely Pittsburgh, PA., graduated from Penn State with a double major in women's studies and journalism and tacked on an English minor for kicks. Her saucy, caffeine-addled writings have popped up in *Venus*, *Pittsburgh Magazine* and Penn State's *Daily Collegian*, but she's pretty new to this journalism thing and promises more credits to wow you soon.

**Eric Grossman** is *Citysearch*.com's Boston editor. A published author, the Boston native has sung on stage with Coldplay, shared beers with the Kings of Leon and is quietly plotting to join Hanson.

**Chris Hassiotis** is the music editor of *Flagpole*, the alternative weekly newspaper of Athens, GA. He has lived there for eight years; he very much likes elephants.

**Matt Hendrickson** lives in Columbia, MO where he owns his own editorial consulting company, Big Swede Media. His writing has appeared in *Rolling Stone*, *Life,* and *Men's Journal*.

**Gil Kaufman** is a freelance writer based in Cincinnati, Ohio. His work has appeared in *Wired*, *Rolling Stone*, *Spin*, *Blender,* and *iD* magazines and on MTV.com, VH1.com and Rollingstone.com.

**Jeff Klein** is a narcissistic yet self-loathing singer-songwriter who has reluctantly lived in the fine city of Austin, Texas since 1999. He's about to release his second album, *The Hustler*, on One Little Indian Records.

**Ryan Lenz** lived in Indianapolis from 2000 to 2003 and covered arts and entertainment in the city and state for the Associated Press.

**Jennifer Maerz** is the music editor at the Seattle alt-weekly the *Stranger*. Over the years her work has also appeared in *Vice*, *Salon.com*, *Thrasher*, *Paper Magazine*, *Spin*.com, the *Washington Post*, and *Alternative Press*, and *Blender*.

**Melissa Maerz** is the senior arts editor at *City Pages*, an alt-weekly in Minneapolis and St. Paul, Minnesota. Her work has also appeared in *Spin*, the *Village Voice*, and the *Chicago Reader*, among others.

**Bob Massey** lives in Chocolate City, which lies just across the Earned Income Tax Credit from Washington, DC. He can't say that college was a total waste of time, but he recommends you buy a sturdy backpack instead.

*Baltimore City Paper* music editor **Bret McCabe** is a lapsed Catholic, lapsed vegetarian, lapsed smoker, and prone to occasional lapses in judgment, but has never given up on the good times.

**Kyle Munson** has been music critic for the *Des Moines Register* since 1997. His work also has appeared in such magazines as *No Depression*. He sheepishly admits to playing accordion.

**Brian Orloff** lives in Evanston, IL where he's finishing school at Northwestern University. His work has appeared in the *St. Petersburg Times* in Florida, the *Chics*, *Rolling Stone* online and *Harp Magazine*.

**Randall Roberts** is a staff writer and weekly columnist at the *Riverfront Times* in St. Louis, where he covers ice cream trucks, private investigators, booze, messy divorces, city planning and the East St. Louis crunk scene. His award-winning music writing has appeared in *Salon*, the *Dallas Observer*, *SF Weekly*, the *St. Louis Post-Dispatch*, and elsewhere. He can be found online at www.glorygloryglory.com.

**Micah Salkind** was born and raised in Lawrence, Kansas but has moved east and now calls the Ocean State his home. His work has appeared in the *Fader*.

Atlanta resident **Craig Seymour** has written about music for the *Washington Post*, the *Atlanta Journal-Constitution*, the *Village Voice*,

*Entertainment Weekly, Vibe,* and others. He is the author of *Luther: The Life and Longing of Luther Vandross.*

**Ryan Sult** publishes Detroit music website Motorcityrocks.com and runs the management firm Sultan Management. He also works at *All Music Guide* and has contributed writing and photography to *NME* and the *Detroit Metrotimes.*

East Coast native **Gemma Tarlach** has been covering music in Milwaukee since 1998 and is currently pop music critic at the *Milwaukee Journal Sentinel.* Her work has also appeared in *Time Out New York.*

**Otis R. Taylor Jr.** has lived in Columbia, South Carolina, for five years and is the music editor for the *State* and *Columbiatunes*.com.

Dedicated to bad music, **Sanden Totten** has spent the last three years hosting a radio show for Oberlin's WOBC station featuring loud music by bands no one likes. You can catch interviews he has done with un-famous musicians occasionally broadcasted there as well. He has been featured as a reporter for Cleveland's *IndyMedia* and works sound for rock shows in his spare time.

**Nathan Turk** lives just outside of Syracuse, New York, where he cut his teeth as the music editor of the *Syracuse New Times.* He writes regularly for *Signal to Noise* and has also appeared in *DIW.*

**Carl Young** lived in Charlottesville, Virginia, on and off for eleven years, while earning his BA, M.T., and Ph.D. at the University of Virginia. He also deejayed at WTJU and sold many records as a Plan 9 employee. Currently, he teaches at Virginia Tech, and his work has also appeared in *English Journal, Contemporary Issues in Technology and Teacher Education,* and *Tough Times Companion.* He still compiles a yearly best of list and looks forward to early retirement so that he can sink his pension into opening a record store.

# Acknowledgments

I am deeply indebted to the many people whose advice, encouragement and elbow-grease made this book a reality. To Wenner Books editor Bob Wallace, whose guidance and unflagging sense of humor carried me through from start to finish; to *Rolling Stone* founder and editor Jann S. Wenner, who gave me a job and then let me leave it; to my agent, Dan Mandel at Sanford J. Greenburger and Associates; to Elizabeth Goodman, who let me dump a buttload of work on her and never once complained; to my friends Fabrizio Moretti and Brett Kilroe, who designed the cover of *Schools That Rock* and whom I owe at least a magnum of champagne each; to Brian Orloff, who has got to be sick of writing about college music departments by now. To my colleagues Nicholas Weir-Williams, Kate Rockland, Laurence Mintz and Mayapriya Long. To those who contributed research and writings for *Schools That Rock*: Steve Appleford, Ricardo Baca, Kimberly Chun, Eric Danton, Dominic Devito, Zach Dundas, Kelly Fitzpatrick, Steve Forstneger, Peter Gershon, Richard Gintowt, Caralyn Green, Eric Grossman, Chris Hassiotis, Matt Hendrickson, Gil Kaufman, Jeff Klein, Ryan Lenz, Jennifer Maerz, Melissa Maerz, Bob Massey, Bret McCabe, Kyle Munson, Randall Roberts, Micah Salkind, Craig Seymour, Ryan Sult, Gemma Tarlach, Otis Taylor, Sanden Totten, Nathan Turk, Carl Young, Jessica Adams, Arielle Baer, Andy Greene, Erin Hall, Joel Hoard, Joey Hood, Adam Jardy, Brent Johnson, Hilary Lewis, Alix McAlpine, Amy Meyer, Jeremy Schmidt, Vanessa Schneider, Eddie Shoebang, Jeffrey Terich, Chris Tucillo, Harold Valentine, Sam Weiner, April Williamson. To Veronica York at LaGuardia High School for the Performing Arts for her insight. To Pete Townshend, John Mayer, Nikki Sixx, Tommy Lee, Ben Kweller, and Nathan Followill for their kind words. Thanks also go to *Rolling Stone* music editor Joe Levy, my mentor and friend; Jason Fine, who witnessed many 3:30 meltdowns over the years; Nathan Brackett, who taught me how to be Zen, even when the shit is hitting the fan; and sweet, sweet Austin Scaggs, who made me tacos and kept me from becoming a shut-in. And, to those without whose love and tireless support I'd be lost, Susan Harmon, Sharon Goodman, and Jarrod Gorbel.

# Appendix

Full Sail Center for the Recording Arts (Orlando, FL)          219
George Washington University (Washington, DC)          300
Gustavus Adolphus College (St. Peter, MN)          256
Hampshire College (Amherst, MA)          300
Harvard University (Cambridge, MA)          44
Howard University (Washington, DC)          300
Indiana University, Bloomington (Bloomington, IN)          131
Indiana University, Indianapolis (Indianapolis, IN)          135
Ithaca College (Ithaca, NY)          137
Johns Hopkins University (Baltimore, MD)          32
Juilliard School (New York, NY)          200
Lewis & Clark University (Portland, OR)          235
Loyola Marymount University (Los Angeles, CA)          145
Loyola University (New Orleans, LA)          193
Middle Tennessee State University (Murfreesboro, TN)          176
Minnesota State University (Mankato, MN)          257
New England Conservatory (Boston, MA)          46
New York University (New York, NY)          199
Northwestern University (Evanston, IL)          122
Oberlin College (Oberlin, OH)          212
Ohio State University (Columbus, OH)          99
Pennsylvania State University (State College, PA)          283
Pomona College (Claremont, CA)          154
Princeton University (Princeton, NJ)          187
Reed College (Portland, OR)          236
Rhode Island School of Design (Providence, RI)          243
Rice University (Houston, TX)          311
Roosevelt University (Chicago, IL)          71
Rutgers University (New Brunswick, NJ)          182
St. Louis University (St. Louis, MO)          248
St. Olaf College (Northfield, MN)          256
San Diego State University (San Diego, CA)          248
San Francisco Conservatory of Music (San Francisco, CA)          263
San Francisco State University (San Francisco, CA)          264
Seattle Pacific University (Seattle, WA)          273